The Media and Sino-American Rapprochement, 1963–1972

The Media and Sino-American Rapprochement, 1963–1972

A Comparative Study

GUOLIN YI

Louisiana State University Press
Baton Rouge

Published by Louisiana State University Press
www.lsupress.org

Designer: Michelle A. Neustrom
Typeface: Minion Pro

Cover photos courtesy National Archives and the Richard Nixon Presidential Library
and Museum.

Portions of this book first appeared in "The *New York Times* and *Washington Post* on Sino-
American Rapprochement, 1963–1972," *American Journalism* 32.4 (2015): 453–75, and are
reprinted by permission of *American Journalism*.

Portions of this book first appeared in "'Propaganda State' and Sino-American Rapprochement:
Preparing the Chinese Public for Nixon's Visit," *Journal of American–East Asian Relations* 20.1
(2013): 5–28, and are reprinted by permission of the publisher, Brill.

Library of Congress Cataloging-in-Publication Data

Names: Yi, Guolin, 1976– author.
Title: The media and Sino-American rapprochement, 1963–1972 : a comparative study / Guolin Yi.
Description: Baton Rouge : Louisiana State University Press, [2020] | Includes bibliographical
    references and index.
Identifiers: LCCN 2020017949 (print) | LCCN 2020017950 (ebook) | ISBN 978-0-8071-7265-0
    (cloth) | ISBN 978-0-8071-7466-1 (pdf) | ISBN 978-0-8071-7467-8 (epub)
Subjects: LCSH: China—Foreign relations—United States. | United States—Foreign relations—
    China. | Mass media—Political aspects—China—History—20th century. | Mass media—
    Political aspects—United States—History—20th century. | China—Foreign public opinion,
    American. | United States—Foreign public opinion, Chinese. | Mass media and history—
    China. | Mass media and history—United States.
Classification: LCC E183.8.C5 Y or G (print) | LCC E183.8.C5 (ebook) | DDC 327.51073—dc21
LC record available at https://lccn.loc.gov/2020017949
LC ebook record available at https://lccn.loc.gov/2020017950

To my wife, Lin
my son, John
and my parents, Youju Yi and Lanying Zhao

Contents

Acknowledgments

I would like to express my sincere gratitude to Melvin Small, who contributed the most to my successful completion of the doctoral program at Wayne State University. He inspired me as a conscientious mentor in studying Sino-American relations and a faithful friend in life. I have greatly enhanced my training in modern Chinese history and politics under the guidance of Alex Day (now at Occidental College) and Yumin Sheng. Alex Day, Aaron Retish, and Hans Hummer have introduced me to World History theories and influenced my teaching from the global perspective. I would also like to thank Denver Brunsman (now at George Washington University) and Sandra VanBurkleo, who offered me generous support and warm friendship at Wayne.

While revising the manuscript, I have benefited tremendously from the advice of Robert Ross from Boston College and Ralph Thaxton Jr. from Brandeis University, two fellow Associates in Research at the Fairbank Center for Chinese Studies at Harvard University. I could not thank Ross more for his consistent and selfless help in my professional career over the years. I would also like to thank Mark Kramer, Program Director of the Cold War Studies at Harvard, for inviting me to share this project by giving a talk cosponsored by the Fairbank Center and the Davis Center for Russian and Eurasian Studies at Harvard in November 2014.

I am obliged to John Lynch of the Television News Archive at Vanderbilt University, Dai Xiaolan and Ma Xiao-he at the Harvard-Yenching Library, and Wang Li, Curator of East Asian Collection at Brown University Library. They have offered generous assistance when I did archival research at their institutions.

I am also grateful to the understanding and support of my boss, David Blanks, the Department Head of History and Political Science at Arkansas Tech University. He has helped me tremendously in navigating the responsibilities of scholarship, teaching, and service at the university while completing this work. I have also benefited from conversations with departmental colleagues such as Jeff Woods, James Moses, and Aaron McArthur. The Professional Development Grant of Arkansas Tech has enabled me to present part of this project at different conferences. I would also like to express my heartfelt thanks to former colleagues, such as Lisa Rosner and Sharon Musher at Stockton University as well as Chris Rasmussen and Bruno Battistoli at Fairleigh Dickinson University, for their encouragement and backing during my growth as a scholar and professor.

Parts of this book have been published in the *Journal of American–East Asian Relations* and *American Journalism*. I appreciate Brill and *American Journalism* for allowing me to use this material in this book.

I am indebted to my parents, Youju Yi and Lanying Zhao. My father's efforts in bringing me from a small village to a factory town have had a lasting impact on my life. That major step laid the foundation for my future development. Lastly, my heartfelt appreciation goes to my wife, Lin Zhang, my closest friend and a source of happiness. She not only has helped me with the materials but also has spent endless hours chatting with me when we had to go through the challenges and uncertainties in life. As a productive scholar herself, she has sacrificed so much for the family and has been a consistent driving force and an inspiration for my academic research. I owe much to my son, John, whose birth has brought new meaning to my life and endless blessings to my family. His sweet personality has lighted my path. As a father, I wish I could spend more time playing with him and witness every moment of his growth.

A Note about Chinese Names and Places

All Chinese names and places throughout the text are rendered in the Pinyin system of transliteration, except where they occur in different forms in quotations. As with the tradition in East Asia, the family name generally goes before the given name for Chinese people, except for those who have adopted English names. For widely accepted terms, such as "Chiang Kai-shek" and "Canton," I put their English equivalents in brackets after their Pinyin spellings.

The Media and Sino-American Rapprochement, 1963–1972

Introduction

The Sino-American rapprochement of 1972 is regarded as one of the most important events of the Cold War. President Richard Nixon's meeting with Mao Zedong not only ended two decades of hostility between the world's most powerful country and its most populous country but also caused a reshuffle in the triangular relations with the Soviet Union as the third player. In a self-congratulatory tone, Nixon claims that it was "the most dramatic geopolitical event since World War II." Historians Chen Jian and David Wilson consider it and the Sino-Soviet border clashes "two of the most important events in the international history of the Cold War."[1] Thus far, scholars of the Sino-American rapprochement have examined the Cold War international setting, domestic politics, and the policy making of the two governments.[2] With most work focusing on the political aspect, we now know more about diplomacy and triangulation. However, we still know very little about how people in the two countries came to learn about the change in relations and how each nation prepared its people for the dramatic rapprochement. We can learn about these developments by looking at the media in the two countries.

The media are important for studying U.S.-China reconciliation for several reasons. As the chief means by which the public gathers information about current issues, the media have the power to influence public opinion. Here "the public" refers to those who demonstrate an interest in a particular issue or in politics in general.[3] Harold Lasswell describes media transmission as a process involving "who says what to whom through which medium with what effects."[4] The media effects concern not only the story and the audiences but also what happened in the transmission process.

1

What people know about an event from the media does not necessarily mirror what actually happened. Instead of reporting the information "objectively," media transmit information to the public through a subjective process of selectivity, placement, images, and opinions. They can prioritize issues that the editors or publishers think are more important and suppress stories or opinions that they do not like. In their coverage, they may use symbols or images that have particular effects. Even for the same event, different media may pick varying emphases and come up with dramatically different interpretations. Therefore, the media's representation of events relating to the two countries might have influenced their audiences' perception of Sino-American relations.

Because of their possible influence on the audience, I am interested in how the media in both countries covered Sino-American relations at different time periods. While most other scholars treat the media as tools or purveyors of government policies in studying the Sino-American rapprochement, I take the media themselves as my objects of study. My focus is not so much on "why" Sino-American rapprochement could happen but on "how" it came about in the media.

Media affected American public officials "indirectly," through their impact on opinion registered in polls, and indirectly, through official media monitors' "impressionistic evaluations" of a story or a newscast.[5] Their influence on public opinion is best reflected in their ability to set the agenda. Bernard Cohen, one of the earliest scholars to study the relationship between the press and U.S. foreign policy, claims that the press is not only a "purveyor of information and opinion" but also has agenda-setting functions. As he argues, the press may not be successful in telling people "what to think," but it is generally successful in telling the audience "what to think about."[6]

Cohen made the claim at a time when newspapers were the dominant channel through which people learned about current affairs. Since the 1960s, television has replaced newspapers as the dominant medium. The development of television consolidated the media's power to set the agenda for political issues. In terms of foreign policy, media could place an issue or region on the government's agenda that was not already there or move an issue or country presently on the agenda to a higher level of policy consideration. As President Jimmy Carter once said, sometimes a particular event "may not warrant preeminent consideration, but because of the high publicity assigned to it, the government officials, including the President, are almost forced to deal with it in preference to other items that might warrant more attention."[7] In another example, as the Lyndon Johnson administration faced increasing criticism for its rigid China policy, Secretary of State Dean Rusk grudgingly complained that the media kept focusing on the question of China's admission to the United Nations (UN) while not giving, in his words, "adequate reproaches" to its "aggression" in Southeast Asia.[8]

Media could also function as cultural institutions that reflect and influence the political culture of a certain period. As David L. Altheide argues: "History speaks through the media in use. And conversely, the media in use during a historical epoch help shape that epoch." According to him, besides the traditional approach of finding evidence of "political/ideological infusion into the media process," we can also look at the media as "cultural items" that contributed to the "values, beliefs, meanings, and symbols that define our social world."[9] The linguistic as well as visual symbols and the discourse in the media created a unique culture that reflected and influenced Sino-American relations. When relations between China and the United States were frozen, the U.S. media insisted on using "Red China" or "Communist China" in referring to the regime on the mainland. With the thaw in relations, they dropped "Red" and "Communist" and even started using its proper name, People's Republic of China. In the Chinese media, on the other hand, the rhetoric that the American "imperialists" were the "most dangerous enemy to people all over the world" also gradually gave way to "heroic" or "friendly" Americans. The change of these discourses concerning the other side both reflected and contributed to the thaw in the relations.

This study is important because it deals with a monumental geopolitical event during a crucial period for the two countries as they both experienced great transformations in their internal as well as external fronts. While the United States was embroiled in the civil rights movement and the Vietnam War, China went through the tumultuous Cultural Revolution and conflicts with the Soviet Union. By using a multinational perspective that involves not only China and the United States but also the Soviet Union and Vietnam, it enriches the study of Sino-American rapprochement through the lenses of the media, an understudied but vital institution that reflected and influenced the two publics' perceptions of the relations. It not only readdresses the issue of the government-media relationship in the United States but also maps out how the Chinese people learned about the developments in Sino-American relations at different time periods.

This book also contributes to the field of political science because it sheds new light on the role of the media and domestic environments in the politics of foreign policy making in Maoist China. By looking at how the decisions of Chinese leaders were passed from the top through the middle-level bureaucracy down to rank-and-file Chinese Communist Party (CCP) members and finally the general Chinese population, this book is among the first works to systematically study the Chinese communication system when it comes to foreign relations. In his article in *China Quarterly* in 1974, Michel Oksenberg examined the communications within the CCP bureaucracy through written documents and meetings at different levels,[10] but he did not touch upon the unique roles of internal publications. By dividing the Chinese communication system into three levels—the classified Party documents, the internal circulations, and the open media—this book demonstrates how people at different levels of the political hierarchy accessed different kinds of information.

In their study of foreign policy making in China, scholars generally do not consider domestic public opinion because the assumption is that Chinese leaders do not need the input of the general public. Even though it might be the case, leaders in Beijing might have to consider people's response to a sudden policy change, particularly if it was related to a country that China's media had consistently called its "number-one enemy." This study shows that on the issue of improving relations with the United States, Chinese leaders not only considered the general public but also took active steps to cultivate them in that direction from a very early period.

This book seeks answers to the following questions: What techniques did the media in both countries apply in their coverage of the events that showed the change in relations? How did they prepare their respective domestic audience and send signals to the opposite side? In other words, I want to see how the media in both countries dealt with the prospect of a thaw in relations. Did the U.S. media pick up the clues of Washington's move toward Beijing? Could a reader of the Chinese press see the revolutionary change in relations coming, especially in the late 1960s as the Soviet Union replaced the United States as public enemy number one?

Comments on Sources: Media under Study

In order to answer these questions, I select some of the most influential media in both countries to examine. Among the U.S. media sources, I look at newspapers, magazines, and television news programs. Among newspapers, the *New York Times* and *Washington Post* were the most influential during the period under study because other major newspapers, magazines, and television networks often accepted their definition of "what was 'news.'" The *New York Times* is especially important because of the prominence it had gained since the 1940s when it invested heavily in foreign affairs reporting, a neglected field of journalism at the time. Since then, the *Times* has had the largest, if not the best, staff of foreign correspondents. The importance of the *Times* can also be shown when several scholars use it as the major source to represent the American media when they study foreign policy reporting.[11] In addition, *Time* and *Newsweek,* among magazines, and the evening newscasts of the three national networks, CBS, ABC, and NBC, were also important sources for Americans. Students of American journalism would agree with Presidents Lyndon Johnson and Richard Nixon, who believed that these seven media institutions were the most important in the United States.[12]

Among sources in the Chinese media, I mainly use *Renmin Ribao* (People's Daily) and *Cankao Xiaoxi* (Reference News) because they represented two levels of the Chinese communication system, one in the form of open media, the other the internal publications.[13] *Hong Qi* (Red Flag), the "ideological journal" of the CCP,[14] appears in my narrative occasionally when it published joint editorials with *People's Daily.* My original plan was to examine the *Jiefang Daily* (People's Liberation Army Daily) as well. However, after checking a number of key events, such as Beijing's 1968 statement offering the renewal of the Warsaw Talks and Mao's photo with Edgar Snow in 1970, I found that its articles were identical to those in *People's Daily,* so I decided not to single it out for analysis.

I do not use Chinese electronic media for several reasons. First, TV programs were not transmitted on a regular basis, and the number of televisions available to the Chinese public was quite limited in the 1960s. Second, archives of telecasts and radio programs in China are not easy to access. The third and most important reason is that the centralized nature of the Chinese media—their control by the Propaganda Department—decides that voices of all public media in China should be generally identical. Important news and commentaries in TV and radio appeared in *People's Daily* as well.

As the official organ of the Chinese Communist Party, *People's Daily* has been the most important newspaper in China, and scholars often use it in studying the Chinese media. It is tasked with disseminating the Party line and policies to the public. Each edition had a wide readership when it was circulated in local work units or put on bulletin boards in public areas. *People's Daily* published commentaries in the following forms: editorials, which were the most commonly used; short general commentaries and articles by the paper's own commentators, which were very brief and usually more locally oriented; articles by the paper's editorial department, reserved for more abstract subjects; articles by political observers dealing with foreign affairs; and articles by various key figures representing the voice of the CCP. Despite the variation in names, they all reflected the position of the Party and the Chinese government. News stories were secondary to editorials in the newspaper. The importance of editorials is exceeded only by directives, Party resolutions, and Mao's words. In a highly politicized culture, it was a common practice among local branches of the CCP or various work units to hold regular meetings to study the editorials of *People's Daily*.[15]

Reference News was an internal newspaper that few scholars have used in studying Sino-American relations. Founded in 1931, it was originally a classified intelligence service read only by top CCP leaders and military commanders. Its circulation was around fifty in the 1930s and two thousand after the establishment of the People's Republic of China (PRC) in 1949. In 1957, Mao decided to turn it into an internal newspaper, with its authorized readership expanded to Communist cadres above the county level and a limited number of non-Communist intellectuals who worked with the CCP. By running news stories that were not fit to publish in the open media, Mao wanted the newspaper to function as a tool to inform the Chinese cadres about world affairs and foreign opinions about China, both positive and negative. In his words, "By letting the cadres know about how our enemies criticize us, *Reference News* would function as a vaccination that promoted their immune system and judgment." Its circulation was 200,000 in 1957 and 400,000 in 1964. When China was moving toward the United States, *Reference News* became even more important in preparing the Chinese cadres for the possible new relationship. On July 5, 1970, the Central Committee of the CCP issued a notice that dramatically increased its circulation to around five million.[16]

As David Bonavia of the *New York Times* wrote in July 1975, *Reference News* carried "accurate though often abridged" translations of reports from the main world news agencies to keep readers informed of trends in foreign public opinion rather than to propagate the news of the Chinese leadership, although he admits the existence of a "slant." He put it in sharp contrast to the Soviet equivalent, a weekly publication that presented only foreign materials favorable to Moscow's propaganda line and that regularly distorted or misinterpreted the contents of the originals for political purposes.[17]

Due to its internal nature, subscriptions to *Reference News* had to be approved by the Party. Foreigners were not allowed to access it until the late 1970s. At one time, permission to read this newspaper had been regarded as a privilege or a sign of social status in China. The header of each issue used to carry the notice "*neibu kanwu, zhuyi baocun*," which means "internal circulation, please handle with discretion." Even its used copies had to be recycled to prevent it from flowing to the public. After *Reference News* became a newspaper, people gave it the nickname *xiao cankao* (Small Reference) to differentiate it from the daily internal publication called *Cankao ziliao* (Reference Materials), or *da cankao* (Big Reference), which published about a hundred pages with a morning issue and an afternoon issue. As the nickname *da cankao* suggests, the *Reference Materials* was read only by the "big shots"—officials of the CCP at the very high level.[18] As *Reference News* was the main channel for the cadres to learn about the outside world, it offers a window into the foreign policy of China. Stories in this newspaper also enable readers to verify whether signals from the Nixon administration had been received by the Chinese.

Media Comparisons

When studying the different media forms in the two countries, this book makes comparisons at three levels: the first level is between the U.S. and Chinese media; the second level is between different forms of media, such as newspapers, magazines, and television; and the third level is between different media organizations within the same country, for example, the differences between the *New York Times* and *Washington Post* in their coverage of China and the differences between *People's Daily* and *Reference News* in their coverage of the United States' and China's position in the world. At the first level, the U.S. government does not have much direct control over the media, except that radio and TV stations are federally licensed. Under the protection of the First Amendment, the media have a relatively freer hand in news reporting and editing. Also, the influence between the American media and foreign policy makers is mutual, which means that whereas the government may try to affect the media through public announcements and selective leaking, the media's prioritized coverage of certain news and their editorial positions might force the government to respond and address those issues.[19]

In China, on the other hand, to serve its "totalitarian ideology," the Communist Party controls the media through its Propaganda Department and uses them to make known its policy direction and to manipulate public opinion.[20] This influence is one-way, from the government to the media. Directors of the Xinhua News Agency and chief editors of *People's Daily* enjoyed high status within the Party and were heavily involved in its policy making. A typical example is Wu Lengxi, who headed both Xinhua and *People's Daily* from 1957 to 1966 and regularly attended the meetings of the Politburo even though he was not a member.[21] Moreover, Mao kept a tight control over the propaganda machines by appointing people he trusted to lead them. Besides Wu, Hu Qiaomu, who headed Xinhua in 1949, and Chen Boda, who controlled *People's Daily* and *Red Flag* during the Cultural Revolution, had all been loyal to Mao because of their previous service as his personal secretaries.[22] Therefore, we can assume that, during most of the time under study, the Chinese media spoke for the Party and the government.[23]

Another difference between the media in the two countries is that information in the American media is more explicit because its political and journalist culture requires open and straightforward articulation. In China, by contrast, the government might deliver political or diplomatic messages with extreme subtlety. For example, when Zhou Enlai arranged for Edgar Snow to stand next to Mao on the Tiananmen balcony on the October Day national celebration in 1970 and had their photo published later, U.S. officials as well as journalists did not realize that it was a message from Beijing that it wanted to do business with Washington. Moreover, the Chinese government often makes propagandistic statements that do not reflect its actual policy. Mao and Zhou Enlai admitted that they usually "fire empty cannons."[24] Therefore, it is more difficult to understand the implications when people read the Chinese media. I would be reading the tea leaves, so to speak.

At the second level, it is worthwhile to note that different forms of media have their own strengths in news reporting. During the time under study, U.S. newspapers and magazines reached far smaller audiences than did the nightly newscasts, had much more space to elaborate a story, relied more on words and language than pictures, and offered far more opinions through editorials and columns.[25] As a visual medium, television is better at presenting events that are "accessible to camera and action." Like radio, it is an "instant" source that reduces the audiences' chance to "check and edit information" before it goes on the air and increases the risk of error or misinterpretation.[26]

Although U.S. television networks are potentially more powerful than newspapers in influencing ordinary people, students of journalism generally agree on the importance of elite newspapers in setting the agenda. Most newspaper editors and television producers relied heavily on the *Times* and the *Post*, the wire services, a few morning columnists, and, more generally, the covers of *Time* and *Newsweek* to decide what was newsworthy. That is why Russ Braley argues that television seldom "discovers" or "initiates" news; it "magnifies" news that others have discovered. Later on, even though television networks became independent gatherers of news, they were limited by time constraints that left them with only about ninety seconds for each story in a twenty-two-minute "news hole" on their thirty-minute nightly programs.[27] They did not have enough space to elaborate on the background, significance, and response relevant to a certain story. For this reason, some correspondents called the nightly news a "headline service" that provided an outline of the day's events. From these "head-lines," viewers could follow up their interests and discover more informa-tion in the newspapers. According to Philip L. Geyelin, the editorial page editor of the *Washington Post* from 1968 to 1979, whereas television news "bombards" viewers with a "shifting series of illusions and deceptive ap-pearances," newspapers tidy things up, examine them so that the stories could make sense.[28]

Moreover, the most influential members of the U.S. public, including policy makers, relied more on the prestige newspapers for serious news than on television, which presented short stories in "sensational packages that lacked context." Therefore, the importance of television in influencing public opinion might be exaggerated. What makes the relationship more complicated is the fact that most officials think that television is more im-portant than print media in affecting public opinion.[29]

Due to the "inherent mechanical need" of television to have images, television reporters were accused of being especially "susceptible to be-ing used" by news sources. Because most stories of foreign affairs con-cerned the White House, and it was more difficult to get decision makers to talk on camera, stories of this kind were mostly "talking heads" and "standuppers"—the White House correspondent, with the White House in the background, talking his story into the camera or even the anchor read-ing the stories in the studio.[30] This was even more true when it came to sto-ries about China due to the lack of images during the period under study.

At the third level, differences exist among media agencies within the same country. For example, a comparison between the *New York Times* and *Washington Post* demonstrates the complicated attitudes toward China in the United States. In China, on the other hand, a comparison between *People's Daily* and *Reference News* reveals important insights about the communication system of the CCP, where people at different levels of the political hierarchy had access to information of various importance or se-crecy level. These differences say a lot about the Cold War culture in the 1960s and early 1970s.

Sampling Method: How to Read the Media

After selecting the media to examine, I set up the chronological boundary, which covers the administration of Lyndon Johnson and Richard Nixon's first term. It starts with Assistant Secretary of State for Far Eastern Affairs Roger Hilsman's major policy speech in 1963, which signified a new U.S. posture toward China, and ends with Nixon's visit to China in 1972. Over this ten-year period, I have selected a number of key events that affected Sino-American relations and examined how they were covered by the mainstream media in their respective countries. The identification of these key events can be subjective. However, I have tried to pick the events whose importance has been agreed upon by most historians. Besides the two just mentioned, other events are the French recognition of China, the escalation of the Vietnam War, and China's nuclear test in 1964; the Fulbright Hearings and the start of the Cultural Revolution in 1966; the Soviet invasion of Czechoslovakia, the beginning of the Paris talks on the Vietnam War, and the Chinese offer to resume the Sino-American Ambassadorial Talks in Warsaw (known as the Warsaw Talks) in 1968; the Sino-Soviet border clashes and U.S. overtures to China in 1969; the resumption of the Warsaw Talks and Edgar Snow's visit to China in 1970; and Ping-Pong Diplomacy and Henry Kissinger's secret trip to China in 1971.

For each event, I briefly describe its development on the basis of secondary accounts and memoirs. It should be noted that several of the events did not happen on a single day but consisted of events that occurred over a long period of time, for example, the Cultural Revolution, the Sino-Soviet conflict, and the Sino-Vietnam split. For these events, I devote more space to their historical background.

After the narration of the event, I examine how the elite U.S. media covered it in terms of headlines, placement, opinions, and the general evaluation of the significance. If there were photos or political cartoons attached, I describe them and interpret their implications, evaluating their possible influence on the audience. If one event that I think is important was not covered by a certain source, it is always worthwhile to explain the reason for the silence. To locate articles from the ProQuest database, I used the search engine on the basis of the date and key words. From the larger sample of articles, I mainly focused on front-page stories, editorials, and columns, eliminating when possible duplicate ideas and arguments. The selection process also involved placement, relevancy, and the reputation of the columnists.

In his study of the media coverage of the antiwar movement in the 1960s, Melvin Small does not look at editorials because he argues that for print media, headlines, lead paragraphs, and pictures on the front pages are more important in influencing the public than editorials or columns, which are usually buried deep. He also believes that editorials of elite newspapers tend to be more conservative than their more objective news articles. Richard Nixon also holds that editorial pages of the newspapers "tilt right," while their reports from the Washington bureau generally "tilt left."[31]

Small's argument is true indeed, but the importance of news articles, especially front-page stories, does not necessarily mean that editorials and columns are not important. According to a report based on research by Belden Associates, on a Newspaper Association of American report detailing a national survey of newspaper readership, on a 1993 study of media and their markets by Simmons Market Research Bureau, and on a review of academic research into readership patterns, editorial readership is second only to general news for adult readers at every level of education and ranks ahead of categories that include sports, business, entertainment, food, and home. Similar studies in 1994 show that 79 percent of adult readers who read newspapers daily read or look at the editorial page. More importantly, these studies show that editorial page readers tend to be "older, more affluent, and better educated," which means their readers are more likely to "hold sway" in public affairs.[32] Moreover, even Small agrees that editorials and opinions in newspapers had more influence on the presidents than news stories because they were given special importance in the news summaries of the Johnson and Nixon administrations. They seemed to think that "publicly expressed opinions" were more important in influencing Americans than front-page news stories.[33]

Time and *Newsweek* are available on microfilm. In order to locate relevant articles on an event, I used *Readers' Guide to Periodical Literature* in combination with the magazines' own indices. As the magazines were published once a week, timeliness was obviously not their strength, which lay in the large number of pictures, political cartoons, and in-depth analyses. Magazines could also prioritize a topic by putting it on their covers.

Then I turned to television programs. During most of the time under study, U.S. television networks did not have many images from China due to their lack of access to the country when interactions between the two countries were extremely rare. Moreover, the Vanderbilt University Television News Archives' videotape collection in Nashville extends back only to 1968. Of the three networks, only CBS maintains an archive for pre-1968 broadcasts. But they are not open to public use.[34] Therefore, I use more sources in the print media, especially the two elite newspapers, than television footage in studying the period between 1963 and 1967. Even though U.S. telecasts become part of my narrative from 1968, it was not until Ping-Pong Diplomacy in April 1971 that they began to play a substantially more prominent role in Sino-American relations. In watching television footage, I mainly look at the direction of the camera, symbols in the picture, and activities and expressions of people featured in the video because these elements could potentially influence the audience's perception of the event. For "talking heads" in the studio, I examine the expression, tone, and arguments of the anchors.

Because of the differences between the media in the two countries, I have come upon different issues in looking at them. In studying the U.S. media, I address the issue of their relationship with the government to see if they played an independent role in America's China policy. When it comes to the Chinese side, evaluation of the media enables me to obtain hints about Beijing's attitude because of their close relationship with the Party and the government.

When reading *People's Daily*, I pay attention to the placement, the headlines, and the format of an article. Usually, editorials appearing jointly in *Red Flag* and *PLA Daily* are more important than articles in other formats. For a specific article, I examine how it characterizes the United States, sometimes in comparison to the Soviet Union, to find clues about official attitudes toward the two countries. From the propaganda, or the "empty cannon," I try to find nuances such as the demonstration of official commitment. With regard to *Reference News*, I mainly focus on the placement of the story and especially how it dealt with the signals from the United States in order to see what kind of information was available to the cadres.

In a more general sense, I look at the differences between media organizations in the same country and try to explain why. For example, the differences between the *New York Times* and the *Washington Post* in their reporting of China might reflect the opinions of different groups in the United States. On the other hand, the different attitude toward the United States in *People's Daily* and *Reference News* reflected how Beijing communicated its foreign policies to people at different positions of the political hierarchy. I am also interested in how the media in both countries responded to each other because usually the reporting of the media in one country would attract the attention of the other. The interpretation of news reporting from the other side could potentially affect the domestic audience. Moreover, I look at the relationship between the actual governmental policy and the media representation. Usually the discrepancy between governmental "words" and "deeds" on certain issues had implications. It is my job to explain the causes of the differences.

Structure of This Book

This book is divided into five chapters. Chapter 1 covers the period from Hilsman's speech in late 1963 to the Fulbright Hearings in the spring of 1966. By working with the critics from academic and congressional circles, the U.S. media contributed to the "depoliticization" of the China issue in the public arena.[35] The Chinese media's attitude toward the United States, on the other hand, changed from moderately hostile to radically hostile during this period. The change in the Chinese media reflects the new developments in China's international environments with the American escalation in Vietnam and the new tensions in the CCP leadership.

Chapter 2 deals with the high point of the Cultural Revolution between 1966 and 1968, during which the Chinese media promoted Beijing's image as a fighter against both "American imperialists" and "Soviet revisionists" in order to inspire the struggle against Mao's political enemies at home. While the voices calling for a more flexible China policy in the U.S. media were overwhelmed by stories of recurrent violence in China, their coverage of its troubles with Moscow and Hanoi presented a disorganized and greatly weakened China that had become less of a threat to the United States. This chapter closely examines the signals between Beijing and Washington during their "tacit agreement" about nonconfrontation in Vietnam and also examines the nuances between what the Chinese government said in the media and what it actually did in Vietnam.

Chapter 3 investigates how the media in the two countries dealt with the opportunity for closer Sino-American relations brought about by the eruption of Sino-Soviet border clashes in 1969 and how Richard Nixon's signals of friendliness were delivered to the Chinese audiences. Whereas

Washington assumed a public posture of detachment, the U.S. media openly elaborated on the benefits of closer ties with Beijing. When Beijing showed a genuine concern for a Soviet surprise attack in its media, *Reference News* started to report on U.S. overtures despite the rigid rhetoric in *People's Daily.*

Chapter 4 looks at the "intricate minuet" between Beijing and Washington from the renewal of the Warsaw Talks in early 1970 to Kissinger's secret trip to Beijing in July 1971. It particularly highlights how the Chinese media demonstrated Beijing's efforts to reciprocate the American overtures by sending signals to the Nixon administration. The U.S. media's positive reports of China, on the other hand, helped to change its image into that of a rational country with which it was possible to negotiate.

Chapter 5 shows how the media in the two countries communicated to their respective public for the thaw in relations and their coverage of the historical summit in 1972. While Nixon started his media campaign to prepare for the show in Beijing, the Chinese government used a variety of media tactics to condition its people for the dramatic change in relations with its former number-one enemy. This chapter also analyzes the "TV spectacle," when massive media coverage contributed to and became part of this success story of public relations.

1

The Depoliticization of the China Issue, 1963–1966

The period between late 1963 and the spring of 1966 witnessed the gradual "depoliticization" of the China issue in the United States.[1] In December 1963, Assistant Secretary of State for Far Eastern Affairs Roger Hilsman made a speech that was received favorably in the United States as a change in government posture toward China. In 1964 China established diplomatic relations with France and successfully exploded its first atomic bomb. These two events dramatically elevated Beijing's international position and posed new challenges to the China policy of the Johnson administration, which faced increasing pressure to include China into the international community.

The U.S. escalation in Vietnam, especially the introduction of ground-combat troops in 1965, raised concern among legislators and journalists about the danger of military confrontation with China. This concern provided a strong rationale for a reappraisal of U.S. policy toward China. During the highly publicized Fulbright Hearings in the spring of 1966, the "containment without isolation" thesis proposed by the academics received overwhelmingly favorable responses in journalistic as well as official circles. The media's coverage of the hearings was important in "legitimizing" the airing of views that would have been considered dangerous in the 1950s.[2]

By looking at the media coverage of the events from Hilsman's speech through the French recognition and the Chinese nuclear test, to U.S. escalation in Vietnam and the Fulbright Hearings, this chapter examines how influential U.S. media acted as vocal critics of the Johnson administration's rigid policy toward China and how they contributed to the "depoliticization" of the China issue. With regard to the Chinese media, this chapter examines how they responded to the new developments in the United States and demonstrated the nuanced differences between the moderates and radicals in the Chinese leadership before the Cultural Revolution.

Sino-American relations were locked in hostility throughout the 1950s. Due to the fighting between the two countries during the Korean War, the "Red Scare" caused by McCarthyism, and the powerful influence of the China Lobby, an interest group mainly consisting of conservative Republicans who supported the Nationalist government in Taiwan, it was politically dangerous for U.S. politicians to talk about improving relations with China. On June 28, 1957, President Dwight Eisenhower's secretary of state, John Foster Dulles, an elder of the Presbyterian Church, made a major China policy speech before the international convention of Lions International in San Francisco, where he used "three Nos"—no recognition, no UN membership, and no cultural exchange or trade—to characterize the U.S. policy toward China. He reasoned that the Communist regime on the mainland was a "passing and not a perpetual phase" and that the U.S. government would work hard to "contribute to that passing."[3] Despite the hostility of Dulles, perhaps the most important accomplishment in Sino-American relations under the Eisenhower administration was the establishment of direct communications between the two governments in the embassies of a third country. They started in Geneva in 1955 and then moved to Warsaw in 1957.[4] Commonly known as the "Warsaw Talks," they were the only channels of direct contact between the two governments until Kissinger's secret visit to China in 1971.

The tension between China and the United States abated a little under the presidency of John F. Kennedy. As a senator, Kennedy had criticized the rigid China policy of the Republican administration in a *Foreign Affairs* article in 1957.[5] In one of his television debates with Richard Nixon during the 1960 campaign, Kennedy advocated forsaking the offshore islands of Quemoy and Matsu, which lay within the cannon range of Chinese forces, to avoid military confrontations with China. Later he had to change his position due to public response.[6] When Kennedy entered the White House, China was ending its disastrous Great Leap Forward. Millions of Chinese had perished due to the famine it caused. Kennedy flirted with the idea of shipping wheat to China, but on the condition that Beijing requested it first. When the Nationalists in Taiwan planned to invade China in 1962, U.S. representatives told the Chinese at the ambassadorial talks in Warsaw that Washington would not support Taiwan's war efforts. As Hilsman claims, Kennedy considered extending recognition to Communist Mongolia as a symbolic gesture foreshadowing a change in China policy, but he did not move ahead due to the opposition of the Nationalists. Hilsman also claims that Kennedy did authorize an attempt to open the door to a normalization of relations with China not long after the Cuban Missile Crisis and the signing of the Limited Test Ban Treaty in 1963.[7] Because of his assassination on November 22, 1963, Kennedy failed to accomplish much improvement in U.S.-China relations.

Hilsman's Speech

Though Sino-American relations did not improve much during the Kennedy administration, there had been a reformist sentiment among higher-level officials dealing with the China policy. In addition to Hilsman, these officials included James Thomson Jr., special assistant in the Bureau of Far Eastern Affairs who had been born to missionary parents in China; Robert Komer of the National Security Council (NSC); Edward Rice, a China specialist and member of the Policy Planning Staff who became U.S. consul general in Hong Kong in 1964; Chester Bowles, Kennedy's special representative and adviser on African, Asian, and Latin American Affairs; and Edwin Reischauer, ambassador to Japan and a prominent Asian scholar.[8]

On December 13, three weeks after Kennedy's death, Hilsman made a speech on China policy in his address to the Commonwealth Club in San Francisco, the same city where Dulles had made his "three Nos" policy statement on China. Hilsman stated that it was time to take "dispassionate" stock of the difficult China problem and that the United States would like to "keep the door open" to negotiations with Beijing if the Chinese leaders would forsake their "venomous hatred" of the United States. Acknowledging that the Communist regime was not likely to be overthrown, Hilsman expressed hope that Chinese leaders "at the second echelon" would take a realistic approach and that they would realize that the Great Leap Forward reflected "a stubborn addiction to theories which did not work in a modern world." He even claimed to have seen "evidence of evolutionary forces at work in mainland China."[9]

The *New York Times* placed the Hilsman speech on its front page with a byline "KEY POLICY STATEMENT" and also reprinted excerpts of the transcripts on the next page. Calling the speech "a new exposition of policy toward China—the first such major statement from either the Kennedy or Johnson administration," it pointed out that it had been "cleared through higher levels of the administration" and that the text of the speech had been distributed by the State Department. In a news analysis entitled "Looking toward Peking: Washington Shows New Frankness on Policies Long under Discussion" on the third page, Max Frankel, chief of the *Times'* Washington Bureau and its major China watcher, gave the recently assassinated Kennedy credit for taking a "new and realistic view of the problem." He claimed that the most important thing about the speech was that "it was made at all." He described Chinese leaders as "prudent and sensible" and appealed to readers by pointing out that the statement was "aimed at Americans" and that it was a call for their "realism and moderation" in dealing with Beijing.[10] By going out of the way to praise Chinese leaders and to acknowledge the significance of the speech, the *Times* tried to open American audiences to new thinking about handling relations with a Cold War opponent.

The *Washington Post*, in contrast, was not as impressed, placing a story by staff writer Murrey Marder on page five. Even though it contrasted Hilsman's "dispassionate" speech to Dulles's 1957 statement, which it described as having been "couched in tones of outrage and indignation," the article still used "Red China" in its headline and characterized it as the "most populous and most embittered nation in the world." The next day, the *Post* ran an editorial entitled "Open?" Depicting China as a country preoccupied with expansion, it lamented Washington's lack of "fresh policy," which essentially rejected the revolutionary nature of Hilsman's speech. It also criticized Hilsman and stated that he should direct his attention to more important topics such as China's relations with India and Taiwan and the security issue in Indochina.[11] In his 1966 book *Lyndon B. Johnson and the World,* Philip Geyelin, the *Post*'s editorial page editor and a prominent foreign affairs correspondent, argued that the closest reading of Hilsman's address "could not uncover any evidence that U.S. policy had really shifted" and that it was meant to put the blame of Sino-American antagonism on China. In addition, he had called Dulles's "three Nos" policy toward China "legal and moral" even though admitting in private that the policy was "difficult to defend on anything but moralistic grounds—or in terms of practical domestic policies."[12] His evaluations of the speech and America's China policy in general might have explained the cool-headedness of his newspaper's editorial page in contrast to the eager optimism of Frankel's piece.

Newsweek described Hilsman's speech as the administration's "tentative, probing move designed to test the reaction—both at home and in Peking—to a subtle change in its attitude toward China."[13] Interestingly, *Time* was silent on Hilsman's speech. Instead, it featured a story about Chinese premier and foreign minister Zhou Enlai's six-week trip to Africa. Referring to Zhou as "the grandest panjandrum from Peking ever" to visit that continent, *Time* claimed that China obviously wanted to establish "the yellow man's burden" even if it "could not afford to pick it up." Here the word "panjandrum" sounds much more negative than "leader." "The yellow man's burden" smacked of racism when it compared Chinese diplomatic activities in Africa to Western countries' colonial conquest in the nineteenth century. When Hilsman resigned from office in early 1964, *Time* described him as an "aggressive and abrasive" man hindering the teamwork necessary for coordinating policy. It even quoted a State Department official who said that Hilsman's resignation was just a "two-day deal" and that they did not mind.[14] *Time's* gloating over Hilsman's departure explains the weekly's silence on his major speech.

The hostility of *Time* to Chinese officials was closely related to its owner, Henry Luce, who had been born to American missionary parents in China and who became a staunch anti-Communist when he grew up. Luce was so angry about the Communist victory in China that he liked to tell friends that the only ambassadorship he would take was to a "restored democracy in China." His strong championing of the Nationalists was evidenced by the fact that, by the time they were driven out of the mainland, Jiang Jieshi (Chiang Kai-shek) had appeared on the cover of *Time* more often than anyone else—even more than Franklin Roosevelt or Winston Churchill or Adolf Hitler.[15] Luce was a leading member of the China Lobby, in which the most important group was known as the Committee of One Million, a nationwide bipartisan organization founded in 1953 aiming to mobilize sentiment against any "appeasement of Communist China." Two weeks after Hilsman's speech, the *Times* reported that the Committee attacked him for "departing from" official U.S. policy by promoting a "two-China" solution. The article in the *Times* was a short piece buried deep that described the Committee as an "Anti-Peking group."[16] Although the *Times* did cover some negative responses to Hilsman's speech, it did not give them as much priority as it did to other positive stories.

In his memoir, Hilsman describes the birth of his speech as more like a reformist movement from below rather than something initiated from above. According to him, James C. Thomson Jr.; Lindsey Grant, officer in charge of mainland China affairs; Allen S. Whiting, director of the Office of Research for Far Eastern Affairs who would later teach at University of Michigan; Joseph W. Neubert, also a special assistant in Far Eastern Affairs; and Abram Manell, public affairs adviser for Far Eastern Affairs, were all involved in drafting the speech. In order to make sure the American people understood its significance, he pointed out, Whiting had briefed the press, the two wire services, the two local Washington papers, and especially the *New York Times*, telling them the speech signified a "departure of historical significance," especially from Dulles's China policy statement of 1957. As a former professor and a graduate of West Point with ten years of service in the army, Hilsman believed he could "blunt" the criticism from the far left as well as the far right.[17]

Hilsman stated that the speech had been cleared by the Defense Department, various branches of the State Department, and the White House staff. However, it was George Ball who read and approved the speech as the acting secretary because Dean Rusk was away for weekend.[18] In reality, Rusk was shocked by the speech and expressed reservations about it in private.[19] Moreover, President Johnson did not read or comment on the speech. As Hilsman claimed, by being "not too closely and personally identified with the decision to make it," Johnson could avoid taking responsibility if it backfired.[20] Hilsman's resignation in February 1964, to some extent, suggests that his China approach was not widely shared by the major policy makers of the Johnson team. It does not matter, however, whether the speech was Hilsman's own initiative or it had been approved by the White House. What matters is that the audience got the impression that the U.S. government was considering a new posture toward China. Here the impression created by the media is more important than the actual positions of the policy makers.

Hilsman claimed that his speech could serve as a "test balloon" of public reaction at very little risk to the Johnson administration's future choice about the China issue.[21] In the recommendations to his boss, National Security Advisor McGeorge Bundy, James Thomson was impressed by what he considered the generally positive response of the press. He argued that it suggested "a dramatic ebbing of passions" on the China issue.[22] If Thomson were not being too optimistic, the ebbing of passions would open the door for more reasonable talk about a more flexible China policy. Meanwhile, it seems that the elite media were ahead of the general public in thinking about better relations with China.

The original response of *People's Daily* to Hilsman's speech was mild. Despite the sarcastic title "Hilsman Whining, Trapped in the Dead Alley of Anti-China, the U.S. is Attempting to Play Double Sides to Avoid Defeat," the article covered the main ideas of Hilsman's speech: the United States had to acknowledge the Communist government was here to stay and expanding its influence; the United States was not ignoring the seven hundred million Chinese but trying to talk to them through channels like Warsaw; the two-Chinas policy; an "open door" policy to push China to give up its rigid policy and accept a diversified world. There was neither a vicious attack on the American policy nor any commitment to an official position. One thing noticeable is that it omitted the wording about Chinese leaders of the second echelon.[23] Eliminating this part serves to deny the existence of leaders who might disagree with the radical path of Mao and to avoid the impression that there might be disagreement within the Chinese Communist Party (CCP) leadership.

Two months later, *People's Daily* published a much longer editorial by "Observer" strongly attacking U.S. officials' recent talks about a possible "open door" to China. It reiterated the Chinese support for the national liberation struggles in Asia, Africa, as well as Latin America, and warned the United States to give up any hope that the Chinese leaders of the second echelon would surrender their commitment to class struggle. It even drew a parallel to 1949 and mocked Washington placing unrealistic hope in the "lovers of individual freedom and democracy" in China back then. Finally, it argued that the change in U.S. policy served as a good "negative example" that would only "reinforce the confidence and determination" of the Chinese and Asian people in their fight against American imperialists.[24] The tone of this article was much more hostile than the one two months earlier. It was a clearer rejection of the new posture from the United States.

Articles by "Observer" in *People's Daily* convey opinions on issues that presumably are highly important but that do not carry the full support of the Party. They cannot be said to reflect official policy and are not as authoritative as editorials.[25] The two-month delay in criticizing Hilsman's speech showed uncertainty or at least confusion in the leadership of *People's Daily*. From 1962 to 1965, Mao lost control of *People's Daily* as he temporarily left the power to moderates like State Chairman Liu Shaoqi, Premier Zhou Enlai, Party Secretary Deng Xiaoping, and Chen Yun, a Politburo member and an expert in economy, due to the grave consequences caused by the Great Leap Forward. Hilsman was hoping that these people would bring positive changes to China's foreign policies.

When *People's Daily* was in the hands of the moderates, *Red Flag*, the theoretical magazine of the CCP, was controlled by Chen Boda, a radical and staunch supporter of Mao. On March 22, 1964, the *New York Times* claimed to have spotted an article in *Red Flag* that it interpreted as a sign that the CCP was concerned that China's young leaders might be subverted by Western influences because the article urged older Party members to educate future leaders in revolutionary traditions.[26] Actually, the article the *Times* referred to was a general piece entitled "Hold on to the Revolutionary Character of the Proletariat Forever" written by Zhao Han, who was then the deputy head of CCP's Central Organization Department in charge of training Communist cadres. It was meant to pay tribute to Liu Shaoqi's famous piece "On the Training of Communists" published a year earlier.[27] Even though the article mentioned the importance of vigilance against peaceful transformation by Western powers, it mainly paid tribute to Liu Shaoqi.

Zhao's article was only one of many *Red Flag* articles dealing with the possible transformation of leaders of future generations. More important pieces appeared after July. It can be seen from an editorial entitled "The Training of Successors Is an Important Task for Our Revolutionary Cause for Thousands and Tens of Thousands of Years to Come." This editorial pointed out that "the American imperialists" were resting their hope on the possibility that the "peaceful transformation of China" would be done through the "degeneration and change" of leaders of the third or fourth generations and that preventing the revisionism of Khrushchev's kind from happening in China was a crucial issue concerning the life and death of the Party and the country. This article was later followed by a longer one written by An Ziwen, the head of the CCP's Central Organization Department. It was a leading article this time.[28]

The timing of the *Red Flag* articles is important because it was in the middle of 1964 that Mao started to emphasize the importance of training "revolutionary successors" and to list the prevention of revisionism as the most important task.[29] Mao's worry about revisionism is closely related to the Sino-Soviet split that turned public after July 1963, when the Soviet Union signed the Limited Test Ban Treaty with Britain and the United States, which China viewed as a betrayal. Between 1963 and 1964, *People's Daily* published nine polemics spelling out the major differences between the two Communist parties. In the ninth and most important polemic against the Communist Party of the Soviet Union, published on July 14, 1964, *People's Daily* and *Red Flag* ran a joint editorial by their editorial departments entitled "On Khrushchev's Phony Communism and Historical Lessons for the World." There was a line, "In order to guarantee that our party and the country would not change their color, we need not only the right guideline and policy, but also the training of thousands of successors for our revolutionary cause." According to Wu Lengxi, who headed both Xinhua and *People's Daily* from 1957 to 1966, Liu Shaoqi and Zhou Enlai did not attend the sessions that Mao presided over in drafting the ninth polemic. At the end of these sessions, Mao particularly talked about the American hope for the peaceful transformation of Chinese leaders of the third and fourth generations and emphasized the importance of preventing revisionism of Khrushchev's kind from happening in China.[30] Roderick MacFarquhar and Michael Schoenhals argue that the ninth polemic contained the essence of what would become the Cultural Revolution.[31] Mao's behavior and the editorials in *Red Flag* reveal his concern over whether his successors would carry on the revolution in the ways he wanted.

The Chinese media's response to the Hilsman speech provides another perspective from which to view the differences between moderates and radicals in the Chinese leadership in 1963 and 1964. As Mao's designated successor, Liu Shaoqi probably wouldn't want to make a big deal about the

American hope for changes in future Chinese leaders because it would not serve him politically. In reality, Liu might have scarcely any disagreement with Mao over China's foreign relations. Nevertheless, he did not want to be viewed as someone deviating from Mao's hopes. On the other hand, Mao's worry about peaceful transformation in the hands of his successors was real. Using the American hope as well as the Soviet precedent in which Khrushchev attacked Stalin in the "Secret Speech" in 1956, Mao could warn the future leaders of China and restrain them. This case also shows that U.S. officials' open statement about their preferences in Chinese politics might have the opposite effect to the one intended. Their expressed hope in leaders at the second echelon probably alerted radicals in the Chinese leadership and unwittingly undermined the position of the moderates.

The French Recognition of China

If the Hilsman speech was the result of initiatives from inside the United States, the recognition of China by the French government in early 1964 constituted a challenge to the Johnson administration from the outside. Rumors of a Sino-French understanding had been afoot since June 1963, when both countries rejected the Limited Test Ban Treaty.[32] Both countries were close to testing their nuclear devices. After that, the U.S. media reported frequent diplomatic and economic exchanges between China and France from October to December 1963. Among them were visits to Beijing by prominent French businessmen and high-level officials such as Senator Edgar Faure, a former premier close to President Charles de Gaulle.[33]

As a man of vision, de Gaulle was convinced that sooner or later China, with its reserves of manpower and resources, would become a major power.[34] He thought it was wise to deal with the nation before being forced to do so when it grew. De Gaulle may have been the first Western statesman to appreciate the importance of the Sino-Soviet split, and he decided to take advantage of it. His analysis of the grand strategy is one of the reasons why Richard Nixon admired him so much.[35]

Paris and Beijing made the official announcement of mutual recognition on January 27, 1964. The French government informed U.S. Ambassador Charles Bohlen of its decision with twenty days' notice.[36] The

recognition of Beijing by a major Western ally just one week after Johnson's inauguration was an embarrassment to the United States. Before the
official announcement came, the White House chose to leak the information to the media. On January 18, the *Times* and *Post* broke the news
on their front pages, based on "authoritative" and "informative" sources,
respectively.[37] Leaking the news to the media could reduce the shock to the
American public.

When Johnson was asked to comment on the French recognition of
China in a press conference on January 25, he simply said, "We gave them
our views and the general effect it would have on the alliance and on the
free world, and it is a matter for them to decide." In responding to the Sino-
French joint announcement two days later, the State Department called the
French move "an unfortunate step when the Chinese Communists were
actively promoting aggression and subversion in Southeast Asia and else-
where."[38] The U.S. government kept a low profile, probably out of frustration that its repeated attempts to stop the French move had failed. Moreover, making a big deal of the issue might trigger more discussions on U.S.
policy toward China, which might embarrass the White House in return.

In private, Johnson was much more sincere. In a phone conversation
with his "mentor" Senator Richard Russell (D-GA) on January 15,[39] Johnson said he would send a low-key protest for the record. When Russell said,
"The time's going to come when we're going to have to recognize them,"
Johnson admitted, "Yeah, I think so—don't think there's any question
about it." Russell pointed out that it was "poison" politically at the time.[40]
Russell was right. In a Gallup Poll in February 1964, 71 percent of the respondents opposed the admission of China into the United Nations (UN).
In another poll in April, when people were asked which country would
be a greater threat to world peace, Russia or China, 27 percent picked
Russia and 56 percent picked China.[41] As a cautious politician, Johnson
was unwilling to make moves that might endanger his own position.

While the official U.S. attitude toward the French recognition of China
can be described as unhappy if acquiescent, the U.S. media showed more
passion over the issue. The *Times* front-page article described the French
move as a "personal policy of General de Gaulle" and a "defiant challenge"
to the United States and asserted that Washington was "informed," not
"consulted." It argued that the "reaffirmation" of France's role as a "great

independent world power" was the motive behind the move. C. L. Sulzberger, the foreign affairs correspondent of the *Times* and part of the family that owned the newspaper, in his column "Foreign Affairs," claimed that de Gaulle "jabbed" the United States at a time of "maximum inconvenience." In his column "Washington," James Reston, the associate editor of the *Times,* maintained that the "weakness and the greatness" of Charles de Gaulle was that "he is so sure that he is right." He called the general a man who was "least sensitive to the personal feelings of other men."[42] The *Post* editorial argued that de Gaulle's reputation made people suspect that he approached China not for any legitimate goal or because of any serious calculation but merely to "play out his private dream for France and to irk the United States en route."[43]

Unlike newspapers, magazines used more dramatic language and cartoons in order to attract readers' attention. *Time* claimed that de Gaulle had "detonated a political bomb that scattered fallout from the Formosa Strait to Washington's Foggy Bottom." In its summary of the world response, the newsweekly paid more attention to negative ones from West Germany, some African countries, and especially the Chinese Nationalists, who referred to the situation as a "state of war," predicting that a "showdown was not far off." Its political cartoons pictured de Gaulle as "a buzzing gadfly, a silly rake wooing an Oriental tart, a kook cutting loose a dangerous dragon."[44] In contrast to the general hostility of *Time,* the response of *Newsweek* was milder. It described the French decision as being as "troublesome" as America's enemies. Its political cartoon featured an arrogant de Gaulle riding a horse side by side with a silly-looking Mao on a small donkey, with a subtitle "Don Charles and Sancho Mao: Who Is Leading Whom?"[45] It was more of a mockery of de Gaulle's decision than outright repudiation of it.

The elite U.S. media did not just blame de Gaulle for embarrassing the United States; they also put Johnson's policy of deliberately ignoring the existence of China under scrutiny. In another *Newsweek* cartoon, for example, de Gaulle bends over to poke at the body of a fat Mao while an angry Johnson in cowboy dress stands far away yelling, ". . . I say he doesn't exist." The article underneath the cartoon argued, "Though officials in the U.S. pretend Communist China doesn't exist, it has long been recognized that eventual admission of Peking into the world community was inevitable."[46] Similar to *Newsweek,* an editorial in the *Times* also argued that American policy toward China was "equally in need of reappraisal" since forty-nine countries had recognized the Communist regime. It maintained that UN membership might be a "restraining influence" and that a negotiation including China might help solve the problem in South Vietnam.[47]

In his Pulitzer Prize–winning column "Today and Tomorrow" in the *Post,* Walter Lippmann tried to find the silver lining in the Sino-French mutual recognition, arguing that the United States would benefit from the French move in the long run because it would sustain the Sino-Soviet quarrel and test the "taming effects of diplomacy and commerce" on China. As he claimed, the French recognition was a good thing because it "opens the door, or at least unlocks the door," to acceptance that the government of Beijing was in fact the government of China. He shrewdly pointed out that even though the U.S. government would go through the "formality" of protesting the French move, Americans should be grateful because "it takes the situation off the dead center."[48]

The story of French recognition remained in the spotlight for a much longer period than Hilsman's speech. An important reason was the media's obsession with the prospect of China's UN membership caused by the French move, which the Johnson administration was unwilling to talk too much about. The United States hoped that Taiwan would not be too hasty to cut off relations with France so that it would reduce the accomplishment of the Chinese government. On the day when the French government informed the United States of its decision to recognize China, McGeorge Bundy suggested to Johnson that if Taiwan did not break relations with France, it would "put the monkey right back on Peking's back."[49]

The U.S. media wanted to see how the idea of "two Chinas" would play out because it would open a door to solve the problem of China's membership in the UN without sacrificing Taiwan. Noting that Beijing did not ask Paris to break off relations with Taiwan as a precondition for recognition, the *Times* called it a "Communist concession," which it regarded as the reason why France moved so rapidly. Similarly, the *Post* called attention to the fact that the French government used the word "establishing" instead of "re-establishing" relations in the communiqué. It interpreted this nuance as a sign that Paris was leaving the possibility open that Taiwan could retain ties with it. Its news analysis argued that the French recognition might lead to similar moves by other nations, as the "tactical concession" of Beijing could enable it to pick up more recognitions and get closer to UN membership.[50]

The U.S. journalists' hope for "two Chinas" turned out to be wishful thinking. In an editorial celebrating the establishment of diplomatic relations between China and France, *People's Daily* especially attacked the U.S. media's speculation that China had become "soft" on the "two-China" policy and reiterated Beijing's determination to "liberate Taiwan."[51] On February 10, 1964, when the French Foreign Ministry announced that its government no longer regarded the Nationalists as representing China in Paris, Taiwan announced its break of relations with France. Taipei's initiative to break relations not only solved the problem for de Gaulle but also dashed the hope of those who supported "two Chinas."

France was the first major Western power that extended full diplomatic recognition to China since the Korean War. It was the second Western ally, after Britain, to break away from U.S. goal of isolating the People's Republic since its establishment in 1949.[52] Though the media under study generally did not like de Gaulle's personality and the way he embarrassed President Johnson, they voiced criticism of the administration's rigid policy of isolating or simply ignoring China. Their voices constituted a pressure on the Johnson administration to move toward a less rigid policy on China.

Chinese Nuclear Test

On October 16, 1964, one day after Soviet premier Nikita Khrushchev's fall from power, China successfully exploded its first nuclear bomb. The entrance of China into the nuclear club raised the specter of nuclear proliferation. How to involve a government with no diplomatic ties with the United States in talks of nuclear nonproliferation constituted another challenge to the Johnson administration.

The official U.S. reaction was to discount the military significance of the Chinese explosion and to reassure the American public that Washington was prepared for it. In a television address, President Johnson said that China still needed many years to build a stockpile of reliable weapons with effective delivery means and that the "free world nuclear strength will continue to be greater." He also stated that the bomb was a "tragedy" for the

Chinese people because the government used its scarce resources, which might be better used to improve their lives, to build a "crude nuclear device" that would only "increase the sense of insecurity of the Chinese people."[53] Secretary of Defense Robert McNamara said at a news conference that the "long-anticipated" explosion of a "primitive nuclear device" in China did not require any change in U.S. strategic plans.[54] In its official declaration, Beijing labeled the test-ban treaty a "fraud" intended to keep the three powers' "nuclear monopoly" and proposed a world summit conference to discuss the "total banning" and "complete destruction" of nuclear weapons.[55] The State Department called Beijing's statement a "sucker proposal" that was "neither serious nor constructive." Dean Rusk simply dismissed it as a "propaganda smokescreen."[56]

While it was easy for the White House to dismiss the *military* impact of the Chinese bomb, it was hard to deal with the *political* fallout, particularly when it was dramatized by the media. The U.S. media showed two major concerns in evaluating the significance of the Chinese bomb: the threat caused by the Chinese bomb and the pressure to include China in the international community due to the danger of nuclear proliferation. In its editorial response, the *Times* argued that the successful nuclear test by an "industrially underdeveloped" country like China raised the specter of nuclear proliferation because other countries might follow suit quickly. It urged older nuclear powers, including the United States, to talk directly with China in order to stop the spread of nuclear weapons.[57] The *Post,* in contrast, advocated a tougher policy. Claiming that China's bomb would enhance the power image that it was "desperately trying to project in Southeast Asia, at Moscow and around the world," it called on Washington to display its "resolve to uphold American responsibilities in Asia."[58] *Newsweek* published a cartoon with a dragon looking at itself in the mirror with a new tooth, the nuclear device.[59] *Time* called the Chinese nuclear test a "fateful firecracker," which Mao had genuine reason to consider a "triumph." It argued that the United States and Russia "share one dilemma"— that they would have to "do something about the China problem" sooner or later.[60] While showing concern about the Chinese nuclear capability, the comments of *Time* also suggested a closer relationship between the United States and the Soviet Union vis-à-vis China after the Sino-Soviet split became public in 1963.

As the prevention of nuclear proliferation required the participation of all countries with nuclear capabilities, how to include China became an issue for the United States because it was the only nuclear power that had no diplomatic relations with China. On October 17, Senator John Pastore (D-RI), chairman of the Joint Congressional Atomic Energy Committee, was reported as saying that the Chinese nuclear test "means the necessity of including Red China in any and every inspection condition attached to any nuclear agreement America might take."[61] On October 18, Johnson again went on TV to comment on the recent ouster of Khrushchev and the U.S. position on the Chinese nuclear bomb. Among the basics of U.S. policy, he stated that China should join the nonproliferation agreement in the framework of the Limited Test Ban Treaty, and he reiterated the U.S. commitment to support any country against "nuclear blackmail."[62] In covering Johnson's speech, the *Times* headline was "President Terms Strength of U.S. the Key to Peace," and the *Post* headline was "Johnson Warns Peking on Nuclear Blackmail,"[63] again demonstrating its support for a tough policy toward China.

The Johnson administration was further put in a "defensive propaganda position" on October 23 when the *Times* and the *Post* reported on their front pages UN Secretary General U Thant's proposal that the five nuclear powers, including China, meet in 1965 to discuss a ban on nuclear tests and measures to prevent nuclear proliferation. One day earlier, the Cambodian representative had submitted a proposal to the UN to include China in the United Nations and had gotten the endorsement of many other nonaligned Asian and African nations. They maintained that no general disarmament was possible until China became a UN member. The *Times* also reported on its front page that Patrick Gordon Walker, the British foreign minister of the newly elected Labor Party administration, declared after a meeting with U Thant that his government supported Thant's proposal and that Britain would vote to seat China in the United Nations at the 1964 session of the General Assembly.[64]

Washington did not respond enthusiastically to the proposal of the UN secretary general. State Department officials said that new international talks were unnecessary because there were already many channels through which Beijing could communicate with the other four nuclear powers, including the United States. As to the disarmament talks in Geneva, the spokesman conceded that "at some stage" China would participate in arms-control agreements.[65] With regard to China's UN membership, a State Department official complained that the international community was using a double standard in dealing with the United States and China: "If the U.S. had made an atomic test in the air, there would have been cries to expel us from the U.N. The Chinese explode one and people want to bring them in. These are the dividends of being a bastard."[66]

During the same period, the United States was also conducting nuclear tests, but under the ground. So was the Soviet Union. On the very day of the Chinese test, the United States conducted one in Nevada, and another, more powerful, bomb was exploded in Mississippi on October 22. On October 25, the United States detected a Soviet underground test.[67] A couple days earlier, when Secretary U Thant claimed that the Chinese test conflicted with the General Assembly resolution adopted in 1962, he condemned all nuclear tests, including underground ones.[68] The tricky thing was that the UN resolution "condemned" all nuclear tests but did not prohibit them. The actual wording was "the effective control of underground tests."[69] The nuclear tests of the United States and the Soviet Union made the issue of the Chinese bomb more complex. When these stories came out, the two superpowers did not seem to enjoy much of a moral high ground over China.

Washington's rigid position on nuclear nonproliferation and its response to U Thant caused criticism of the elite U.S. media. An editorial of the *Times* cited McNamara's warning that there would be ten or twenty atomic powers in a decade or two if no action were taken. Urging Washington that "the moment is now," it also argued that a five-power agreement on nuclear nonproliferation might mark a first step in bringing China out of its isolation.[70] The *Post* also advocated giving Thant's proposal "the widest and broadest consideration" because a flexible U.S. policy would keep the world's attention focused on China. It also criticized the U.S. nuclear tests as "ill-timed" because they had taken the mind of the world off the Chinese blast. Similar to the *Times*, it urged the Johnson administration that "the months and years immediately ahead" might be the "very last chance" to prevent nuclear proliferation and tests.[71] Different from the *Times*' attention to the end of China's isolation, the *Post* was more concerned with defending American interests.

After the Chinese nuclear test, the urgency of preventing nuclear spread seems to suggest that the inclusion of China in the international community was no longer an option but a necessity. In the *Bulletin of the Atomic Scientists* in February 1965, Arthur S. Lall acknowledged that China's bomb would make it much more difficult to keep China out of the United Nations.[72] Taking advantage of the calls from the science community at home and the pressure from abroad, China experts in the Johnson administration pushed harder for a revision of the policy toward China. As one of the most ardent promoters of policy change, James Thomson recommended to William Bundy, the successor of Hilsman, that the U.S. government should demonstrate its willingness to participate in negotiations of nuclear arms control that included China, arguing that the world position of China would change rapidly and that it would "very probably" be voted into the UN in 1965 regardless of U.S. policy. He also proposed approaches different from containment and moral preachment, for example, using goods, people, and ideas whose corrosive value had been proven in dealing with other totalitarian regimes.[73] Harlan Cleveland, the assistant secretary of state for International Organizational Affairs, also pointed out in his letter to Dean Rusk that even though the opposition to China's behavior was not eroding, the traditional tactics of the U.S. government were "eating away its very foundations," particularly when major allies like Britain and France and most other significant allies would not help the United States maintain it.[74] Robert Komer wrote to William Bundy that China's nuclear test underlined that it was here to stay and that it also served as a reason why the United States should enter into a dialogue with Beijing on the issue of arms control.[75]

If the recognition by a major Western power in early 1964 greatly elevated China's international position, its entry into the nuclear club in October constituted another reason that it could not be simply ignored. Even though White House officials tried to minimize the military and strategic impacts of the Chinese nuclear test, the elite media's coverage dramatized its political effects. On one hand, their prominent coverage built up the image of the China threat. On the other, by elaborating on the urgency of preventing nuclear spread, they prioritized the voices at home and abroad that supported engaging China in international talks. These voices would again exert pressure on the rigid policy of the Johnson administration.

U.S. Escalation in Vietnam

The escalated U.S. involvement in the Vietnam War in 1964 provided another opportunity to review the U.S. policy toward China because of the latter's close relations with North Vietnam. After the Gulf of Tonkin Incidents on August 2 and 4, when the USS *Maddox* was allegedly attacked by North Vietnamese torpedo boats in the Gulf of Tonkin, President Johnson authorized retaliatory bombing of patrol-boat bases and a supporting oil complex in North Vietnam. On August 7, Congress passed the Gulf of Tonkin Resolution, granting the president vast power in using American military forces to "head off aggression." From August 8, 1964, to Johnson's inauguration on January 27, 1965, the military and political situations in South Vietnam deteriorated rapidly and the United States had to decide between direct military involvement and the loss of South Vietnam. In February 1965, Johnson initiated the massive bombing campaign Operation Rolling Thunder and sent the first detachment of ground-combat troops—two battalions of marines—to Da Nang. By July 28, 1965, U.S. troops in the theater had risen to 175,000.[76]

The dramatic increase of the U.S. military presence in Vietnam alarmed Chinese leaders. It also changed China's posture toward the United States in its official media. In the first half of 1964, Zhou Enlai and Chinese foreign minister Chen Yi on several occasions had expressed Beijing's willingness to reduce tension with the United States and blamed Washington for refusing to sign two agreements with China: the "peaceful coexistence based on five principles" and the U.S. promise to withdraw all its forces from Taiwan and the Taiwan Strait.[77] Also during this period, *People's Daily* ran several nonpoliticized informational pieces about the United States, describing, for example, the structure of the Department of State, and the national conventions of the Democratic and Republican Parties, in a special column called "World Knowledge."[78] In a July 1 editorial commenting on a statement by the Chinese Foreign Ministry warning the United States against the infringement of its territorial water and airspace, *People's Daily* was still talking about "peaceful coexistence" with the United States.[79] That was the last time the official organ applied the term to the United States. After the Gulf of Tonkin Incidents, this phrase completely disappeared from the discourse of *People's Daily* in reference to the

United States. It would not reemerge until the end of 1968, when Beijing proposed to renew the Warsaw Talks.

Beijing showed its support for Hanoi first through its propaganda machine. An article in *People's Daily* on August 6 threatened that the "invasion of the DRV [Democratic Republic of Vietnam] is an invasion of China" and that "the Chinese people will not sit still [for it]." After U.S. Congress passed the Gulf of Tonkin Resolution, the Chinese government reportedly mobilized twenty million people in mass demonstrations. In covering the demonstrations, *People's Daily* particularly highlighted how the People's Liberation Army (PLA) was prepared "to defend China." What was noticeable in the editorial was that it sent a message to those who wanted better relations with the United States: "The malicious aggression of the United States in Vietnam again reminded the Chinese people that they should not cherish any illusion about the imperialists."[80] The Party organ was using the anti-U.S. protests to warn those who wanted better relations with the United States. It is safe to conclude that the U.S. escalation in Vietnam contributed to the radicalization of Chinese foreign policy. Now it became morally impossible for Beijing to pursue "peaceful coexistence" with a country that it perceived to be committing aggression against a southern neighbor and threatening its own border.

When U.S. ground-combat troops were deployed in South Vietnam, on March 25, 1965, *People's Daily* published on its front-page a statement of the National Liberation Front (NLF) and followed it with an editorial pledging that the Chinese people would employ all their means to provide "necessary material support, including weapons and all war materials, to the heroic people in South Vietnam."[81] This editorial shows an increase in the seriousness of Beijing's warnings and especially its commitment to support the Vietnamese with concrete measures.

Besides the propaganda campaign, Beijing also took military steps to deter the United States from expanding the war to the Chinese border. When Mao learned of the Gulf of Tonkin Incidents, he changed his itinerary of visiting the Yellow River valley. His written instruction on the official statement protesting against the U.S. bombing of North Vietnam read: "There is going to be war. I have to reconsider my (travel) plan."[82] The perception of the threat from the United States also triggered Mao to modify the third five-year plan and initiate the project to move the heavy industry from the coastal areas to the hinterland in the Southwest.[83] On August 13, Mao told visiting North Vietnamese leaders that China had deployed several air force and anti-aircraft artillery divisions to provinces bordering Vietnam and was planning to construct new airfields in this area. Mao specifically said, "We will not make this a secret but will make this open."[84] In April 1965, Mao rescinded the "Six-Point Directive" in January that instructed the Chinese military not to attack U.S. aircrafts that entered Chinese airspace, and ordered them to "resolutely strike American aircrafts that overfly Hainan Island." On April 14, the CCP Central Committee distributed the document throughout the Party structure above the county level, alerting the cadres to the grave danger posed by the American escalation of the war in Vietnam and stressing the urgency of war preparations.[85]

Beyond open statements and military mobilization, the Chinese government also sent serious warnings to the United States through private channels. During his visit to Karachi in April 1965, Zhou Enlai asked Pakistani president Mohammad Ayub Khan to convey three points to Washington: "1. China would not take the initiative to provoke a war against the United States; 2. China meant what it said. 3. China was prepared."[86] In messages through Indonesia's first prime minister Subandrio and the British chargé d'affaires Donald Charles Hopson in May, Zhou added the fourth point: "If the United States bombs China, that would mean bringing the war to China and there would be no boundary to the war."[87] The gist of the "four points" is that China did not want to directly fight the United States unless it were invaded.

Mao expressed his idea about no confrontation with the United States clearly in his interview with the leftist American journalist Edgar Snow on January 9, 1965. When Snow said that there would not be war between China and the United States, Mao agreed and said that China would fight the United States only when it invaded China. Mao was probably expecting the journalist to take the message to Johnson because Snow told him that he would meet with the American president after his return home. Mao also told Snow: "Wherever there is revolution, we issue a statement and hold rallies to show support. . . . We like to fire empty cannons, but we don't send troops."[88] Mao's words show that Beijing was belligerent in words but cautious in actions. The Chinese government was more interested in exploiting the propaganda value of the U.S. "aggression" in Indo-china than engaging the imperialists in the field. Stories in *People's Daily* were meant to showcase China's anti-imperialistic stance to the third-world countries.

On the American side, Johnson made a speech at Johns Hopkins University on April 7, 1965, in which he explained the reasons for sending troops to Vietnam and pledged to keep the conflict from spreading. He also offered "unconditional discussions" and "billion-dollar American investment" in Vietnam after peaceful settlement was under way.[89] Johnson's speech was well received in the U.S. media. The *Times* editorial praised him for opening a "hopeful phase" of the conflict and winning a "moral battle" over China and the Soviet Union that, as it pointed out, either rejected or omitted Johnson's peace proposal in their propaganda machines.[90] The *Post* editorial was much more hawkish. It warned Chinese and Vietnamese Communists to take "sword and olive branch" in the speech very seriously because the American military power had shown just the "thinnest edge," and "there was more where the power came from."[91]

The editorial page of the *Post* strongly supported Johnson's Vietnam policy, which can be seen in articles such as "Why We Are in Viet-Nam . . . in Defense of Self-Determination" and one that went as far as "Viet-Nam Policy: Critics Unwanted."[92] Phil Graham, the publisher of the *Post*, had been deeply involved in politics and had become a close friend of Kennedy and Johnson.[93] With his contempt for the separation between news reporting and editorials, Graham made his newspaper a supporter of Johnson. Ben Bradlee, who had worked for *Newsweek* in the 1950s and the *Post* in the 1960s, claimed that Graham's meddling in *Newsweek*'s Washington bureau after he purchased it in 1961 was "beyond endurance."[94] For the *Post*'s editor position, Graham hired Russell Wiggins, whom Johnson deeply appreciated when he said that the newspaper's editorials were worth "two divisions" to him. Many reporters and their wives thought the paper's editorial support for the war was "morally wrong." When Bradlee returned to the *Post* as the managing editor in 1965, its editorial page became less conservative as he hired several first-rate journalists including David Broder of the *New York Times;* Don Oberdorfer, a foreign affairs expert; and Stanley Karnow, who would become the *Post*'s chief China watcher and the head of its Hong Kong Bureau. The change was complete in 1968 when

Bradlee became the executive editor replacing Wiggins, who had been rewarded with the position of U.S. ambassador to the UN by Johnson.[95]

In order to defend the U.S. policy in Vietnam, administration officials constantly evoked the specter of "China threat." In his Johns Hopkins speech, for example, Johnson referred to the conflict in Vietnam as "the new face of an old enemy . . . the deepening shadow of Communist China," which he described as "helping the forces of violence all over the world."[96] One of the most frequently cited examples of evidence of this "threat" was Chinese minister of defense Marshall Lin Biao's article entitled "Long Live the Victory of People's War," which appeared in *People's Daily* on September 3, 1965. The actual speech was given in August to commemorate the twentieth anniversary of defeating Japan in World War II. The article condemned the Soviet leaders as "betrayers" of the people's war and expressed particular pride in being described as "too militaristic." Lin also claimed that Mao's theory of the "countryside surrounding the cities" could be applied to world revolution because North America and western Europe were the "cities" and the developing countries in Asia, Africa, and Latin America were the "countryside."[97] It was essentially Lin's compliment to Mao's thought on world revolutions, also known as the national liberation movements, and a display of China's commitment to support them.

The *Times* gave high prominence to Lin's speech. In a single issue, it not only covered the story on the front page but also followed it with excerpts of the article. It also ran an editorial that called the speech Mao's "nightmare blueprint for the world's future."[98] The *Post* showed less interest than the *Times* in Lin's speech, wrapping it in a page-four story about PLA chief of staff Luo Ruiqing's speech. Commentaries by Walter Lippmann in his *Post* column were more interesting. Even though he compared the certainty of Lin's revolutionary propaganda to the way Hitler announced that his Reich "would last for a thousand years," he did find nuances in an emphasis on "self-reliance," which he interpreted as a sign that Beijing wanted the war in Vietnam to continue but was unwilling to intervene.[99]

Different from Lippmann, who was able to discern the "soft" messages in Lin's speech, administration officials eagerly picked up its militant side to play up the "China threat." In his speech to block China's UN membership, Ambassador Arthur Goldberg referred to it as China's attempt to "change world order by violence." Dean Rusk, Robert McNamara, and his deputy Cyrus Vance all compared Lin's article to Hitler's *Mein Kampf* and used it as evidence of Chinese expansionism.[100] McNamara explicitly said that the speech signified a program of "aggression" and that the United States should "take the Chinese Communists at their word and develop improved means of coping with their threat."[101] People may wonder whether McNamara was sincere in his claim about the nature of the China threat because, as the secretary of defense, he was well aware of the Chinese capability of projecting its power beyond its border. McNamara, along with many Johnson aides, seemed to be deliberately calling attention to what Beijing *said* rather than what it *did*. Lin Biao's speech, and the *Mein Kampf* remarks by administration officials, when covered in the elite media, served to dramatize the threat of China. In 1965, when the American public's support for the Vietnam War was still high, Beijing's public statements became useful tools for American politicians to justify their policies in Indochina.

Between 1963 and 1965, the U.S. media's call for China policy reform did not turn into "widespread clamoring for change" because it had not been elevated to a pressing issue on the American political agenda. There were strong antireform elements in the Johnson administration. Since his assumption of office in late 1963, Johnson depended heavily on Dean Rusk, McGeorge Bundy, and Robert McNamara on foreign policies. These three advisers, particularly Rusk, were opposed to any modification of the U.S. China policy. Rusk wondered at one time why "the question of Peking's admission to the United Nations had been renewed without adequate reproaches being made over their polices in South East Asia."[102] Moreover, Johnson faced severe restraints from Congress as well as public opinion. On April 19, 1965, the Committee of One Million made a declaration opposing any concessions to China, such as the recognition of it, the admission of it into the UN, or having trade relations with it. The declaration received the endorsement of 321 congressmen—51 senators and 270 members of the House.[103] That was more than half of Congress. What contributed to the negative attitude toward China included its bellicose rhetoric, its support for the Viet Cong, and the threat caused by its possession of nuclear bombs. During this period, the number of Americans opposed to the recognition of China and its entry into the UN in public surveys consistently exceeded half of the total. As a cautious politician, Johnson decided to "stay the course" in his China policy.[104] Up to that point, the media had not been able to make a dent in the rigid China policy of the Johnson administration.

Fulbright Hearings

Since Johnson's escalation in Vietnam, J. William Fulbright (D-AK), chairman of the Senate Foreign Relations Committee, was one of the most vocal critics of his Vietnam policy. On January 26, 1966, Fulbright's committee began a routine hearing on a supplemental aid bill for South Vietnam. He shrewdly transformed the sessions into an inquiry into U.S. policy on Southeast Asia. When General Maxwell Taylor and Dean Rusk engaged in a hot debate with General James M. Gavin, a parachute hero during World War II, and George F. Kennan, the father of the "containment" policy, over the war strategy in Vietnam, the media's attention was attracted, in particular the television networks, which began to cover the sessions live. Johnson became so worried that he hastily held a conference with American military commanders and leaders of South Vietnam in Honolulu to divert the media's attention from the hearings. But it did not work very well. Between late January and March, the hearings remained in the headlines.[105]

In his criticism of Johnson's Vietnam policy, Fulbright repeatedly evoked the danger of a war with China if the conflicts escalated. Contending that reconciliation with China was necessary if the United States wanted to find a solution in Vietnam, he proposed at the hearings that Washington should reach "a general neutralization agreement for Southeast Asia" with Beijing.[106] Beginning in March, he called a review of America's China policy for "education" reasons, asking China experts, including A. Doak Barnett from Columbia, John King Fairbank from Harvard and several others, to testify.

A few months earlier on December 10, 1965, more than one thousand students and several hundred faculty members of Yale had published a full-page advertisement in the *Times* calling for a "nationwide reappraisal" of American policy in the Far East. This advertisement was sponsored by a group called Americans for Reappraisal of Far Eastern Policy, which was started by Yale students. According to the *Times,* the organization sponsored seminars on more than twenty campuses throughout the country on

October 24 to discuss U.S. policy in Asia. An active participant in those meetings, Fairbank also signed the advertisement. The effort by the group probably could not attract much attention because the news article was placed on page twenty-one and the advertisement on page fifty-three.

The media's attention to the Fulbright Hearings provided the academics with a much better platform to present their views. At the hearings, Barnett put forward his famous idea of "containment without isolation," which meant the United States should continue to contain the expansion of China but should adopt measures to end its isolation from the world community. Fairbank criticized U.S. officials who compared Lin Biao's speech to a blueprint of world conquest or a "*Mein Kampf*" type of outline, arguing that the statement was simply "a reassertion of faith" that the "parochial example of rural-based revolution" in China was a model for underdeveloped countries.[107] As *Newsweek* reported, Senators Fulbright and Wayne Morse (D-OR) tried to push Barnett and Fairbank to support their challenge to Johnson's Vietnam policy at the hearings, but they both refused. Even though they were concerned about a clash with China, the two professors supported Johnson's Vietnam policy and the containment of China.[108] In the media the two professors appeared as moderate advice givers, which was in sharp contrast to radical leftists in the streets. Their expertise and moderation made it reasonably easier for the public and those in Washington to consider their views.

Overall, the elite media in the United States covered the Fulbright Hearings prominently, completely, and favorably.[109] Fulbright and the China experts were given prominence when they made the front pages six times in the *Times* and five times in the *Post* in March.[110] Among those who were opposed to the "containment without isolation" policy, George Taylor and David Nelson Rowe, professors from University of Washington and Yale University, and Walter Judd, former Republican representative from Minnesota and a prominent figure in the China Lobby, were called to testify when the hearings were close to the end. They made the front pages of the two elite newspapers only once without any editorial comment.[111] The *Times* placed the testimony of former Assistant Secretary of State for Far Eastern Affairs Walter S. Robertson at the House Foreign Affairs Committee in the last three paragraphs of the jump page of an article, probably because he was an advocate of a hard-line policy toward China.[112]

In their editorial pages, both the *Times* and the *Post* gave favorable reviews of the China debate, especially Barnett's "containment without isolation" thesis. The *Post* praised the hearings for "contributing to public understanding" and particularly endorsed the distinction between "containing" and "isolating" China. The most important factor that led "urgency" to Barnett's argument, as it pointed out, was the danger of U.S. defeat in the UN on the issue of China's admission. While acknowledging the difficulty of ending the isolation of China, it argued that American thought had been turned in that direction through the "ventilation" of those ideas.[113]

The *Times* argued that the Fulbright Hearings had validated its long-held view that "the country was far ahead of the Administration" in openness to new approaches. Citing the fact that a statement calling for a more flexible China policy had recently been supported by 198 scholars and opposed by only nineteen members of the Association for Asian Studies, it claimed to have found where the weight of "informed American opinion" was. It criticized Rusk and McNamara for drawing "fallacious parallels" between China and Hitler's Germany because they might close off a "reappraisal of China policy" for many years. Similar to the *Post,* it showed concern for the "urgency" of the UN issue. As it maintained, America's open attitude would not only send positive signals to a new generation of China leaders but also attract more international support for American policy in Asia and reduce the danger of military confrontation with China.[114]

The newsmagazines also acknowledged the value of the hearings on China. Despite its sarcastic title "Reading the Dragon's Mind," an article in *Time* conceded that the hearings were "all right" for their educational purpose. *Newsweek* regarded the China debate as a subject that permitted legislators a "remarkable degree of rational discussion and agreement."[115]

As James Reston argued in his *Times* column, Fulbright's official "teach-in" in front of TV cameras was the "first serious open debate" on the problems of American foreign policy in years, and the live coverage of congressional debates by TV cameras would be a "powerful influence for understanding and change."[116] By the time the hearings ended, 71 percent of Americans polled had heard about them, and almost 60 percent had seen some parts on television. *Newsweek* described them as the "most searching public review of U.S. wartime policy" since the MacArthur hearings of 1951.[117]

Even though the China policy review was secondary to the discussions on Vietnam policy at the hearings, the administration was pleased with it because many critics of America's China policy supported the Vietnam policy. The consensus on a more open policy toward China looked better than did the division over Vietnam. In his appearance on NBC on March 13, Vice President Hubert Humphrey echoed Barnett, saying that the U.S. policy toward China should be one of "containment without necessarily isolation." He mentioned that the administration had decided recently to allow scholars and writers to travel to China, which he described as the "beginning of a much better relationship."[118] Senator Stuart Symington (D-MO), an ardent supporter of the official policy in Vietnam, said, "I do not see anything that I do not agree with." A White House aide also claimed that the president was pleased with the transcripts of the week's hearings.[119]

The China debate at the Fulbright Hearings, as Michael Lumbers argues, marked "something of a watershed" in U.S. policy toward China. It could test the public reaction to a controversial issue for the government. More importantly, the media's prominent and favorable coverage "legitimized" the airing of views that would have been considered "heresy" in the 1950s and "emboldened" those advocates of China policy reform inside and outside the government to push that agenda.[120]

The media's intensive and favorable review of the China debate at the Fulbright Hearings also played an important role in educating the public about America's China policy. In December 1965, a Gallup Poll indicated that 22 percent of the respondents supported China's UN membership and 67 percent were opposed, while 10 percent had no opinion. In March 1966, the numbers changed to 25 percent and 55 percent with 20 percent without opinion. When asked if China's UN membership would improve relations with the United States, the numbers of "yes" and "no" became 56 percent and 28 percent.[121] Similarly, as reported in the *Post*, a Harris survey in June showed that 57 percent of the respondents favored U.S. recognition of China and 55 percent supported Chinese entry into the UN so long as Taiwan was not expelled.[122] The polling results showed a growing openness to a more flexible China policy after the Fulbright Hearings.

The Fulbright Hearings might also have led to the decline of the Committee of One Million. When Marvin Liebman, the committee's secretary, learned of the hearings, he complained that he had not been given advance notice and that those scheduled to testify represented viewpoints "contrary to the Committee and to the majority of Americans, including Congress."[123] In October of that year, the Committee still managed to obtain the endorsement of 325 members of Congress when it published in a *Times* display ad its opposition to China's UN membership. While publishing its ad, the *Times* carried an editorial repudiating the Committee. As it argued, "It is the opinion of this newspaper that a majority of those Americans" concerned with the question "either favor inviting Peking into the United Nations or would at least "have no serious objections."[124] When Senator Jacob K. Javits (R-NY), who had appeared on the front page of the *Times* during the Fulbright Hearings due to his support for ending the isolation of China, announced his decision to withdraw from the Committee, the *Times* placed his story on the front page, arguing that the China hearings constituted a factor for his move. The *Times* also reported a memorandum sent by Liebman to all congressional members declaring that the Committee would not use their names on letterheads and publication. It interpreted the memorandum as a sign that members of Congress had begun to have doubts about the Committee's policy.[125] Stories in the *Times* left the impression that the rigid position of the Committee of One Million was losing support among congressional members. Even though there might be other factors that led to the decline of the Committee, the newspaper gave extra credit to the impact of the Fulbright Hearings.

A Lost Chance in 1966?

By 1966, the U.S. and Chinese governments seemed to have reached a tacit agreement about no direct confrontation with each other in Vietnam. Washington took measures to reassure Beijing that it wanted neither to attack China nor to destroy the Hanoi regime. In a memorandum to George Ball, William Bundy recommended clarifying the U.S. intention to avoid direct confrontation with China at the next Warsaw meeting on December 15, 1965.[126] On May 10, 1966, *People's Daily* published Zhou Enlai's four points to the United States for the first time.[127] Two days later, when the U.S. Air Force reportedly shot down a Chinese aircraft close to the Vietnamese-Chinese border, Beijing's response was quite restrained. Even though the Chinese Ministry of Defense declared that the Chinese people "are not easy to trifle with" and that "blood would be repaid with blood" in its "strong protest," it reiterated Zhou's "four points."[128] Some people might interpret the "four points" as a warning to the U.S. military not to violate the Chinese sovereignty. Others might view them as a sign of Beijing's unwillingness to directly confront the United States in Vietnam. For example, North Vietnamese defense minister General Vo Nguyen Giap later complained that Zhou's four points "stabbed the Vietnamese in the back" because it was a signal to the United States that "it could bomb Vietnam at will, as long as there was no threat to the Chinese border."[129]

More importantly, the U.S. media's overwhelmingly favorable review of the Fulbright Hearings on China in spring 1966 not only signified the depoliticization of the China issue but also greatly encouraged the Johnson administration to move toward a more conciliatory posture with China. On July 12, 1966, Johnson made what White House officials called his "first major statement" on China in his address to the annual conference of the American Alumni Council. Johnson expressed his hope for the "reconciliation between nations that now call themselves enemies" and maintained that lasting peace in Asia could never come "as long as the 700 million people of mainland China are isolated by their rulers from the outside world." He also mentioned the steps his government had taken to permit American scholars and experts in medicine and public health to travel to China, and particularly a case where Washington issued a passport for a leading American businessman to exchange knowledge with the Chinese on the very day of his speech.[130] This was the first time that Johnson explicitly and openly called for reconciliation with China. It was covered prominently and favorably by the *Times* and the *Post*. The editorial of the *Times* argued that it had laid a new basis for the "concrete measures" that would provide a solution to the problems in Asia. The *Post* editorial claimed that the United States should bring down its barriers in order to "diminish the dangerous isolation" of China from the world.[131]

Considering the two governments' tacit agreement on Vietnam and the favorable environments in the United States after the Fulbright Hearings, Xu Guangqiu, in his book about the relationship between Congress and China policy, claims that "a chance to improve Sino-American relationships was lost" in the 1960s. He cites the memoir of Wang Guoquan, the Chinese ambassador to Poland who represented China in the Warsaw

Talks with the United States between July 1964 and March 1967. Wang wrote, "If the Cultural Revolution had not happened in 1966, the Beijing government might have modified its U.S. policy in that year, and U.S.-China normalization might have started in 1966 rather than in 1972." As far as Xu understands, when congressional leaders called for a change in China policy in the 1960s, the White House escalated the Vietnam War. Therefore, Beijing "suspected" the real intentions of the reform-minded legislators and "misunderstood" their suggestions about a flexible China policy.[132]

Xu and Wang are probably too optimistic about the status of Sino-American relations in 1966. Though the U.S. government was assuming a new conciliatory posture toward China, this mainly served to defuse domestic criticisms. It remains a question how far the Johnson administration was willing to go in changing the status quo. For the Chinese government, its gesture to avoid confrontation with the United States in Vietnam might show a desire for peace, but it does not necessarily mean Beijing wanted to improve relations with Washington. In reality, when Washington was moving toward a more flexible gesture to China from 1963 to 1966, Chinese foreign policy was turning increasingly radical. Back in January 1962, Mao was disgraced when he made a self-criticism for causing the great famine of the Great Leap Forward at the seven-thousand cadres meeting. At the same meeting, Wang Jiaxiang, the head of the International Liaison Department of the CCP, proposed a foreign policy that would ease China's tensions with "imperialists" (with the United States as the head), "revisionists" (notably the Soviet Union), and reactionary forces (in Taiwan), and at the same time would reduce China's support for revolutionary movements in the third world. The rationale was that China could focus more energy on fixing its own problems at home.

Wang thus became the first victim of Mao's counteroffensive when he openly criticized Wang's foreign policy as revisionist by labeling it as "san he yi shao" (three moderations on the enemies and one reduction on the friends) at the Tenth Plenary of the Eighth Congress of the CCP in August 1962. At the same time, Mao claimed that parallel to the "three moderations and one reduction" on foreign policy, there was a policy of "three selfs and one contract" at home. What he was referring to were policies adopted by moderates to revive the economy damaged during the Great

Leap Forward: more small, privately farmed plots for peasant households, more free markets with prices determined by the buyers and sellers, more enterprises with profit and loss borne by the management, and farms contracted to households at fixed output quotas. Arguing that the former was the international program and the latter the domestic program of some Party members, Mao attacked both of them as a package of "revisionist line."[133] Essentially, Mao used his attacks on Wang's moderation in foreign policies to curb what he considered the "revisionist" tendency in the economic reconstruction at home. His attacks gave little room for his colleagues to moderate the Chinese foreign policy, which would become even more radicalized with the opening of Sino-Soviet split after the Limited Test Ban Treaty in 1963 and the dramatic increase of U.S. military presence in Vietnam in 1964.

When the Fulbright Hearings were held in 1966, the Chinese government did not misunderstand the messages from the United States. For Beijing, "containment without isolation" was no better than "containment and isolation" because "containment" was still being emphasized as a key U.S. policy and "isolation" by the United States did not bother Chinese leaders at all because it was largely their own choice. In its editorials, *People's Daily* mocked the speakers as "clowns" and the hearings as a "farce of illusion" because the Johnson administration was "at its wit's end" in dealing with China. While attacking Humphrey's "unusual friendliness" to China as "dream talking" and the "kiss of Judas," the official organ particularly pledged that the Chinese people would become more vigilant regarding the "trickery of the American imperialists."[134] As the Chinese foreign policy was turning more radical, "containment without isolation" might be viewed with more suspicion by those who were bent on revolution because of its perceived ability to subvert the Chinese revolution through "peaceful transformation." After all, the "softening of" future Chinese leaders' revolutionary commitment had been one of Mao's major concerns. Therefore, it is not surprising that *People's Daily* still frequently referred to the United States as the "most dangerous" or the "worst enemy" to people all over the world in the first half of 1966.[135]

Chinese attitude toward the American flexibility can also be seen in stories in *Reference News*. In reprinting articles on the Fulbright Hearings on China in March 1966, it featured titles such as "Promoting a China Policy Backed up by Force," "Both Sides in the Debate Agree on the Containment of China," and "Fairbank and Others Support the Containment Policy."[136] These titles generally highlight the American containment of China while playing down or simply ignoring the information about ending the isolation of China.

When Johnson assumed a more flexible gesture toward China, stories in *Reference News* did not give him much acknowledgment either. At a press conference on March 22, 1966, for example, he was asked about Vietnam and his China policy in view of the recent congressional hearings on China. In the full text of the article in *Reference News,* Johnson's gesture was much more conciliatory when he expressed a willingness to engage China more frequently. However, the title of that story was "Johnson Was Bragging about the High Morale of the American Military." A few days earlier, the internal newspaper even ran a story reprinted from Hong Kong's pro-Beijing *Wenhui Daily* that claimed that Johnson was planning to "start an all-out invasive war against China."[137] Moreover, when Johnson made his first major speech on China on July 12, 1966, in contrast to the excitement of the American media, neither *Reference News* nor *People's Daily* covered it. Overall, even though stories in *Reference News* were more "objective" and insightful, they generally emphasized hostility and conflicts between the two countries. As such, the domestic and international environments for both countries were not ready for an improvement in relations in 1966 even without the Cultural Revolution.

Conclusion

As this chapter shows, between 1963 and 1966, many U.S. journalists criticized the Johnson administration's rigid China policy. Though Hilsman's speech in late 1963 was not initiated by high-level policy makers in the Johnson team, it worked as a test balloon. The media's positive review of the administration's new posture toward China signified an ebbing of emotions over the issue and suggested an opening for reasonable talk. In the case of French recognition of China, while the elite media did not like the "timing and manner" of de Gaulle's decision, they also criticized Washington's rigid posture and called for a move toward a "two China" solution before a U.S. defeat in the UN. When China joined the nuclear club, the U.S. media elaborated on the dangers of nuclear proliferation and urged Washington to use creative means that could include China in international agreements on nuclear nonproliferation. In both cases, the elite U.S. media called for China's inclusion in the international community. When the United States expanded its military operations into North Vietnam, congressional critics of Johnson's war policy found themselves allied with academics and the elite media because of their common concern over military confrontation with China. Media discussions on these issues created a platform for public deliberations of America's China policy.

By the end of 1966, more than half of the American people still opposed the recognition of China as well as its admission into the UN, and a majority in Congress endorsed the Committee of One Million's China policy. However, influential U.S. media moved ahead of public opinion and pushed for a flexible China policy by prioritizing the critical voices from the academic community and Congress on their front pages and making their own critiques in editorials. Because of the media's prominent and intensive coverage, critical voices at the Fulbright Hearings were legitimized and accepted more widely in the public sphere, which created a favorable environment for Johnson to ease the rigid policy toward China. Essentially, if the Hilsman speech set off the "depoliticization" of the China issue, the Fulbright Hearings symbolized the culmination of this process.

Unfortunately, while U.S. journalists were calling on Washington to adopt a more flexible China policy between 1963 and 1966, Chinese foreign policy turned increasingly radical. In this context, the rhetoric of the Chinese media toward the United States changed from moderately hostile to radically hostile. Between 1962 and 1965, anti-American propaganda coexisted with the moderate voices of "peaceful coexistence" with the United States in *People's Daily*. After the Gulf of Tonkin Incidents, however, this discourse completely disappeared in the Chinese media. In the mid-1960s, Beijing had no desire to improve relations with Washington whatsoever. It rejected the idea of flexibility as put forth by U.S. academics and officials, attacking it as "hoax" and a tool of peaceful transformation. Even though stories in *Reference News* provided more insights about the flexibility in the American attitude, they did not demonstrate Beijing's interest in improving relations with Washington. When Mao was mobilizing the Chinese people for his "continuous revolution" and the ideological polemics with the Soviet Union, Washington became a convenient "whipping boy" in the Chinese media.[138] Maintaining cold relations with the United States would serve his domestic agenda.

2

"All under Heaven Is Great Chaos," 1966–1968

Between 1966 and 1968, the heyday of the Cultural Revolution coincided with the high point of U.S. involvement in the Vietnam War. Mao frequently described this period as "all under heaven is great chaos" when he talked about China's domestic and international conditions.[1] The Cultural Revolution turned out to be a watershed for Sino-American relations because several conditions that allowed for Nixon's opening to China came into being during this chaotic period.[2] Among these conditions were the reduction of tension between Beijing and Washington, the replacement of the United States by the Soviet Union as China's primary enemy, and Beijing's open rift with Hanoi. This chapter examines how these conditions played out in the media of both countries. It looks at the Chinese media's handling of the United States, the Soviet Union, and the Vietnam War as well as the U.S. media's coverage of the factional struggles in China, Sino-Soviet polemics, and Sino-Vietnamese discord.

Due to the media's favorable coverage of the Fulbright Hearings in the spring of 1966, President Johnson adopted a much more conciliatory tone toward China in his first major policy speech on China in July. In his State of the Union address on January 10, 1967, Johnson again stated that the United States would "continue to hope for a reconciliation between the people of mainland China and the world community" and that the United States would be "the first to welcome a China which decided to respect her neighbors' rights."[3] This time, the *Times* and the *Post* did not pay special attention to his remark about China. James Reston noted Johnson's conciliatory tone in his column a few days later, but he did not assign it too much importance except to argue that it showed Johnson's cautious attitude about the convulsions in China.[4] By that time, Johnson's concilatory tone seemed much less significant to the U.S. media than the extraordinary turmoil in China because of the Great Proletarian Cultural Revolution.

The Great Proletarian Cultural Revolution: The Cultural Aspect

The Chinese history from May 1966 to Mao's death in September 1976 is generally known as the Cultural Revolution. It was the last of Mao's major campaigns to shape the development of China according to his own thoughts. The most radical stage of the movement, however, was between 1966 and 1968, when the Red Guards' activities were at their peak.

When analyzing the causes of the Cultural Revolution, scholars generally focus on Mao's dissatisfaction with State Chairman Liu Shaoqi, who supposedly introduced material stimulus and private lots to fix the damaged economy and on Mao's efforts to regain the power that he perceived as slipping out of his own hands after the Great Leap Forward.[5] Another important reason that Mao started the Cultural Revolution has to do with what he considered capitalist tendencies in the Chinese media. Very few scholars have paid attention to the cultural aspect of Mao's revolution.

Mao's ideas on the media are perhaps best reflected in his "Talks at the Yan'an Forum on Literature and Art," a speech given on May 2, 1942, during the Yan'an Ratification Campaign. In this historic document, Mao argues that literature and art are never neutral and that they should serve the "revolutionary masses," which was a veiled reference to the Chinese Communist Party (CCP), instead of the bourgeois or the class enemies of the people. In order to justify the censorship of dissenting views, Mao particularly attacked individualism and liberalism in literature and art.[6]

Between 1961 and 1964, a group of intellectuals, who were also Party officials in the Beijing Municipal Government, emerged as the critics of the local cadres' working style, which they implied had caused the mass famine during the Great Leap Forward (GLF). This group was organized around Deng Tuo, who was the alternate secretary in CCP's North China Bureau in 1960 and the secretariat of CCP's Beijing Party Committee in charge of Culture and Education when he was relieved from the position as the editor in chief of *People's Daily* in 1958;[7] Wu Han, the deputy mayor of Beijing and a prominent historian of the Ming dynasty; and Liao Mo-sha, head of the United Front Department of the Beijing Party Commit-tee. These intellectuals published satirical essays in a column known as "Yanshan yehua" (Evening chats at Yanshan) in *Beijing Evening News* from March 1961 to September 1962; "Sanjiacun zhaji" (Notes from a three-family village) in the fortnightly magazine *Qianxian* (Frontline) from Oc-tober 1961 to July 1964; and "Chang duan lun" (Long and short commen-taries) in *People's Daily* from May to December 1962. At the same time, Wu Han wrote a play, *Hai Rui Dismissed from Office,* which dealt with the dismissal of an honest official who cared about the sufferings of the people during years of difficulty caused by an irresponsible emperor.[8] The flour-ishing of satirical articles in the Party newspapers of Beijing is a sign that Mao had lost control of them in the early 1960s.

For Mao, criticizing the Great Leap Forward is tantamount to criti-cizing himself. He viewed these satirical essays with hostility. In July 1964, Mao ordered the establishment of a Central Cultural Revolution Group, also called the Five-Man Group, to lead a revolution in the cultural sphere. The group was headed by Peng Zhen, the Party boss of Beijing and the fifth-ranking member of the Politburo of the CCP. The other members in-cluded Lu Dingyi, head of the CCP Propaganda Department; Wu Lengxi, who succeeded Deng Tuo as the editor in chief of *People's Daily;* Zhou Yang, who had established himself as the guardian of literary and cultural orthodoxy; and Kang Sheng, a close associate of Mao since the Yan'an era.[9] The subsequent developments show that Mao was not happy with this group's supervision over the cultural sphere.

In addition to the cultural sphere, Mao also became increasingly un-happy about his successor, State Chairman Liu Shaoqi, particularly after the Socialist Education Movement (SEM) started in 1963, because Liu op-posed Mao's demand to make the Party apparatus the target of the move-ment. In other words, during the SEM, Liu was not very cooperative in answering Mao's call to remove those in the Party in authority who were "taking the capitalist road." As discussed in chapter 1, the conflicts between Liu and Mao during this period happened at the same time when Hilsman was hoping the "second echelon of Chinese leaders" would become more flexible and Mao openly talked about his concerns about the successors of Chinese revolution. The conflicts ultimately led Mao to make his decision in early 1965 to remove Liu, as he told Edgar Snow during his visit to China in 1970.[10]

Being very familiar with the court intrigues in Chinese history, Mao engaged in political maneuvering, using the purge of the cultural sphere as a means to remove Liu Shaoqi. The first target of his maneuvering was Wu Han, a subordinate of Peng Zhen, who was a political associate of Liu. In a top-down system where the power of the lower level derives from the above, the mistake of a lower-level official would imply his direct superior's incapacity to either pick the right person for the job or to prevent the wrongdoings of his subordinates. Therefore, as long as Mao could nail Wu for any activity deemed "counter-revolutionary," which was a very broad term and difficult to define, he would be able to bring down Peng Zhen and then implicate Liu Shaoqi.

Having lost control of the newspapers in Beijing, Mao had to use *Wenhui Daily*, a newspaper in Shanghai, to start his offensive in the cultural sphere. In late 1965, Mao authorized Yao Wenyuan, one of a group of radical Marxist theorists in Shanghai associated with his wife, Jiang Qing, to publish an article in *Wenhui Daily* entitled "Comments on the New Historical Play *Hai Rui Dismissed from Office*," which Mao had revised three times before publication.[11] The article alleged that the play was a "poisonous weed" that attacked the policies of the Great Leap Forward (GLF) and that it was an attempt to rehabilitate "someone," by whom it meant Marshall Peng Dehuai, the commander of Chinese troops during the Korean War who was dismissed from office by Mao in 1959 because of his blunt way of pointing out the problems caused by Mao's radical policies during the GLF. The article shocked Peng Zhen not only because of its strong criticism of his own subordinate but also because of its violation of the Party principle that public criticism of a high official needed the approval of Party organs. Working with Lu Dingyi and other members of the Five-Man Group, Peng successfully blocked the reprinting of Yao's article in any central or Beijing municipal newspapers. It was not until after the personal intervention of Premier Zhou Enlai that the article appeared first in the *PLA Daily*, and then in *People's Daily*.[12]

At a Central Work Conference in late March, Mao harshly criticized Wu Han and Peng Zhen and managed to enlist the support of Zhou Enlai and Deng Xiaoping. The enlarged meeting of the Politburo between

May 4 and 18 was a landmark of the Cultural Revolution when Wu Han, Peng Zhen, Lu Dingyi, and Zhou Yang were purged. In their places Mao installed people loyal to himself and set up a new Central Cultural Revolution Group (CCRG) under the Standing Committee of the Politburo.[13] The meeting came up with a circular on May 16 that would be known as the "May 16 Circular" or "May 16 Notification." Alleging that "bourgeois ideas" did not exist only in the cultural sphere but also among ranking Party and state officials, the document shifted the movement from one principally targeting intellectuals to one aimed at the whole Party bureaucracy.[14] The "May 16 Circular" was categorized as "highly classified" at first and circulated only among high-level CCP officials.[15] It did not go public until a year later, on May 17, 1967, when *People's Daily* and *Red Flag* described it as something that had "sounded the marching bugle" of the Cultural Revolution in their joint editorial celebrating the first anniversary of the movement.[16]

The main tool Mao employed in his attack on the Party establishment and intellectuals was to mobilize popular participation in which the Red Guards would play a dominant role. Between August 19 and November 26, Mao reviewed the Red Guard rallies at Tiananmen Square eight times. The rallies greatly promoted the prestige and publicity of the Red Guards.[17] In response to Mao's urge to "destroy the old order," the Red Guards beat up intellectuals as well as Party officials and destroyed a large number of cultural vestiges. The attacks forced Party establishments to defend themselves by forming their own Red Guard organizations. These organizations fell into factional struggles and developed into armed fighting, bringing China to what Mao later called an "all-round civil war."[18]

Chinese Media during the Cultural Revolution

In the guiding document of the Cultural Revolution, the "Sixteen Points Decision," which was passed at the eleventh plenum of the CCP's Central Committee on August 8, 1966, a statement of Mao's is quoted: "To overthrow a political power, it is always necessary to first of all, create public opinion, to do ideological work. This is true both for the revolutionary classes as well as for the counterrevolutionary classes."[19] Being well aware of the function of the media for the success of the Cultural Revolution,

Mao sent his former secretary Chen Boda, who was also the editor of *Red Flag* and the head of the CCRG, to seize control of *People's Daily* on May 31, 1966, after the purge of his perceived opponents.

During the Cultural Revolution, *People's Daily* played an important role in mobilizing the masses and causing chaos. After Chen Boda's take-over, the newspaper no longer reflected the views of the Central Committee of the CCP, but the ideas of Mao himself. According to Ma Jisen, an employee at the Chinese Foreign Ministry during the Cultural Revolution, when the Cultural Revolution started, Acting Foreign Minister Ji Pengfei told his staff, "Now the newspapers lead the Cultural Revolution movement. *People's Daily* presents the guiding principle." He told them to read it carefully when it came out because it would "give the tenor of the movement." The newspaper, with its provocative language such as "sweeping away all Oxen, Ghosts, Snakes and Demons (OGSD)," "eliminating all class enemies," and many others, had become "a source of turbulence."[20]

Because one of the most important goals of the Cultural Revolution was to struggle against "capitalist roaders" at home, struggling against capitalist countries abroad would conveniently serve the domestic agenda. Naturally, Beijing not only rejected the friendly gesture from the Johnson administration but also escalated its anti-American rhetoric in its official media.

In order to serve its anti-American agenda, Beijing also reduced its contacts with Washington in Warsaw. When the American representative at a Warsaw meeting talked about Washington's offer of trade and travel relaxations, Chinese ambassador to Poland Wang Guoquan turned them down, arguing that it was "absolutely impossible to improve Sino-American relations" if the Taiwan issue was not solved. Wang charged that the United States was trying to "deceive" the Chinese people and "lull their fighting spirit" with proposals for contacts so that it can "impose war on Chinese people at the appropriate time."[21]

From 1966 to 1968, the Chinese side deliberately lengthened the gap between the meetings despite American requests to meet more frequently.[22] While in both 1964 and 1965 they met five times, the number of meetings decreased to three in 1966, two in 1967, and only one in 1968. Moreover, the contact was lowered to the level of second secretary between meetings. On May 18, 1968, the Chinese embassy sent a letter to the U.S. embassy saying that it wanted to postpone the 135th meeting until mid- or late November because "there was nothing to discuss." Though Rusk was worried at one time that China might break or suspend the meetings, U.S. representatives in Warsaw felt that Beijing wanted to retain the channel of communication.[23] The Chinese side was also deliberate in putting off the meetings as agreed upon by both sides. In 1967, *People's Daily* published three stories about the postponement of Sino-American meetings for "institutional" reasons. The 134th meeting, in particular, was put off by two months from November 8, 1967, to January 8, 1968.[24] Through these gestures, the Chinese government wanted to show the world how it downgraded the importance of the meetings and how it slighted Washington.

Beijing's reduction of contacts with Washington also reflected its effort to avoid the political embarrassment of dealing with the Americans in secret when it attacked Moscow for "colluding" with the American "imperialists." Since the beginning of the Cultural Revolution, Beijing's official protests against U.S. military operations in Vietnam were usually accompanied by attacks on the Soviet Union. In response to the U.S. bombing of Hanoi and Haiphong in June 1966, for example, while *People's Daily* labeled the American "imperialists" as the "most dangerous enemy" to people all over the world, it also charged the Soviet Union with acting as the "number-one accomplice of American imperialists." When *People's Daily* charged the Americans with a "war provocation" for bombing Chinese civilian facilities close to the Vietnamese border, it blamed the Soviet Union for "cooperating with and instigating" the Americans in their plot to "spread the war to all of Indochina."[25] Beijing's tactic was to embarrass the Soviet Union as much as possible when it attacked the United States.

According to *People's Daily,* the Soviet official organ *Pravda* in July 1966 insinuated a "Sino-American deal" by publishing American ambassador to Poland John Gronouski's remarks about a Sino-American meeting in an interview. In order to show Beijing's position, *People's Daily* published on its front page the full texts of Wang Guoquan's opening statement and his remark to the media after the meeting. On both occasions he used strong language repudiating both the United States and the Soviet Union.[26] Off the record, Wang complained several times to Gronouski about the leak of the meeting contents by the American side.[27]

In January 1967, both the *Times* and the *Post* featured on their front pages a story by a French editor, who claimed that a Chinese diplomat in

Paris a year earlier had asked the French Foreign Ministry to relay Beijing's message that China would not enter the Vietnam conflict so long as the United States observed three conditions. Taking into account the performance of U.S. military operations in North Vietnam, both newspapers concluded that the two countries had reached an "accord" about no heads-on collision in Vietnam.[28] The story was soon picked by the press of the Soviet Union and India. In response to "rumors" of "understanding" or "tacit agreement" between Beijing and Washington, *People's Daily* attacked the "slandering" of China by the Soviet and Indian press as the "enemies' ploy to sabotage" the close friendship between the Chinese and Vietnamese people.[29] As mentioned in chapter 1, up to May 1966, when the U.S. Air Force downed a Chinese plane, *People's Daily* was still talking about Zhou Enlai's "four points." After that, the "four points" vanished from *People's Daily.* With the beginning of the Cultural Revolution, the Chinese media eliminated any sign that could be interpreted as a "compromise" with the United States.

In order to consolidate Beijing's revolutionary credentials, the Chinese media promoted conflicts between China and the United States. Between 1966 and 1968, *People's Daily* carried stories where Chinese fishermen were killed or the Chinese embassy in Hanoi was hit by U.S. bombs.[30] More importantly, it carried several stories where the Chinese military downed U.S. aircrafts.[31] On August 21, 1967, when the Chinese Air Force shot down two U.S. Navy jets straying into the Chinese air space and captured a pilot named Robert Flynn, *People's Daily* published the photos of Flynn as well as the plane wrecks, arguing that the PLA's punishment of U.S. "aggressors" would inspire the Cultural Revolution at home.[32] In this instance, the Party organ was truthful.

At the Warsaw Talks, when Gronouski proposed a joint investigation of the incidents, Wang rejected it as "unnecessary" and called the proposal an American effort to "cover its crime" and "deceive the people." In one incident where the U.S. military rescued several Chinese fishermen in December 1966 on the basis of their testimonies in Saigon, Wang accused the U.S. side of "maltreating" them and of attempting to "recruit them as spies or defectors to Taiwan."[33] Just as Chinese officials in Warsaw were instructed not to give the United States credit for saving Chinese sailors, *People's Daily* would not help the U.S. government score a possible propaganda victory. Instead, it gave higher priority to the protests of the Chinese Foreign Ministry when U.S. bombing allegedly caused the injuries and deaths of Chinese fishermen.[34] Beijing's rejection of joint investigations suggested that it wanted to avoid dealing with the United States as much as possible. More significantly, whether those incidents actually happened or how they were solved was much less important to the Chinese than their propaganda value showing Sino-American conflicts.

While the front pages of *People's Daily* highlighted the "conflicts" between China and the United States, its interior pages featured many stories highlighting the domestic problems in the United States, such as the antiwar protests, race riots, and inflation. In its short comments on Johnson's State of the Union address in 1967, *People's Daily* cut out his message about China, describing him as being "engrossed in problems at home and abroad."[35] *Reference News,* the internal newspaper with stories more objective and less propagandistic due to its mission to educate midlevel cadres about the outside world, reprinted a story from a Hong Kong newspaper asserting that the American desire to build connections with China had been rejected by the CCP, but its abridged version of Johnson's address retained his friendly message to China. The internal publication wanted Chinese cadres to know about the United States' conciliatory gesture but framed it in a way that suggested that the United States was in a state of decline and that its offer of friendliness simply showed its weakness.[36]

The Cultural Revolution also severely damaged China's relations with other countries and its information about the outside world. Under the pressure of the Red Guards, China recalled all its ambassadors except for Huang Hua in Cairo and most of the senior embassy staff members to take part in the Cultural Revolution. At home, radicals took control of the Foreign Ministry and even put Foreign Minister Chen Yi through public criticism sessions.[37] Under the influence of xenophobic propaganda, the Red Guards targeted people with foreign connections or foreigners themselves in China. For example, the Red Guards broke into the British mission office in Beijing on August 22, 1967, and set it on fire after the British rejected a Chinese ultimatum demanding that it release Chinese agitators in Hong Kong and lift the ban on two pro-Chinese newspapers.[38] As China's relations with most countries including its former allies deteriorated, Albania was among the very few remaining friends of China. In the foreign affairs page of *People's Daily,* China's diplomatic activities seemed still very "busy," but it is not hard to find that most of them related to Albania only.

The isolation of China due to its militant and chaotic foreign policies can be better reflected in *Reference News.* In early 1967, for example, it covered the frequent exchanges and cooperation between the Soviet Union and North Korea. There was even a report that Pyongyang "had warned Beijing not to take unfriendly actions toward North Korea" and another one explicitly stating that the recently concluded Soviet–North Korean Agreement showed that "Pyongyang had returned to the arms of Moscow."[39] In another case, while *People's Daily* consistently praised Prince Sihanouk of Cambodia and the traditional friendship between the two countries,[40] *Reference News* covered many of his unfriendly remarks about China. In September 1967, for example, it featured a story that claimed Sihanouk had asked two pro-Beijing cabinet members to resign and attacked China for "interfering with its internal affairs." Sihanouk was also reported as having said that the clashes between "white Communists" and "yellow Communists" showed that the international Communist movement was "nothing but a farce." It even published stories asserting that Sihanouk had requested the United States not to leave Asia, which would cause Cambodia to "fall into the hands of China."[41] From *Reference News,* people could clearly see that China had far fewer friends than indicated in *People's Daily.*

The Cultural Revolution also provided ordinary people the chance to peek into Chinese politics through classified documents due to the freedom of speech created by Mao's encouragement of big-character posters and the full airing of views. Before the movement, the CCP adopted a dual system of communication by which the latest Party directives were transmitted through the internal system and were released to the public later in an always revised version in order to cushion the possible negative impact. During the Cultural Revolution, this system broke down when Red Guard newspapers and wall posters openly carried fresh directives from the central authority. What was more, in some places the Red Guards broke into Party archives and accessed classified documents in search of "black materials" that went against the Party leaders. They would disclose the secrets, sometimes in "distorted" versions, through Red Guard newspapers and wall posters.[42] These newspapers and posters became important sources for foreign correspondents in China in their reporting of the Cultural Revolution.

Response of the Johnson Administration
to the Cultural Revolution

When the Cultural Revolution broke out in the summer of 1966, Washington persisted in sending peace signals to Beijing. In January 1967, the State Department advised all U.S. diplomats and consular staffers stationed abroad to emphasize the limited objectives of the United States in Vietnam and to "seek ways of recognizing the past and potential greatness of China and the history of friendly relations between the American and Chinese peoples." When Romanian premier Ion Gheorghe Maurer, who was on good terms with Chinese leaders, visited the United States in June 1967, Johnson asked him to convey his message to Beijing that the United States did not want war with China or to change its system and that "all we want to do is to trade with China and get along with her to the extent that she will permit."[43] Publicly, Johnson's conciliatory gesture toward China promoted the administration's peace image to the "restless" and "war-weary" American people and shifted the blame for the Sino-American deadlock to Beijing for "domestic and international consumption."[44]

In responding to the chaos of the Cultural Revolution, senior U.S. officials believed that the United States had limited ability to shape events in China and that any hint of U.S. interference in Chinese politics might "unwittingly" undermine the position of pragmatic elements in Beijing. Therefore, they refrained from making comment on either China's state of affairs or the administration's preferred outcome. National Security Adviser Walter Rostow later recalled that Johnson deliberately refrained from condemning Mao in public. By refusing to publicly take sides in China's internal struggle or to gloat over its troubles, the Johnson administration tried to reduce Chinese hostility as well as its "siege mentality."[45] As the main China hand in the National Security Council (NSC), Alfred Jenkins acknowledged the U.S. posture of "quiet reasonableness" and the "hope for ultimate reconciliation." But he recommended postponing even "the minor policy changes" until Washington could "make a better judgment as to the course of events in China."[46]

While Jenkins was mainly concerned with the proper timing of China policy reform, Rusk consistently believed that the United States' "firm posture in Asia" was crucial and that any significant "concessions" to Communist China would be "seriously misunderstood in key quarters, not to mention the Congress." Ultimately, due to Rusk's opposition, in addition to other factors including the great domestic turmoil caused by the antiwar movements in 1968, Johnson's search for a negotiated settlement in Vietnam, the distraction of the general election, and Beijing's cold attitude, the Johnson administration did not make much progress in improving relations with China.[47] The uncertain situation in China also did not favor a bolder move from the U.S. government.

U.S. Media Coverage of the Cultural Revolution

When the Cultural Revolution broke out in China, the U.S. media were confused and did not pay much attention to the "cultural" aspect in the Chinese official propaganda. However, the downfall of Peng Zhen, a key member of the Politburo and one whom they viewed as a possible successor to Mao, became a headline in the *Post* and the *Times*. Because Mao had disappeared from public view since November 1965, they speculated that he had lost control of the situation.[48] The *Post* published A. Doak Barnett's speculation that Mao was probably dying and the current turmoil was a power struggle around his succession.[49] The *Times* first learned of the official name of the campaign—"Cultural Revolution"—on June 18, when Zhou Enlai informed leaders of Romania of it during his visit to that country.[50]

During his disappearance, Mao was pulling the strings behind the scenes and orchestrating the offensive against Wu Han. Once he secured a complete control over the key posts in the propaganda apparatus, Mao staged a triumphant reappearance by swimming in the Yangtze River on July 16, 1966. For some unknown reason, the Chinese media chose not to release the story of Mao's swim until July 25. With several pictures on its front page, *People's Daily* claimed that Mao had swum thirty *li*, approximately nine miles, within an hour.[51] That would be a stunning performance for a seventy-two-year-old. The writers of the CCP's propaganda were so eager to extol Mao's strength that they may have forgotten about the laws of physics. Or perhaps Mao was actually able to pull it off with the help of the swift current of the Yangtze River.

Due to the wide speculations about him, Mao's dramatic reappearance naturally caught the attention of media around the world. While the *Times* featured a story entitled "Mao's Long Swim in Yangtze Is Hailed by China," the *Post* published a piece with the title "'Ailing' Mao, 72, Swims 9 Miles in Choppy River" by Karnow with a byline, "Stops to Teach Young Woman the Backstroke," a scene many American audiences would probably find to be odd. The *Post* also alluded to the negative side of Mao's swim by claiming that the mass swimming demonstrations held at Mao's bidding had caused mass drowning due to poor preparation. Despite their different tones, both newspapers agreed that Mao's reappearance showed that he was in good health and had been in full control of the Party and the purge from the beginning.[52]

While agreeing with the two elite newspapers on the political signif-icance of Mao's swim, newsmagazines also jabbed at the exaggerations in the Chinese media. *Time* magazine titled one article "The Great Splash Forward," using a type of wordplay that had been employed frequently in the U.S. media since the disastrous Great Leap Forward.[53] It pointed out that Mao's performance of swimming nine miles in one hour was four times the world record of marathon swimming, implying it could be hardly possible. *Newsweek* used the title "No Ordinary Swim: New Light on the Great Purges as Chairman Mao Surfaces." It showed skepticism by reprinting a *London Daily Mirror* commentary that suggested Mao might have been held up "by inscrutable Chinese frogmen."[54] Western media has a natural tendency to be cynical about the grand schemes in Communist countries, particularly if they are used to extol their leaders.

With the Cultural Revolution increasing in intensity, stories of mass violence caused by the Red Guards appeared frequently in the U.S. me-dia. This is not surprising because of the media's "penchant for drama."[55] The U.S. media were deeply disturbed and horrified by the government-supported "xenophobic frenzy" in defiance of diplomatic norms when the Red Guards targeted Western life styles as well as foreign nationals in re-sponse to Mao's call to "eliminate the bourgeois influence." In August 1966, for example, the *Times* and the *Post* reported on their front pages how the Red Guards in Beijing had attacked churches in Beijing. Western journalists received a rare firsthand experience of the Red Guards' brutality when eight expelled nuns crossed the border into Hong Kong. As *Newsweek* described it, when an eighty-five-year-old nun fainted, she was "unceremoniously dumped faced down on a baggage cart" and wheeled across the border while scores of Red Guards stood nearby and jeered. Both *Time* and *Newsweek* presented a photo of the sister being wheeled across the border. The story that the sister died in a Hong Kong hospital the next day added horror to the scenario.[56]

To solve the problem of no direct access, U.S. media agencies used the stories of other countries with journalists stationed in China, such as Canada, Japan, the Soviet Union, and Czechoslovakia. Journalists of these countries often used wall posters or Red Guard newspapers as their source of information. One merit of these unofficial channels was that they provided news that would never appear in the Chinese official media, such as stories about the bloody fights and casualties, personal attacks on Mao's wife, Jiang Qing; Lin Biao; and even Mao himself. One big problem was that information in these posters could not be verified. For example, a *Post* front-page article reprinted dispatches from Japanese and Czechoslovak correspondents who used information from wall posters to claim that fifty-four persons had been killed during a riot in Nanjing. As to the number of the injured, the Japanese report was six thousand whereas the Czechs listed sixty thousand. The Czech news agency also quoted Red Guard leaflets circulated in Beijing that described the torture of their own members by opposing factions: "Their fingers, noses, and ears were chopped off and their tongues were cut off." The *Post* admitted that there was no eyewitness to such events.[57] These leaflets might have deliberately exaggerated the atrocities of the opposing factions in order to arouse anger and hatred. Even though some of the stories from foreign media sources could not be confirmed, the American audience got a sense of the chaos in China from them.

In covering the Cultural Revolution, the *Post* seemed to present more graphic and sensational pictures than the *Times*. Whereas the *Times* used "Red Guards" or "Maoists," the *Post* mostly used "mobs." When reporting the Red Guard harassment of Soviet women and children at the Beijing airport in February 1967, for example, the *Times* used the headline "Soviet Dependents Harassed in Peking." It claimed that the Chinese demonstrators at the airport were "evidently under a measure of discipline" because the Red Guards' fists "stopped within inches of Russian face." The *Post*, in contrast, used a headline "Soviet Wives Forced to Crawl in Peking," featuring how Soviet officials were pushed and manhandled when they tried to protect their women and children who "had to crawl" beneath the portrait of Mao.[58] The *Post* also seemed to be more impressed by the provocative rhetoric of the Cultural Revolution, which could be shown in its headlines such as "Peking Declares War of Annihilation" and "Mao Urges Crushing of Foes."[59] The *Post*'s reporting of the Cultural Revolution was in line with its somewhat tougher position on Beijing in general.

For all the differences on their front pages, the *Post* and the *Times* both expressed disgust at the Red Guards in their editorials. The *Times* compared the "officially organized violence against foreigners" in China to Empress Dowager Cixi's endorsement of the Boxers in 1900.[60] The *Post* argued that the image of China had become dominated by "a steadily darkening ugliness" and that the "young fogeys of Peking are frightening."[61]

Stories in the U.S. media often misread Cultural Revolution propaganda when they took the Chinese newspapers at face value. For example, in a story entitled "Lin Piao Is Made Red Guards' Head: Chou Enlai and Ho Lung Also Named to High Posts in Chinese Youth Unit," the *Times* reprinted a Japanese story based on the monitoring of a Beijing broadcast. As the story went, Zhou Enlai said, "I will join your picket corps and will serve as an adviser" when the Red Guards placed an armband on him. The radio also said Marshals He Long and Lin Biao had agreed to serve as chief of staff and commander in chief of the Red Guards when the youth asked them.[62] During the Cultural Revolution, there was never any official Red Guard organization with Lin as the commander in chief, Zhou as the adviser, and He Long as the chief of staff. What the Japanese picked up from the Chinese radio was nothing but propaganda aimed to show the endorsement of the Red Guard movement by the top leaders. It was more like impromptu support in spirit without any possibility of implementation. Actually, in its coverage of the Red Guard rallies, *People's Daily* consistently called Mao the "paramount commander." Mao and his wife had much more influence on the Red Guards than did Lin, Zhou, and He, who probably would have had reservations about their rampages.

Because the Chinese media repeatedly attacked Liu Shaoqi as Mao's chief opponent, the U.S. media also described him as the "rallying point" of "Mao's foes." The *Times* considered Liu and Deng as either "fence-sitters" or "leaders of the reported opposition."[63] *Time* reprinted the Chinese propaganda that "Liu's faction" had tried to "vote Mao out of power."[64] *Newsweek* maintained that "pitched battles between the supporters of Mao and Liu" had become almost a daily occurrence.[65] In the summer of 1967, when Deng Xiaoping came under attack, the *Post* speculated that he was "a major figure functioning behind the scenes to mobilize Mao's adversaries."[66] In a typical example, *Time* magazine identified photos of Mao, Jiang Qing, and Lin Biao as "Heroes" in the left column, and those of Liu Shaoqi and his wife, Tao Zhu, Peng Zhen, Deng Xiaoping, Li Xuefeng, and Zhou Enlai as "Villains" in the right column.[67] The list revealed the American media's tendency to oversimplify the struggle in China into one between Mao and his alleged "enemies," or one between "good cops" and "bad cops."

The reality in China was much more complex because the factions fighting against each other all claimed to be followers of Mao. Those who were purged more recently might have been beneficiaries of previous purges. They were purged later merely because they were unfortunate enough to have fallen out of Mao's favor or might have stood in the way of his political maneuvering. In the above list of "villains," Tao Zhu and Li Xuefeng had been promoted to replace Peng Zhen and Wu Han, who had been purged earlier. As for Zhou Enlai, even though the Red Guards attacked him for being "too soft on Mao's foes,"[68] he was not purged because Mao needed him to ensure the functioning of the country in the middle of the "civil war." Another case was the PLA. While Mao wanted it to "support the left" and seize power from the Party establishment and organize revolutionary committees, local military forces did not cooperate well with mass representatives supported by the radical Cultural Revolution Group.[69] In many cases, the military had to suppress the radicals. Therefore, the PLA was more of a stabilizing force most of the time during the Cultural Revolution.

When the U.S. media linked all opponents to radicals together into a consolidated bloc that was anti-Mao in nature, the result was the exaggerated strength of "Mao's opponents." In an article "Some Doubt Survival of Present Peking Setup" published on the eve of the Chinese National Day in 1966, the *Post* speculated that Mao and Lin Biao could be overthrown by an opposition that had "grown significantly." The *Times* editorial also maintained that the turmoil in China had raised questions about the "stability of the Peking regime" with signs denouncing Mao.[70] On the cover of a January 1967 issue, *Time* magazine featured a large picture of Mao's head wound up by a dragon of the Great Wall with a subtitle "China in Chaos." The accompanying article described China as reaching the final stages of the "legendary dance of the scorpion—just before it stings itself to death."[71] Considering the widespread instability in China, it was natural for foreign observers at the time to speculate about the downfall of Mao's rule or the survival of the Communist regime. Some of these stories might contain elements of wishful thinking. However, the troubles inside China, as James Reston argued, reduced the possibility of China's military intervention in Vietnam.[72] The external threat of China was thus reduced in American perceptions.

The U.S. media's misunderstanding also included projecting U.S. values on Chinese realities. When the Cultural Revolution started, for example, a *Post* editorial speculated that the movement might signify another "Great Leap Forward" modernization.[73] In March 1967, another editorial claimed that Mao was retreating from his Cultural Revolution and the central issue now was "how to modernize China," which would require help from the outside world. Therefore, it argued, Beijing in its weakness would be "receptive to arrangements with Washington."[74] The *Post* was probably too optimistic about China's need for modernization as a driving force for it to seek reconciliation. It well reflects the prejudices of the "modernization theory" at the time, which posited that every country had to go through "development," defined by "progress" in technology and economy among many other things.[75] Being embroiled in power struggles, Mao was probably much more interested in revolution than in "modernization." Moreover, even if China needed modern technologies, it could find ways to obtain them from other Western countries rather than the United States due to ideological considerations. Later, when Chinese leaders made the decision to reconcile with the United States, modernization counted for little.

Despite the chaos in China, U.S. newspeople persisted in criticizing the rigid China policy and pushed for more flexibility. The newspapers were more straightforward than the administration in expressing their preference. The *Post* argued that the United States had a "stake" in the outcome and that a flexible American posture would give encouragement to moderate forces in China. The *Times* also maintained that it was in the interest of the United States to encourage the "rational" faction in China by "holding open the door wherever possible."[76]

In July 1967, those who disapproved of Johnson's handling of the Vietnam War exceeded 50 percent for the first time in the Gallup Poll.[77] In face of the rising criticism of the Vietnam War, the Johnson administration mounted its offensive on the critics in the fall of 1967. Many administration officials responded to media interviews with "predominantly hawkish advice"[78] and invoked the specter of the "China threat" in their defense of the administration's Vietnam policy. A typical example was Dean Rusk at a press conference on October 12, 1967. When asked to elaborate on why U.S. security was at stake in Vietnam, Rusk responded that in another ten or twenty years, "there will be a billion Chinese on the Mainland, armed with nuclear weapons, with no certainty about what their attitude toward the rest of Asia will be."[79] In their front-page stories reporting Rusk's press conference, the two elite newspapers obviously did not agree with him. The *Post* mentioned Rusk's "unwarranted obsession about Communist China." The *Times* noted that his "usual calm tone was missing," emphasizing the irrational side of his comments. In a column, James Reston argued that Rusk's remarks were "good theatre but bad policy" and that the reporters liked his "loyalty, optimism, and appealing conviction" but simply could not "believe he was right."[80] Rusk's remarks caused more controversy when Senator Eugene McCarthy (D-MN) accused him of obscuring the issue by invoking the "yellow peril." Even though Rusk denied it promptly, it made headlines in both the *Times* and the *Post*. In his *Post* column article entitled "Rusk's Raising of Yellow Peril Is Truly Dangerous Escalation," Joseph Kraft argued that Rusk had put his country in a position that had "elements of madness."[81]

Dean Rusk was not the only administration official who used the "China peril" to defend the administration's Vietnam policy. When speaking at the National Shrine of Our Lady of Czestochowa in Pennsylvania on October 15, Vice President Hubert Humphrey reasserted that the U.S. security was at stake in Vietnam and that the "current threat to world peace is militant, aggressive Asian communism, with its headquarters in Peking,

China." The *Times* seemed to be more critical of the "hawkish" remarks of administration officials than the *Post*. It placed Humphrey's speech on its front page whereas the *Post* did not.[82] Interviewing specialists on China affairs and U.S. diplomacy, the *Times* published an article entitled "Some Specialists Say U.S. Aides Exaggerate Peking Threat."[83]

As the U.S. media watched the rise and fall of unrest in China, their call for better Sino-American relations was soon submerged by new stories of Red Guard violence. In March 1967, both the *Times* and the *Post* claimed to have found signs that Mao's Cultural Revolution was subsiding. A *Post* editorial was so optimistic that it claimed a "propitious moment" had come to "assay the small steps with which America's eventual reconciliation with China must begin."[84] A month later, world-famous violinist Ma Sicong and his family arrived in the United States seeking asylum after they fled China. Their arrival caused much interest because the Ma family was among the very few Chinese witnesses of the Cultural Revolution to set foot on American soil.[85] After learning of Ma's mistreatment by the Red Guards, an editorial in the *Post* condemned the Communist madness, predicting that such a system would not "persist long enough to imperil for generations the safety and security of millions of people."[86] While both newspapers claimed to have noticed signs that the Cultural Revolution was coming to a close as early as October 1967, *Time* and *Newsweek* reported that bodies were still flowing down the Pearl River to Hong Kong and Macao in July 1968.[87] With stories of recurrent violence, China seemed too unpredictable to work with diplomatically. For the American people, the media's coverage of Red Guard brutalities and their violent xenophobia and fanaticism must have alienated them.

For all their inaccurate reading of the domestic politics in China, the U.S. media were right in deducing from the struggles Mao's weakness in keeping the country under control. Mao's use of the military to deal with his opponents, as the *Times* saw it, was an "admission of weakness."[88] In response to the mutiny in Wuhan in July 1967, which ran out of control and almost threatened Mao's life,[89] the *Times* argued that if Mao could not even "liquidate his opponents in so central an institution as the armed forces," it only showed that he was not "fully the master in his own realm." The *Post* also maintained that the incident suggested Mao was failing in his effort to impose the "discipline and purity of his Cultural Revolution across his distressed land."[90] The resistance and obstruction to Mao, although exaggerated by the U.S. media, destroyed the myth of an "impenetrable" Chinese leadership.[91] The media's coverage of the chaos indeed presented the image of an irrational China. However, stories of chaos also created the impression that China was preoccupied with domestic troubles, which reduced the likelihood of overseas adventures.

The U.S. Media on the Escalation of Sino-Soviet Polemics

The Cultural Revolution witnessed the deterioration of the Sino-Soviet conflicts because offensives against "revisionists" abroad would serve Mao's domestic agenda—the attacks on revisionists at home. This position can be seen in the "Sixteen Points Decision," where "struggle against the Soviet Union" was adopted as an official policy.[92] Liu Shaoqi's nickname in the Chinese media, the "Khrushchev sleeping by our side," is a perfect combination of revisionists within the Party and without. Spurred by the strong anti-Soviet propaganda in China, the Red Guards targeted the Soviet embassy for mass rallies and demonstrations in August 1966. The Chinese government's failure to rein in the Red Guards' attack on the embassy annoyed Moscow, whose protests only served to add fuel to the Red Guards' frenzy. As the quarrels between the two Communist giants escalated and turned dramatic at times, the U.S. media watched with great interest. During the Cold War, the coverage of quarrels among Communist countries would no doubt undermine their credibility and be interesting to American readers.

Sino-Soviet quarrels reached their peak with the "Moscow Incident" in January 1967. On January 24, sixty-nine Chinese students studying in Europe arrived in Moscow on their way back to Beijing to take part in the Cultural Revolution. When they requested to present a wreath to Stalin's grave, they were rejected by the Soviet authority but allowed instead to pay tribute to the Lenin Mausoleum, which was also at Red Square. After laying the wreath, the students refused to leave, and together they read aloud quotations from Mao that included anti-Soviet slogans. Clashes broke out when the Soviet police tried to stop the Chinese students. In protest, the Red Guards laid siege to the Soviet embassy in Beijing for several weeks. In retaliation, the Soviets besieged the Chinese embassy in

Moscow, but only for several days. When tensions in Beijing caused the Soviets to evacuate their women and children, as mentioned earlier, many of them were harassed by the Red Guards on their way to the airport. In Moscow, Soviet citizens broke into the Chinese embassy complex, grabbed the display items inside, and beat up Chinese diplomats. These "tit-for-tat" struggles caused the Sino-Soviet tension to worsen and sent it on a no-return track.[93]

What complicated the Sino-Soviet "war of words" was the tension along their disputed border. Since the Cultural Revolution started, violence against Soviet diplomats and the anti-Soviet hysteria in China further aroused Moscow's fear of war with China. In a Communist Party of the Soviet Union (CPSU) plenum in December 1966, several key Party leaders complained that Chinese leaders had put struggle against the Soviet Union in the first place. As a result, Moscow accelerated its military buildup along the Sino-Soviet and Sino-Mongolian borders in 1967 and 1968. From 1965 to 1969, the number of Soviet divisions reportedly increased from seventeen to twenty-seven. Leonid Brezhnev, the secretary-general of the Central Committee of the CPSU, assumed that more troops would reduce the danger of military confrontations.[94]

In Xinjiang, an autonomous region in central Asia, the chaos caused by the Red Guard movement and their hunt for Soviet sympathizers triggered large numbers of Uyghurs and Kazakhs to flee to the Soviet Union, in numbers the Soviet press reported as several hundred thousand in January 1967. In response, Mao ordered all border forces on the Soviet frontier to be alerted on February 11. In the same month, Moscow reported a withdrawal of Chinese troops one hundred miles from the Soviet and Mongolian borders.[95] In late 1966, *Reference News* reprinted Western media stories about increasing Soviet troop deployment, frequent military drills, and Soviet leaders' anti-China indoctrination during their visit to the Sino-Soviet border.[96] All news of Sino-Soviet border tensions was censored in *People's Daily*, though. The withdrawal of Chinese troops from the border and the silence of *People's Daily* on these tensions show that Chinese leaders were not expecting a real war against the Soviet Union when the Cultural Revolution was raging. Mao was mainly interested in using the ideological differences with Moscow to serve his domestic struggle against "revisionists."

American journalists covered the Sino-Soviet polemics with prominence and not without drama. They published vivid stories of the "war
of words" emanating from Moscow and Beijing in early 1967. Under the
headline "Moscow and Peking in Loudspeaker War," the *Times* described
a scene where large Soviet loudspeakers mounted on two trucks blared
against two smaller ones installed by the Chinese embassy.[97] The *Post,
Time,* and *Newsweek* placed pictures of demonstrators burning effigies of
Soviet leaders in Beijing side by side with the Russians shouting "shame
on Mao" in Moscow. In an article entitled "Mao Baits the Russian Bear,"
Newsweek reported the clashes at the Red Square with an amusing anec-
dote. As the story went, when the Chinese embassy in Moscow produced
two of the "allegedly injured students at a press conference, one of them
spoiled the whole effect by becoming so excited that he unwittingly ripped
off his bandages to reveal an unblemished face."[98]

While the U.S. media admitted that Beijing was more provocative than
Moscow, they did not appreciate the "quiet self-congratulation" of the Soviets.[99] For example, the *Times* claimed that the Soviet press was "more
graphic about unrest and violence in China than many Western papers."
James Reston noticed that U.S. officials talked about the Cultural Revolution far less than did the top leaders of the Soviet Union. In an editorial
entitled "Moscow Fishes in Peking," the *Post* argued that the Russians were
conducting an extensive campaign to "dislodge" Mao by putting pressure
on him and making his rule as "arduous" as possible. *Newsweek* pointed
out that Moscow had good reason to be worried by the fact that Beijing
had accorded it the same "arch-demon status" as Washington.[100] During
his visit to Great Britain in February 1967, Soviet premier Alexei Kosygin remarked in a television interview that the Soviet Union sympathized
with Chinese people who were struggling against "the dictatorial regime
of Mao Tse-tung." The *Post* interpreted Kosygin's unusual condemnation
of Mao as a sign that Moscow was giving priority to better relations with
the West. In the editorial "Kosygin Drops the Mask," the *Times* argued that
his remark "in the capital of a capitalist nation" was "counterproductive"
because it only served to inform the West of the "extreme seriousness of
the Sino-Soviet crisis."[101]

The U.S. media also gave prominence to the Sino-Soviet border tensions and speculated about a possible war between the two Communist

giants. In 1966, *Time* magazine had called attention to the border conflict, which it described as a "lesser known and potentially dangerous" aspect of the Sino-Soviet disputes. Citing the increase of Soviet anti-China indoctrination on the border, it claimed that "the war of words" might become an "Armageddon at the summit of the Communist world."[102] Similarly, an editorial in the *Times* argued that by provoking a crisis with Moscow, Mao might be preparing a campaign to win some of the disputed territory in Siberia. With regard to Kosygin's remarks in London, it again raised the question whether it might spark a war between the two Communist powers.[103] On February 10, 1967, journalists from the Japanese news agency Kyodo reported, based on information in leaflets in Beijing, that Mao had given orders to alert all Chinese border troops. The *Times,* the *Post,* and *Time* quickly picked up the story even though they had no means to confirm it. *Newsweek* also talked about the "War of Nerves" on the Sino-Soviet border.[104] By February 1967, the seriousness of the Sino-Soviet conflict had become so clear to newspeople that a permanent split seemed very likely to them.[105] In general, during the Cultural Revolution their coverage of the Sino-Soviet conflict was more accurate than their perceptions of Chinese domestic politics.

As the Sino-Soviet rift developed, it provided a foundation for new thinking for those concerned about Sino-American relations. In February 1967, scholars on China convened a conference at the University of Chicago's Center of Policies Studies. In his speech at the conference, Senator Robert Kennedy (D-NY) asserted that the United States had "widely exaggerated" the threat of China and underestimated the significance of the Sino-Soviet split. He called on administration officials to distinguish between "armed attack and internal revolution," between "Chinese direction of revolutionary forces and Chinese exhortation." Kennedy's speech made the front pages of both the *Times* and the *Post.*[106] The next day, the *Times* covered ideas from the conference with the title "Victory for Mao held Best for U.S.: Experts See Chinese-Soviet Rift as an Advantage."[107]

Several columnists in the *Post* criticized Kennedy. Claiming that the senator's proposal had existed inside as well outside the government for some time, Joseph Alsop complained that Kennedy had appeared on the front pages too often and that he was given too much credit for pressing a so-called "brand-new" China policy. William S. White, in his article

"Who's Advising Bobby? . . . China Proposals Shock Associates," criticized Kennedy by reemphasizing the Chinese "aggression" in Korea and Vietnam. He attacked the senator for "becoming a part-time dove" on Vietnam where his brother JFK had been a "resolute hawk." He also described Kennedy's academic advisers as "splendid" writers but not "wise politicians."[108] Though not shared by all, these criticisms of Kennedy reflected conservative opposition to reforms in U.S. China policy during the Cultural Revolution.

In reality, the United States had been much closer to the Soviet Union than to China since the early 1960s. This was especially the case during the Cultural Revolution when the Soviet leadership was truly alarmed by the Chinese anti-Soviet hysteria. In January 1967, the Soviet Politburo approved a policy to maintain Soviet-American relations on a certain cordial level to help the Soviet Union avoid fighting on two fronts.[109] At the Glassboro Summit in June 1967, though Kosygin and Johnson did not reach any concrete agreement, the intimate atmosphere was interpreted by the *Times* and the *Post* as the beginning of a better Soviet-American relationship.[110] At the fiftieth anniversary of the October Revolution in 1967, Harrison Salisbury, a prominent journalist on the Soviet affairs and the assistant managing editor of the *Times,* wrote a column "China Tops Soviet List of Potential Dangers," arguing that the United States had dropped to the third place on the list of potential threats to the Soviet Union, with China and West Germany the top two.[111] Officials on the Johnson team appreciated the Soviet cooperation over the Paris talks on Vietnam. They were unwilling to exploit the Sino-Soviet rift because of their fear of alienating the Soviets, whom they believed might help find a settlement in Indochina.[112]

The U.S. Media on Sino-Vietnamese Relations

The U.S. media not only followed the Sino-Soviet polemics, they were also interested in the relations between Beijing and Hanoi because any rift between them could affect the U.S. war efforts in Vietnam. As one of the greatest victims of the Sino-Soviet disputes, Sino-Vietnamese relations had started to strain after Moscow increased its role in the Vietnam War when Kosygin's visit to Hanoi in January 1965 started the flow of more sophisticated weapons from the Soviet Union. In his later visit to Beijing when Kosygin proposed a Sino-Soviet "joint action" to support Vietnam, Mao dismissed his proposal, asserting that China's argument with the Soviet Union would "continue for another 9,000 years."[113] Beijing's obstinate rejection of the "joint action" proposal for world Communist countries to support North Vietnam severely embittered Hanoi. Several years later, when China invaded Vietnam in 1979, Hanoi listed "sabotaging the united action" as one of China's "crimes" in its publication of the history of Sino-Vietnamese relations.[114]

Beijing not only rejected the joint-action proposal but also demanded that Hanoi take sides in the Sino-Soviet quarrel and repudiate Soviet revisionism. In his March 1966 talks with Le Duan, the general secretary of the Vietnamese Workers' Party (VWP), for example, Zhou Enlai emphasized that opposing American imperialists must go hand in hand with opposing Soviet revisionism and that the two things could not be separated. He also complained that Vietnamese newspapers were carrying stories about Chinese aggression against Vietnam in the past. When he failed to convince the North Vietnamese to distance themselves from the Soviet Union, Zhou insisted that mentioning the Soviet aid together with the Chinese aid was an "insult" to China. On another occasion, when the CCP's hot-tempered General Secretary Deng Xiaoping met with Le Duan in April, the atmosphere was more intense. Deng said: "Why are you afraid of displeasing the Soviets, and what about China? . . . Vietnamese comrades have some other thoughts about our methods of assistance, but you have not yet told us. . . . Are you suspicious that China helps Vietnam for our own intentions? . . . We will withdraw our military men at once."[115] These actions only alienated the North Vietnamese and pushed them further toward the Soviets.

As the rift between Beijing and Hanoi developed, the *Times* had spotted the sign as early as May 1966, when Albanian premier Mehmet Shehu visited China. From the joint announcements made by Chinese and Albanian leaders that there could be no "neutrality" or "middle of the road" in the struggle against Soviet revisionism, it sensed "thinly veiled attacks" on Hanoi's leaders. When the Cultural Revolution erupted, *Newsweek* speculated that Hanoi might have been "disillusioned" by the upheavals in China because they might affect its war effort. During the Glassboro Summit in June 1967, the *Post* featured a story entitled "Talks Said to

Cool Hanoi-Peking Ties" arguing that the gap between Beijing and Hanoi would widen when the Soviets' increasing influence on Hanoi would facilitate its role as a "high-level broker" between the United States and North Vietnam.[116] In other words, a closer Soviet-American tie would alienate the relations between Hanoi and Beijing because of Hanoi's closer relations with Moscow.

When the Paris talks started in May 1968, *People's Daily* remained silent and reduced coverage of Vietnam, especially on its front pages. The *Post* interpreted Beijing's continued silence as an indication of its unhappiness with Hanoi. In a front-page article, "Hanoi and Moscow Appear to Mesh Tactics on Talks," the *Times* noted that China had been excluded from policy formulation over negotiations. It also featured an editorial entitled "Hanoi and Peking: They Don't Always See Eye to Eye." Seeing China's upgrading of the Viet Cong mission in its capital, *Newsweek* interpreted it as Beijing's effort to "drive a wedge" between Hanoi and the Viet Cong if the Paris talks went on.[117]

Moreover, both the *Times* and the *Post* reported stories of Chinese demonstrations in front of North Vietnamese consulates in Chinese cities. The *Post* even obtained information from a Red Guard bulletin in Guangzhou (Canton) claiming that Red Guards had stormed the North Vietnamese consulate and taunted its diplomats in Nanning, the capital of Guangxi province adjacent to North Vietnam, on June 2, 1968.[118] In July, the two newspapers reported that Chinese leaders including Zhou Enlai blamed the factional strife for halting the shipment of Soviet and Chinese aid to Vietnam. They speculated that the Red Guards might be deliberately blocking the transportation to show their discontent with Hanoi.[119] Stories of discord between Beijing and Hanoi reduced Beijing's role in Vietnam, which to some extent weakened the China threat.

Different from the silence of *People's Daily* on the Paris talks, *Reference News* had been following their progress closely since the Vietnamese representatives arrived in Paris in May 1968. It not only reprinted the full texts of the speeches given by Vietnamese representatives at the negotiations but also ran stories reporting that Hanoi's chief negotiator, Xuan Thuy, would visit Moscow en route to Paris.[120] Since many Red Guards came from Communist cadre families, they probably had read stories about the Paris talks in *Reference News* and became angry at the attempts of North

Vietnam to seek "compromise" with imperialists and at the closer relations between Hanoi and Moscow.

Impact of the Soviet Invasion of Czechoslovakia

In the last year of the Johnson administration, the domestic and international environments for both the United States and China moved in a direction that favored a better relationship between them. As the chaos in China showed apparent signs of decline, Johnson also started his deescalation plan through negotiation. Moreover, the China Lobby in the United States had been severely weakened with the Committee of One Million losing the endorsement of congressional majorities.[121] Candidates of both parties no longer took it as a taboo to publicly talk about negotiating with China.[122] Most important of all, the Soviet invasion of Czechoslovakia in August 1968 and the introduction of the "Brezhnev Doctrine," which used the conception of "limited sovereignty" to justify the Soviet military intervention in another socialist country, greatly increased Beijing's concern about the Soviet threat. Slowly, Beijing started to turn its attention away from Vietnam to the mounting threat from the north.

In denouncing the Soviet invasion of Czechoslovakia, *People's Daily* described Moscow as "having degenerated into a socialist-imperialist and socialist-fascist" state.[123] The change from "revisionist" to "socialist-imperialist" in the Chinese official discourse symbolizes that the Soviet Union had shifted from an "ideological opponent" to a "strategic threat."[124] In September 1968, the official organ began to publicize strategic threats from the Soviet Union. For example, *People's Daily* for the first time revealed tensions along the Sino-Soviet border by publishing a Foreign Ministry protest against Soviet intrusions into China's air space in the past, particularly in August. In October, it published Zhou Enlai and PLA chief of staff Huang Yongsheng's public speeches with reference to Soviet troop deployment and "provocations" on the Sino-Soviet and Sino-Mongolia borders.[125]

People's Daily also singled out Moscow when it attacked countries that it considered part of the "anti-China strategic circle." In an article entitled "Warning to the 'Heroes and Fellows' in the Anti-China Circle" from the PLA's point of view, it listed recent "anti-China activities" conducted by the Soviet Union.[126] Between September and November 1968, while *People's*

Daily ferociously attacked the "Soviet socialist imperialists" on its front pages, it only briefly referred to the American military "failures" in Vietnam and great civil disturbances at home in interior pages. It seemed that Beijing was more concerned with a threatening Soviet Union than a weakened United States.

Reference News displayed clearer signs that Beijing started to view Moscow as its "principal enemy" after the Soviet invasion of Czechoslovakia. A front-page article entitled "Soviet Revisionists Are Playing the Leading Role in the Anti-China Circle with the Approval of the United States" argued that the Soviet military drills between 1965 and 1967 reflected that China had become the "number-one imaginary enemy" of the Soviet Union after Moscow had effectively reduced tensions with the West. As it stated, while the "anti-China circle" put together by the United States had collapsed due to the resistance of the Vietnamese in the first stage of the Soviet-American understanding, the Soviet Union had taken up the leading role in the second stage, by containing China from both sides with "the two claws of the crab."[127]

After the Paris talks began, Hanoi's refusal to repudiate the Soviet invasion of Czechoslovakia further weakened Sino–North Vietnamese relations. During the National Day celebration of 1968, *People's Daily* placed Vietnamese representatives after guests from Albania, Pakistan, Burma, Indonesia, and New Zealand when it reported the state reception held by Zhou Enlai. Lin Biao totally ignored the conflict in Vietnam in his speech at the Tiananmen Square celebration the next day. On the same occasion a year earlier, Vietnam had been ranked after only Albania and the Democratic Republic of the Congo, and Lin had expressed warm support for the Vietnamese.[128] The *Post* read Lin Biao's speech as a sign that Beijing had shifted its focus away from Vietnam to the danger of a possible collision with the Soviet Union.[129]

Beijing's public attitude toward the Paris talks began to change in October 1968, when *People's Daily* for the first time ran a front-page article pointing out that the talks had reached their "delicate stage" after twenty-six formal negotiations since their beginning in May. As it reported, "more and more signs show that the stalemate at the Paris talks might have been broken" because Johnson had applied the "fraudulent trick" of a comprehensive halt to bombing in order to push for an agreement. It also grudgingly claimed that the news needed to be "further confirmed as the situation develops."[130] As the *Times* correctly pointed out, Beijing chose to disclose the Paris talks at that moment because it needed to prepare its public when progress was "imminent."[131] It did not want the Chinese people to be too surprised if a settlement was reached in Vietnam.

When Johnson declared in a television address on October 31 a complete halt to the bombing, *People's Daily,* to the surprise of the foreign media as indicated in *Reference News,* published the full text of his address.[132] *People's Daily* also published Hanoi's official declaration that it was ready to join the quadripartite talks that included the National Liberation Front (NLF) and the government of South Vietnam, along with Ho Chi Minh's message to the Vietnamese people. On November 18, it published the statements of the U.S. State Department and the Foreign Ministry of North Vietnam (DRV) on their positions in the recent Paris talks.[133] In Beijing's strategic consideration, if Hanoi's support for the Soviet invasion of Czechoslovakia was a sign that it had "lost out in its competition with the Soviet Union over Hanoi's allegiance,"[134] the beginning of the quadripartite talks in November consolidated the Soviet victory. By publicizing Hanoi's negotiations with the United States, Beijing seemed to be discrediting Hanoi and preparing for its own disengagement from Vietnam. While in private Mao dropped his opposition to negotiation and switched to endorse Hanoi's "fighting and talking" strategy when he met with DRV and NLF leaders in November 1968, China started to withdraw support troops from North Vietnam at the same time.[135]

More importantly, in November, Beijing signaled to Washington its wish to renew the Warsaw Talks. When the United States proposed to put off the 135th meeting to February 20, 1969, a month after the inauguration of Richard Nixon, the Chinese Foreign Ministry responded positively with a statement that was unusually long and more detailed than any previous ones. The statement, with its attack on the "typically imperialist" attitude of the United States, stated that China would like to talk with the United States based on two principles: the U.S. withdrawal from Taiwan and its willingness to sign an agreement with China based on "the five principles of peaceful coexistence."[136] By that time, the war in Vietnam was no longer among the high priorities of the Chinese government.

The reemergence of the discourse of "peaceful coexistence" with the

United States in Beijing's public statements was an important sign of friendliness to Washington. The Chinese government could have just sent a letter to the U.S. embassy and published a statement when the meeting was over, as it normally had done. Publishing a lengthy response before the meeting could show Hanoi and Moscow that China had its own options. At the same time, it could also demonstrate to the domestic audience that the Chinese government was not afraid of talking to the "imperialists" in a rational manner.

In the United States, the *Times* was the most excited about the Chinese response, granting it front-page prominence. It argued that the "peaceful coexistence" clause might signify "a possible shift in the Chinese foreign policy from belligerency back to the flexible policy of the 1950s." Considering Beijing's "overture of coexistence" and the starting of quadripartite negotiations over Vietnam, its editorial pages expressed great optimism about peace prospects in Asia at the end of 1968.[137] The *Post* was not too impressed by Beijing's proposal at first, when it placed the story on page sixteen and did not read too much meaning into the Chinese statement. In December, it was "amazed" to find that the United States was being "wooed" by both Beijing and Moscow.[138]

Of the three TV networks, only CBS reported the Chinese story in the evening news of that day. It put the story at the end of a clip showing the recent activities of President-elect Richard Nixon, whose foreign policy adviser Robert Murphy was reported as saying that he was "pleased but not excited" about the Chinese offer to talk.[139] ABC reported the news a week later, claiming that the change in the Chinese attitude might be an opportunity for Nixon to make concessions in his China policy.[140] NBC reporting came out three weeks later, after it had time to weigh the significance of the Chinese announcement. While showing the film of Mao's recent meeting with the Pakistani president, the anchor said that Mao wanted to test the temper of Nixon by using the "five principles of coexistence," which could have been condemned as "rank revisionism" a year ago. It concluded that Nixon was the "first beneficiary of the Cultural Revolution."[141]

Of the two newsweeklies, Henry Luce's *Time* described the signals from Beijing as "erratic, vague and contradictory," but it acknowledged them as a positive sign that China's relations with the world could expect to become "more rational and more flexible." *Newsweek* did not cover the Chinese call for talks until February of the next year.[142] It took the U.S. media several weeks to gradually dwell upon the positive significance of the Chinese call for the renewal of the Warsaw Talks. As is often the case, the evaluations of the *Times* may have exerted some impact on other media outlets or were at least ahead of many of them.

The Johnson administration responded to the Chinese offer with restrained optimism. In his memo to National Security Advisor Walt Rostow, Alfred Jenkins argued that he did not believe it was much of an "invitation for rapprochement." He thought it was probably a signal of Beijing's "readiness" to listen to any interesting change in policy from the new administration. Rostow and Dean Rusk recommended that President Johnson approve a change in trade regulations and permit U.S. subsidiaries abroad to sell a limited range of nonstrategic goods to China. Rusk believed that this change was a useful move prior to the scheduled meeting with the Chinese in Warsaw. Rostow thought that they could set up a "modest precedent" that Nixon could either follow or ignore, but it would reduce the significance if Nixon initiated it.[143] The Johnson administration ended up leaving the initiative to Nixon.

Conclusion

As this chapter indicates, the Cultural Revolution was a watershed in Sino-American relations.[144] While the U.S. escalation in Vietnam caused the Johnson administration to cautiously reduce tensions with China through tentative bridge-building gestures, the Cultural Revolution witnessed the dramatic escalation of Sino-Soviet tension and the open rift between Beijing and Hanoi. By the end of 1968, moreover, the American preparation to disengage from Vietnam also reduced China's perception of this threat. When the Soviet Union replaced the United States as the number-one enemy of China, it created a condition for Chinese leaders to reconsider China's strategic position, which can be seen from Beijing's willingness to restart the Warsaw Talks. All these developments laid the foundation for a better relationship between the two countries.

At the height of the Cultural Revolution, the Chinese media promoted Beijing's image as a fighter against both "American imperialists" and "So-

viet revisionists" in order to inspire the struggle against Mao's political enemies. The contrast between Chinese words and deeds shows that Beijing
did not want to fight either of the superpowers while China was in a state
of turmoil, if ever. The Chinese media played an important role in provoking the Soviet Union and intensifying the Sino-Soviet polemics. As they
continued the ideological invectives against the United States, the Chinese
media displayed Beijing's slight of Washington by repeatedly delaying the
already reduced contact in Warsaw. In order to protect China's revolutionary credentials and to dispel the "rumor" of its "understanding" with
Washington on Vietnam, they eagerly took advantage of the propaganda
value of the "conflicts" between the two countries in the air and on the
high seas close to the Chinese border. Their attacks on "U.S. aggression"
usually served the additional purpose of embarrassing the Soviet Union,
which the Chinese media constantly labeled as the "number-one accomplice" of the United States.

In comparison with *People's Daily,* which covered China's "normal"
diplomatic activities, such as its "busy" interactions with Albania, stories
in *Reference News* presented a more realistic picture of China's worsening
international relations. There were timely and detailed reports on the escalating Sino-Soviet border disputes and clear indications that Hanoi was
tilting toward Moscow. With the start of the Paris talks in May and the
Soviet invasion of Czechoslovakia in August 1968, both *People's Daily* and
Reference News demonstrated Beijing's unhappiness with Hanoi and its
increasing concern with the Soviet Union as a greater strategic threat. By
educating the domestic audience about the problems in China's strategic
position, the Chinese media could lay the groundwork for a more flexible
public stance toward the United States if the government chose to move in
that direction in the future.

On the American side, while the Johnson administration refrained
from making public comments on the domestic politics of China, the U.S.
media's penchant for drama caused them to prominently cover the power
struggles and Red Guard violence in China. These stories unavoidably
caused the decline of China's image among the American audience. Due
to their lack of access to China and their simplified reading of Chinese
propaganda, U.S. journalists tended to oversimplify the situation in China
and to project their own wishful thinking on the Chinese reality. Their

coverage of the resistance to the Cultural Revolution, however, suggested the weakness of Mao's control and shattered the myth of a united Chinese leadership. Despite the chaos in China, some commentators persisted in criticizing the U.S. government's rigidity and pushed for a more flexible policy. The chronic violence in China, in turn, shattered the optimism about improvement in Sino-American relations.

In comparison to their coverage of Chinese domestic politics, U.S. media agencies were more accurate in assessing China's international relations, especially the Sino-Soviet and Sino-North Vietnamese rifts. The seriousness of the Sino-Soviet split discussed in the media encouraged those concerned with Sino-American relations to think more seriously about exploiting the conflicts, even though the lame-duck Johnson team did not move in that direction. Accounts of the rift between Beijing and Hanoi demonstrated Beijing's reduced role in Vietnam. Essentially, the U.S. media pictured a disorganized and greatly weakened China with deep domestic as well as international troubles, which made it look less threatening and probably easier to deal with. At the end of 1968, when Beijing offered to renew contacts in Warsaw, the U.S. media were looking for a more promising Sino-American relationship in the coming Nixon administration.

3
The Sino-Soviet Crisis

DANGER AND OPPORTUNITY IN 1969

The year 1969 witnessed the opportunity for a thaw in Sino-American relations. When Richard Nixon came into office, he encountered much more favorable domestic and international attitudes toward dealing with China than Lyndon Johnson had. Not only had the China Lobby been severely weakened, but China entered into a period of stability when the Ninth Congress of the Chinese Communist Party (CCP) in March 1969 put an end to the most radical stage of the Cultural Revolution. Moreover, Beijing had openly expressed its desire to renew talks through the Warsaw channel. Most important of all, the Sino-Soviet tensions suddenly intensified into military conflict. In the Chinese language, the word for "crisis"—*weiji*—has two characters: "danger" and "opportunity," a notion Nixon also used in his book *Six Crises*.[1] The crisis not only brought about the "danger" of a large-scale war between the two Communist giants but also provided an "opportunity" for Washington and Beijing to move toward each other.

This chapter looks at how the U.S. media responded to the Sino-Soviet crises and especially how they dealt with the prospect of Sino-American accommodation in the new context. It also studies the media's role when Nixon sent clear signals to Beijing about the American intention to improve relations. On the Chinese side, by looking at the performance of its media, this chapter examines how Beijing responded to Nixon's overtures and slowly changed its attitude toward the United States.

Cancellation of the Warsaw Talks

On January 20, 1969, Richard Nixon was inaugurated as the thirty-seventh president of the United States. He was presented with an opportunity to improve Sino-American relations because the previous November Beijing had offered to renew talks in Warsaw. The Chinese Foreign Ministry stated in 1968: "We totally understand your proposal because the new president is coming into office. And it would be easier for you to make a decision by the time we meet next time when the new president would have been in office for a month."[2] This statement could be viewed as a Chinese gesture to the incoming Richard Nixon inviting better relations.

The Chinese media did not assign too much importance to Nixon's inauguration. For a week, *People's Daily* kept it off the front pages without publishing any major editorial comments against the American president. It reported only a few demonstrations in Washington, D.C., and a small one in Austria in the interior pages.[3]

A week later, on January 28, a campaign against Nixon suddenly started in the Chinese media when *People's Daily* and *Red Flag* published a joint editorial, "A Confession in an Impasse: Comments on Nixon's Inaugural Address and the Shameless Flattering of the Soviet Revisionists." It depicted the United States as a "failing, yet brutal and aggressive system over which Nixon presided as a frightened ineffectual front man." Mocking Nixon's peace proposal as a "façade for further aggression," it claimed that he was "beset with difficulties at home and abroad" and that he would "not fare any better than his predecessor." In the following days, the Party organ published many stories about how Chinese workers and soldiers who, upon learning of the editorial, swore to repudiate Nixon and the Soviet Union. Many of these articles used titles containing personal invective against Nixon such as, "Let Nixon's 'Benevolent Rule' Go to Hell!," "Dump Nixon into the Trash of History!," and "Get Rid of Nixon's Junk Ideas." To highlight the importance of the editorial, the article claimed that leftist organizations in Japan and Africa had expressed their support after reading it.[4] The sudden escalation of invective against Nixon in the official organ seemed to suggest something unusual in Beijing.

What happened in that week? On January 24, Liao Heshu, the chargé d'affaires of the Chinese embassy in the Netherlands, defected before seeking asylum in the United States.[5] The defection of one of its own officials to capitalist countries was deeply humiliating to the Chinese government. Before the incident was known to the world, China might have started the media campaign against the United States in order to show its tough position. It could also give the impression that it was not forced to do so when the news was broken to public.

Beijing remained silent on Liao's defection in order to avoid the embarrassment. On February 4, however, the U.S. State Department announced that he had been admitted to the United States.[6] In response, *People's Daily* published Beijing's strong protest, attacking Washington for "deliberately engineering" the serious anti-China incident in collusion with its "little flunky," the Dutch government. It claimed that the incident showed that Nixon and his predecessor, Lyndon Johnson, were "jackals from the same den" in terms of their hostility toward China. What was noteworthy in the statement was a line that the Chinese representative at Warsaw had filed a strong protest to American ambassador to Poland Walter Stoessel, demanding Liao be handed back; otherwise the United States would have to "bear any serious consequences" it caused.[7] On February 18, two days before the scheduled meeting, the Chinese Foreign Ministry announced the decision to back out, stating that the "undeniable crime" of the United States against China in inciting Liao's defection rendered the atmosphere "unsuitable" for diplomatic talks.[8] Liao's defection could not have occurred at a worse time, and Washington probably had not expected it to happen either, but since he was already on American soil, the U.S. government could not go against its own values. So it had no choice but to take Liao. Beijing's response was understandable because it needed to save face and also show the world that China was not courting the United States at whatever cost.

American officials did not expect that the defector incident would cause Beijing to cancel the meeting because Chinese officials had still come to Warsaw when a similar case occurred in 1966. Moreover, Chinese officials in Warsaw did not show any intention of canceling the meeting in the initial days after the U.S. announcement of the defection. On February 5, for example, when Stoessel asked the Chinese whether the official meeting should be held in the U.S. or Chinese embassy, they responded that the usual venue was fine. Stoessel described the atmosphere of their brief discussion as "relaxed and pleasant." In addition, a State Department Bureau of Intelligence and Research (INR) report claimed to have detected from the Chinese protest a departure from its standard accusations against Lyndon Johnson because it had not accused Nixon of wanting to "wage war on

China" or using Vietnam to threaten China's security. INR concluded that these "significant holes in Beijing's propaganda" suggested its willingness to give Nixon a chance.[9] With these conditions, National Security Adviser Henry Kissinger did not change the plan and sent a memo to Nixon making recommendations about the coming Warsaw Talks as late as February 12. As to Beijing's abrupt decision to cancel the meeting, INR interpreted it as the "latest and most striking evidence of disagreement and indecision at the highest levels of the Chinese leadership."[10]

While the U.S. media were still talking about Chinese moderation signaled by its calling for the renewal of the Warsaw Talks, they were taken aback by its sudden cancellation. The networks connected the Chinese announcement with the defection. The *Post* blamed China for cutting the tie, alleging that it seemed to be "less interested in being accepted" into the international society than in "reasserting its traditional role as the great power, paid tribute to by countries nearby." *Newsweek* quoted a China specialist who described Washington as an "innocent victim" of Beijing's leadership problems.[11]

With many first-rate China watchers, like Tillman Durdin, who headed its Hong Kong bureau, the *Times* was probably the least shocked because it had sensed bad omens from the Chinese media in the past. When Beijing started the campaign against Nixon a week after his inauguration, the *Times* interpreted it as a "calculated blow at détente with the United States" because the attacks had been withheld for several weeks. It thus suggested that the outlook for the Warsaw meeting on February 20 would be "less favorable." Moreover, when Washington announced Liao's defection, the *Times* had displayed its worry that the announcement might become a source of "potential diplomatic embarrassment" for the two governments. On the Chinese cancellation, the *Times* not only talked about the possible leadership problems in Beijing but also criticized the Nixon administration for the lack of initiatives toward China. Along with the *Post*, it argued that the U.S. government should not limit itself to the Warsaw channel in seeking accommodation with China.[12]

Though Beijing canceled the Warsaw meeting, there were signs of flexibility in the Chinese media. One noticeable thing that escaped the U.S. media's attention was that *People's Daily* published the full text of Nixon's inaugural speech in the same issue as the joint editorial attacking him. What was more interesting was that other major newspapers all over China, following the general practice during the Cultural Revolution of reprinting the editorials of *People's Daily,* also published Nixon's address. This was unprecedented in the history of the PRC.[13] There was evidence that Mao had personally ordered the publication of Nixon's address. When editors of *People's Daily* and *Red Flag* sent their editorials to Mao for approval, his instruction was: "Publish the article as it is. Nixon's [inaugural] speech should also be published."[14] It seems that Mao wanted some of Nixon's messages to be known to the Chinese audience.

Nixon did not specifically mention China in his inaugural address, but his meaning was not hard to perceive when he stated: "Let all nations know that during this administration our lines of communication will be open. We seek an open world—open to ideas, open to the exchange of goods and people—a world in which no people, great or small, will live in angry isolation."[15] Mao's head nurse, Wu Xujun, said that Mao, who had been impressed by that line, asked her to keep it in mind.[16] The phrase "angry isolation" echoed Nixon's 1967 *Foreign Affairs* article in which he famously stated: "We simply cannot afford to leave China forever outside the family of nations, there to nurture its fantasies, cherish its hates and threaten its neighbors. There is no place on this small planet for a billion of its potentially most able people to live in angry isolation."[17] There is evidence that Mao not only had read the article but also had shown it to Zhou Enlai. When Senate majority leader Mike Mansfield (D-MT) visited China in 1972, Zhou told him: "It is Chairman Mao's decision to open up Sino-U.S. relations. Actually, he has read an article written by Nixon before he won the presidential election in 1968."[18] Mao might have inferred from the article a possible change in U.S. China policy if Nixon were elected president.

Nobody knows for certain Mao's motives. Chen Jian argues that Mao might have ordered the publication of Nixon's address in full text to reveal that "he had noticed Nixon's message."[19] Or Mao might have had other considerations. While brainstorming on Sino-American relations, he might have wanted to keep different options open by letting the Chinese people know about Nixon's original meaning.

Another sign of Chinese flexibility was reflected in how *People's Daily* treated Nixon's first press conference on January 27. When asked about his China policy, Nixon said his administration would "continue to oppose Communist China's admission to the United Nations." Among the reasons, he cited the Chinese lack of interest in joining the UN, its refusing to abide by the UN Charter, and its insistence on the expulsion of Taiwan, which Nixon described as a "responsible member of the international community." Though he expressed interest in what China had to say at the next Warsaw meeting, Nixon concluded that he saw no immediate prospect of any change in U.S. policy "until some changes occur on their side."[20] The remarks about China worried the U.S. press when *Newsweek* claimed that they could have been "eagerly cited as proof of America's evil intentions." The *Times* also called it the "the most disappointing section" of his press conference because he chose to ignore the fact that the Chinese initiative in calling for the Warsaw Talks was itself a change of its earlier stance.[21] Interestingly, however, neither *People's Daily* nor *Reference News* cited Nixon's "disappointing" lines in their coverage of the press conference. Headlines of *People's Daily* criticized the Soviet Union for "shamelessly flattering" Nixon and "colluding" with him.[22] Interestingly, the Chinese media seemed to be covering for Nixon. Another possibility is that for China at the time, the coming Warsaw Talks were much more important than a seat at the UN, which they had lived without for almost two decades.

The performance of the Chinese media over the renewal of Warsaw Talks from December 1968 to February 1969 shows that at a time when the Sino-Soviet and Sino-Vietnamese relations were both deteriorating, Mao was actively brainstorming and looking for ways to improve China's own international position. He seemed to be exploring what kind of opportunities would arise with a new president in the White House. Despite the Chinese media's invective against the U.S. government and Nixon himself, closer reading could reveal nuanced signs of flexibility, which can be particularly seen in their handling of Nixon's inaugural address and his early press conferences. The conflicting signals in the Chinese media show that, even though Beijing sent out feelers to test the attitude of the new administration, Chinese leaders were not ready to substantially change the relations with the United States.

Eruption of Sino-Soviet Border Clashes

Even though the initial probing between Washington and Beijing failed, the eruption of Sino-Soviet military conflicts provided an opportunity for the two sides to make bolder moves toward each other. The fighting that broke out on March 2, 1969, was a culmination of Sino-Soviet border tensions that had been brewing for years, especially over two small islands, Zhenbao and Qiliqin, on the Wusuli (Ussuri) River. In the wake of the Soviet invasion of Czechoslovakia and the CCP's twelfth plenum in the second half of 1968, tensions rose sharply in this area. Between December 1968 and February 1969, several incidents occurred in which Soviet armored vehicles landed on Zhenbao Island and its soldiers beat up Chinese soldiers with sticks or caused injuries by other means. After careful preparation, Beijing authorized its border troops to teach the Soviets a "bitter lesson." On March 2 and 15, they inflicted heavy casualties on Soviet forces in the two battles at Zhenbao Island. When clashes broke out, neither China nor the Soviet Union seemed to be considering a large-scale war. Soviet leaders did not even change their foreign visit itinerary upon learning of the first clash. After the second battle on March 15, Mao's order was: "We should stop here. Do not fight any more."[23]

In their immediate response, the *Times* and the *Post* were both surprised not by the fighting but by the fact that it was promptly announced by both governments. They knew there had been skirmishes along the border for years, but Beijing and Moscow had either denied unofficial reports of border incidents or dismissed them with vague references. The *Post* said that the conflict was as "important for being announced as for being fought." The *Times* claimed that the territorial issue was only a "sidelight" that could be turned on or off as the overall climate changed.[24] *Time* magazine blamed China by arguing that it had put its border clash with Russia to use "in a new domestic campaign" similar to the Great Leap Forward.[25] *Newsweek* gave equal coverage to both sides in terms of their respective versions of what happened during the battle, the background, and the explanations of the other side's motivations.[26] Standing in the middle, the magazine left its readers to judge for themselves.

The three networks used Soviet-provided film showing the memorial service for fallen Soviet soldiers and Chinese border guards violently wav-

ing Mao's Red Books and shouting in the faces of Soviet guards. To add
to the sensation, they all quoted the Soviet Foreign Ministry's statement
that the Chinese had mutilated dead Soviet soldiers with bayonets.[27] The
overall impression was that the Chinese had been more provocative than
the Soviets.

Based on the exchange of words between Beijing and Moscow, the
U.S. media did not find the atmosphere to be particularly intense. Even
in the Soviet-provided film, some Russian civilians, though shouting slogans, looked more relaxed than furious, and some were even smiling. ABC
reporter Irv Chapman described the overall atmosphere of the Soviet-
orchestrated protest as "good-humored." The *Times* claimed that the ban-
ners and shouts of the marchers brought forth by cheerleaders in loudspeaker trucks in Moscow contrasted with "the gay comportment" of
many demonstrators. It described the crowd in Beijing, many of them
women or schoolchildren, as more relaxed and less threatening than in
the earlier protest meetings by the Red Guards, who by now had been
sent to the countryside. The *Post* depicted the Soviet demonstrators as
"restrained" when they passed the Chinese embassy in an "orderly fashion,
six abreast."[28] By contrasting the official fury with the protestors' relaxed
demeanor, the U.S. media seemed to be mocking the two governments for
staging the demonstrations.

Between April 1 and April 24, 1969, the Chinese Communist Party
convened its Ninth National Congress. At the twelfth plenum of the Eighth
Congress that had convened the previous October, Mao said that the Cultural Revolution would probably last three years and might end in the
summer of 1969.[29] Even though Mao never officially declared the ending
of the Cultural Revolution, with the dissolution of the Central Cultural
Revolution Group and the restoration of power to the Politburo, its most
radical stage had ended.[30]

At the Ninth Congress, Chinese leaders seemed to show little concern
about the border clashes either. Though Lin Biao condemned the Soviet
Union in his official report, he stated that the Chinese government was
considering the Soviet request for negotiation. Mao talked about preparing for war, but mainly in a "spiritual sense," which was no different from
his position since the early 1960s. He did not demand special logistical
mobilization or extra alerts to deal with the Sino-Soviet conflict.[31]

In the March/April issue of *Red Flag*, the editorial "About Summing up Experience" was placed before the one attacking the Soviet Union for the border clashes. It declared that the Cultural Revolution had achieved its "great and decisive" victory and called on the Chinese people to work harder on the "fronts of industry, agriculture and education."[32] This editorial, along with another one entitled "Make Revolution, Promote Production, and Win New Victory on the Industrial Front," both reprinted in *People's Daily*, reflected the shift of China's focus from "revolution" to "production." Its placement suggested that for the leadership in Beijing at the time, reorganization of the Party and the shift of its focus were more important than the conflict with the Soviet Union. It also suggested that Beijing was not too worried about the border clashes with the Soviet Union.

As the Ninth Congress was the first key meeting of the CCP in thirteen years and was announced in the 1969 New Year's joint editorial of *People's Daily, Red Flag,* and the *PLA Daily,* the U.S. media were well aware of its importance. At the beginning of the year, the *Times* and the *Post* had managed to obtain the draft of the new Party constitution circulating at the provincial level.[33] When the congress started, they observed on their front pages that it would put an end to Mao's Cultural Revolution. *Newsweek* pointed out that the presence of "military men and career bureaucrats" as the majority in China's top ruling organs was a sign of moderation in Chinese domestic policy. *Time* viewed the Ninth Congress as "China's search for stability," arguing that the fact "that the congress was convened at all showed that Mao had made at least some progress toward domestic peace."[34]

With the general impression that the Ninth Congress would bring stability to China, some U.S. news agencies began to dwell on its significance for Sino-American relations. In an article headlined "Washington Hopes Peking Meeting Leads to Talks with U.S.," the *Times* shrewdly referred to an ongoing China policy review headed by Henry Kissinger as "disclosed" by U.S. officials and Secretary of State William Rogers's recent remark to the Senate Foreign Relations Committee that the Ninth Congress "might result in the formulation of new policies setting the course for China's future developments." NBC went even further than the *Times*. After reporting Rogers's statement that the United States would not exploit Sino-Soviet troubles and that it wanted better relations with both countries, the anchor said that the CCP's Ninth Congress might result in a "softer" China policy and that "diplomatic gossip" in Eastern Europe about a warming of U.S.-China relations gave the Russians "sleepless nights."[35] Although Rogers's statement gave the impression of American neutrality, the anchor's comments pointed toward better relations with China, because of the Sino-Soviet conflict.

Front-page stories in the *Post* played down the Chinese threat and highlighted the Soviet nervousness about a possible thaw in U.S.-China hostility, which can be seen in such titles as "Moscow Is Strident: China Tones down Trouble on Border" and "Chinese Threat Obsesses Table-Pounding Brezhnev." In its editorial pages, while Stanley Karnow, the *Post*'s main China watcher in Hong Kong, advocated tilting toward Beijing in his column "Soviet Anti-Chinese Blasts Provide Openings for U.S," Stephen Rosenfeld, the former chief of the *Post*'s Moscow bureau, argued that the United States should avoid exploiting the Sino-Soviet trouble and develop close relations with both in his column "US Has Dilemma on Ussuri Fighting." Interestingly, the editorial board of the *Post* went along with Rosenfeld's position.[36] The differences in their positions again demonstrate a pattern in which the front-page news stories appeared more liberal than the editorial pages.

On its editorial page, the *Times* reprinted a speech of former White House counsel Theodore Sorensen, who presented evidence to show that Beijing was more hostile in words but Moscow was more threatening in deeds.[37] Sorensen made his address at the National Committee on United States–China Relations conference on March 20, chaired by Edwin O. Reischauer of Harvard, former ambassador to Japan, and Columbia University's China expert A. Doak Barnett. It attracted prominent media coverage due to the attendance of Senator Edward Kennedy (D-MA), who in his keynote address called for "sweeping change" in America's China policy in the context of Sino-Soviet conflicts. After reporting Kennedy's speech on their front pages, the *Times* and the *Post* ran additional stories about how China specialists praised his proposal. In an NBC telecast, the anchor started with, "However improbable it may seem, the United States and China might have an understanding." He then explained that when the New York liberals met to talk about China policy, Russia's *New Time* condemned the meeting because it seemed to "coincide with" the Chinese attack. When he pointed out that the meeting had been planned a year earlier,[38] it looked like a blow to the Soviet accusation and highlighted Moscow's paranoia.

By late 1968, the images projected to the world by the two Communist countries had changed a lot. While the Soviet tanks rolled into Czechoslovakia to crush the liberal reforms, chaos caused by Red Guards in China declined substantially because Mao had sent millions of them to the countryside. In covering the Sino-Soviet conflicts, the U.S. media generally described the Soviets as more aggressive than the Chinese, and many of them argued that the trouble between the two Communist giants provided a good opportunity for Washington to improve relations with Beijing. As with the Fulbright Hearings three years earlier, the media appeared to be again working with academics and Congress to push for a reform in China policy. On the issue of Sino-Soviet conflicts, the U.S. media, unlike the U.S. government, did not have to worry about upsetting the Soviet Union when they openly elaborated on the benefits of moving closer to China. These media stories would feed government officials and justify their policies if they chose to move toward China.

The Four Marshals' Reports

The Ninth Congress of the CCP in April not only ended the most radical stage of the Cultural Revolution but also marked a watershed in China's foreign relations. In its wake, Beijing began to normalize its diplomatic activities by sending out its diplomats again.[39] As early as January 1969, the *Times* had obtained information that a leading tailor shop in Beijing was busy making suits for the Chinese Foreign Ministry, which it interpreted as a sign that Beijing was "contemplating a more active role in foreign affairs."[40] In order to improve relations with other countries, Beijing invited several foreign envoys to join Mao and other Chinese leaders for the May Day celebration at the Tiananmen rostrum.[41]

After the Ninth Congress, a review of China's foreign relations was conducted by four highly esteemed marshals—Chen Yi, Ye Jianying, Xu Xiangqian, and Nie Rongzhen—who had been sidelined because of their complaints about the Red Guard violence in the "February Reverse Current" incident in 1967. When Lin Biao was officially designated as Mao's successor at the Ninth Congress, his followers and radicals headed by Mao's wife, Jiang Qing, won most of the key positions in the central leadership. In order to counterbalance the power of Lin Biao and Jiang Qing, however, Mao inserted several veteran civilian and military officials into the Party leadership. Among these officials were the four marshals whose positions in the Central Committee and as the vice chairmen of the Central Military Committee were kept at the Ninth Congress even though most of them did not have many active duties to fulfill.[42] The most important of the marshals was Ye Jianying, whom Mao used as a counterweight to Lin Biao. He stayed in the Politburo and would play an active role in the Sino-American talks during Kissinger's secret visit to China in 1971.

Under the instructions of Mao, Zhou Enlai asked the four marshals, who were "studying" at factories in a suburb of Beijing, to meet from time to time and discuss current international affairs. Zhou encouraged them not to limit themselves to conventional thinking in their analyses and said that he would pass on their reports to Mao. Zhou also assigned Xiong Xianghui—a spy during the Chinese Civil War and the former chargé d'affaires to the United Kingdom who later acted as Zhou's aide in talks with Kissinger—to assist the marshals with English materials. Between June 7 and July 10, the four marshals met six times and talked in total for nineteen hours about the international situation, especially about the triangular relations among China, the United States, and the Soviet Union.[43]

On July 11, the four marshals submitted their first report. As they argued, even though the United States and the Soviet Union collaborated with each other, the hostilities between them were fiercer than before. They explicitly pointed out that the Soviet Union posed a more serious threat to the security of China than the United States. While they discounted the possibility that Washington and Moscow would start a large-scale war against China, either jointly or separately, they recommended that China should "postpone" conflict with either of them. In terms of China's overall foreign policy, they recommended the enhancement of its offices abroad and the expansion of their diplomatic activities.[44] According to Xiong, the General Office of the CCP distributed their report to officials in the central government as a Party document on July 20.[45] The spread of their report reflected Mao's approval of their evaluations of the triangular politics and China's strategic position with the two superpowers.

Gao Wenqian, a researcher at CCP Central Party Literature Research Center involved in writing the official biographies of Zhou Enlai and Mao Zedong after the Cultural Revolution, mentioned some interesting developments in the Chinese media during the summer of 1969. According to him, when Chinese newspapers in late June 1969 were about to publish their routine editorials attacking the American "invasion" of Taiwan nineteen years earlier, Zhou Enlai proposed at a Politburo meeting that the current focus was the struggle against the Soviet Union and that attacks on the American invasion of Taiwan should be toned down.[46] Given the higher priority of the Soviet threat, Zhou Enlai was not blind to the possible benefits of moving toward a former number-one enemy. Toning down the anti-American rhetoric in the Chinese media could send a positive message to the U.S. government.

Xiong Xianghui pointed out another change in the Chinese media after the Ninth Congress. As he said, even though the report of the congress had described the relations between Washington and Moscow as "competing and colluding" with each other, the Chinese official documents and the media dropped the Soviet-American "competition" and shifted to highlight the "collusion" between them, especially their collusion for anti-China purposes.[47] In June and July 1969, besides reporting more incidents supposedly started by the Soviet Union, *People's Daily* carried several articles charging that the United States and the Soviet Union were collaborating with each other or were working with Japan in carrying out activities against China.[48] During the Cultural Revolution, Beijing had attacked the Soviet-American collusion mainly in order to embarrass Moscow and serve its domestic purpose of struggling against revisionism because the Soviet Union did not constitute a strategic threat to China. The testimonies of Xiong, along with the performance of the Chinese media in June and July, indicate that the Chinese government was indeed worried about the possibility of a Sino-Soviet collusion against China after the Sino-Soviet border clashes in March. In that context, the position of the U.S. government on the Sino-Soviet conflicts became an important factor to move Sino-American relations forward if it could address Beijing's concern.

Nixon's Overtures to China in the Summer of 1969

After the abrupt cancellation of the Warsaw Talks in February, the Nixon administration was not as optimistic as the media in finding signs of moderation in Beijing in evaluating the Ninth Congress. On April 29, Kissinger submitted to Nixon a report prepared by the Central Intelligence Agency (CIA), the Department of State, and the National Security Council (NSC). Referring to the signs that a continued "power stalemate" existed in the Chinese leadership and to the "denigration" of the United States in the Party communiqué, Kissinger claimed to have seen "no indication that the Chinese leaders intend to become less cautious in avoiding foreign commitments."[49]

What triggered the Nixon administration to take more rigorous initiatives toward Beijing, according to Kissinger, was the "heavy-handed" Soviet diplomacy in handling the clashes with China. According to him, when he met with Soviet ambassador Anatoly Dobrynin on March 11, 1969, the latter told him "passionately" that China was "everybody's problem." When Kissinger described the encounter to Nixon that evening, the president was intrigued and talked about how "unexpected events could have a major effect." Kissinger then suggested that the United States had a chance to "gain a great deal strategically." In May, when new border clashes broke out in Xinjiang, where the Soviets had much better logistic lines than the Chinese, Kissinger changed his perception of the two Communist powers and began to view the Russians as more aggressive. What intrigued Washington further was Brezhnev's proposal of "collective security in Asia" in his speech to the International Conference of Communist Parties on June 8, which was obviously directed against China. Kissinger reported to Nixon that these signs showed that the growing Soviet obsession with the China problem had reached the point that it could be turned to the advantage of the United States. When Nixon read the report, he wrote in the margin, "This is our goal."[50]

In July and August 1969, through a series of public diplomatic activities and private channels, the Nixon administration sent clear signals to Beijing of its intention to improve relations. On July 21, 1969, the State Department announced the easing of trade restrictions and the travel ban on China. The timing of the announcement was based on shrewd calculations. Nixon had made the decision in June, but he chose to announce it on the day of his trip to countries that included Pakistan and Romania, both of which had friendly relations with China. In so doing, Nixon hoped that his policy change would be viewed as a friendly gesture by the Chinese leadership. Another reason why the announcement was made in July before the Nixon trip was that a delay might force the United States to deal with "unforeseeable situations" such as the worsening of the Sino-Soviet border situation. It could "preclude" the announcement and thus cause Washington to lose the diplomatic benefits. Also, if Nixon waited to announce the decision until he returned from Romania, which was not on good terms with Moscow, it probably would be tied in with speculation regarding a "putative anti-Soviet" purpose in the "Bucharest stopover." This would give his decision too much "overt anti-Soviet significance."[51]

Nixon's decision to relax trade and travel restrictions with China received a variety of comments in the U.S. media. ABC praised him for dismantling "the most formidable barriers" between the two countries, which showed that he was "really interested" in improving relations. An NBC anchor appeared somewhat skeptical. He said that the United States wanted to be "somewhat friendlier" to China and that the U.S. policy was not "a warm or loving embrace" as the trade restrictions were partly lifted, but not eliminated. He also doubted whether China would respond. CBS just reported the announcement and did not make further comment on the significance of the Nixon policy.[52]

Unlike TV programs, which are limited by time constraints, newspapers have enough space to elaborate on the background, significance, and response to a government policy. Calling attention to the effective date of the Nixon policy, the *Times* referred to the recent China policy review by the NSC and the endorsement of the policy by Senate majority leader Mike Mansfield (D-MT). It concluded that they seemed to signal an "official response to evolving attitudes in the United States toward the Chinese, away from the hostile rigidity."[53] While the *Times* placed the story on the front page, the *Post* assigned it to page twenty, arguing that the Nixon move had "greater symbolic meaning" than any practical application that might result from the changes. Recalling Nixon's tough words about China at his first press conference and the recent Chinese attack on him, it expressed doubt about the possibility of an open door between China and the United States.[54] While the *Times* presented a picture of a favorable domestic environment for a change in relations, the *Post* seemed to emphasize the empty half of the glass. It could also be interpreted as its frustration at the lack of concrete progress in Sino-American relations.

During his trip, Nixon sent public gestures of friendliness to China on several occasions. In his informal conversations with the press in Guam on July 25, he announced what would later be known as the "Nixon Doctrine," by which the United States, despite its promise to honor its commitments in Asia, would "look to the nation directly threatened to assume the primary responsibility of providing the manpower for its defense." He also told the press that China was not nearly as effective in exporting revolution as it was five or ten years ago and that it was playing a "minimal role" in Vietnam as compared to the Soviet Union.[55] Here Nixon was underplaying the China threat in comparison to the Soviet Union to justify his move toward Beijing. During his private visit to the Pacific area four years earlier, Nixon had declared in Australia that the United States should bomb China if it were "so rash as to introduce so-called volunteers [into Vietnam]."[56] Now Vietnam had declined as a major issue between China and the United States in Nixon's rhetoric.

Besides public gestures, Nixon also pushed hard through private channels. During his talk with Pakistani president Yahya Khan, Nixon told him that the United States wished to seek an accommodation with China and would appreciate it if Khan's government would pass on this message to Zhou Enlai when the Chinese premier visited Pakistan. Even though Nixon told journalists in Guam that his trip to Romania should "under no circumstances" be interpreted as "an affront to the Soviet Union or as a move toward China," in his conversation with Romanian president Nicolae Ceausescu, Nixon said Washington would not join in a Soviet arrangement against China in Asia and expressed his hope that Ceausescu would play a "mediating role" between Washington and Beijing.[57]

Due to China's friendly relations with Pakistan and Romania, the U.S. media alluded to the China connection in their coverage of Nixon's trip to these countries. ABC speculated that their leaders might serve as the middlemen between the United States and China. It even reported a rumor that Nixon might meet Chinese officials in Romania.[58] Both the *Times* and the *Post* in their editorials argued that Nixon's visit to Romania, a dissident in the Communist movement, could help the United States open its door to Beijing.[59] Unlike the previous administration, Nixon was creating an atmosphere for much better relations with China, progress of which the elite media were not unaware, even though they were still unclear about the exact details of what was happening behind closed doors.

During Nixon's trip, Secretary of State William Rogers also went on a Pacific tour, visiting Japan, South Korea, Indonesia, Taiwan, Hong Kong, Australia, and New Zealand to explain American policy in Asia, especially its decision to slowly withdraw from Vietnam. On his tour, Rogers openly reiterated the willingness of the U.S. government to talk to China. While he was in Hong Kong, the *Post* featured on its front page a photo of Rogers playing golf at a countryside lodge three miles from the Chinese border. As the *Times* reported, Rogers cited the recent American effort to lift trade restrictions and criticized China for not responding to it. In Australia, Rogers made a major speech declaring that Beijing would "soon" be asked to reopen the Warsaw Talks.[60]

People's Daily responded to Washington's overtures with invective. It attacked Nixon's visit to Asia as a cover for his policy of "aggression and war" and ridiculed his withdrawal from Asia as merely a change in tactics to serve the long-term goal to "occupy" Asia. It reported several demonstrations in countries Nixon visited with people shouting slogans like "Down with Nixon" and "Out with Nixon." In order to justify the U.S. withdrawal from Asia, Nixon had proposed the idea of "collective security" by Asian countries themselves in dealing with aggression as part of the "Nixon Doctrine." The official organ compared it to the Soviet proposal of Asian collective security and used them as evidence of Soviet-American "collusion" in containing China, listing both as the "worst enemies" of the Asian people.[61]

While *People's Daily* attacked the "evil designs" of the Nixon administration, *Reference News* fed higher-level Chinese cadres undistorted stories of Washington's intentions. During the Ninth Congress in April, it reprinted articles introducing the China policy review in Washington along with the U.S. hope that the congress would lead to the moderation of China. The most notable line was the Agence France-Presse's comment that there had never been such an "advantageous moment" to normalize the U.S.-China relations in the last twenty years.[62]

When Nixon's Asian trip was announced in late June, *Reference News* carried a story claiming that Nixon's acceptance of Ceausescu's invitation to visit Romania was aimed at China. On its front pages, it not only featured the State Department's announcement of relaxing trade and travel restrictions to China in an article entitled "The United States Put on a 'Conciliatory' Posture," but it also carried Taiwan's complaints about Washington's change in policy. In covering Nixon's meeting with Indonesian president Suharto, it reprinted Indonesian foreign minister Adam Malik's remark that "Nixon was not interested" in the Soviet proposal of collective security in Asia. It also reported Rogers's statements about Washington's desire to renew contact with Beijing when he visited Hong Kong and Australia.[63] Different from the "empty cannons" in *People's Daily*, these insightful analyses reprinted in *Reference News* provided useful perspectives for the Chinese cadres to consider the significance of Nixon's moves for U.S.-China relations.

Nixon's peace initiatives were understood well in Beijing. On July 16, the Chinese captured two American yachtsmen whose lifeboat drifted into Chinese territorial waters close to Hong Kong. According to Kissinger, Washington decided not to announce it immediately to see if Beijing would use it for anti-U.S. propaganda. When Zhou Enlai learned of the incident, he instructed the Foreign Ministry and the Public Safety Ministry to do a thorough investigation and to be cautious not to attach political meaning to the captured Americans. The Chinese media, under Zhou's instruction, remained silent on the incident. Beijing released the two Americans on July 24 after the U.S. relaxation in trade and travel. Kissinger argued that Zhou Enlai, who had understood the American gesture, also made a move that required no reciprocity from the United States.[64] Kissinger was right. Unlike the meetings at Warsaw, which required the coordination of both sides, sending signals through the media—or through the media's silence in the Chinese case—would be much easier because it did not require any active response from the other side. Even if the feelers did not go through, the political fallout might not be too great. This tactic is also useful when one side cannot verify the exact intentions of the other.

In the Shadow of the War Scare

As the Nixon administration was sending friendly signals to China, Sino-Soviet military conflicts suddenly escalated. On August 13, the Soviet armed forces ambushed a unit of Chinese border patrol in Xinjiang with superior forces consisting of helicopters, tanks, and armed vehicles, which caused heavy Chinese casualties. After the attack, Moscow gave the impression that it was considering a preemptive strike against Chinese nuclear facilities. Besides deploying nuclear strike groups along the border, Soviet diplomats also inquired of diplomats from its Eastern European allies and the United States about what their response would be if the Soviet Union initiated a nuclear attack against China.[65] In response, on August 28, the CCP Central Committee issued the "Order for General Mobilization in Border Province and Regions."[66]

When war fervor began to increase along the Sino-Soviet border in August 1969, the Nixon administration began to seriously consider how to deal with the scenario of a large-scale war between China and the Soviet Union. At an NSC meeting on August 14, Nixon stated that it was against the interests of the United States to let China be "smashed" in a Sino-Soviet war. His view was in line with Kissinger's, who had pointed out that history had shown that it was better to align with the weaker, not the stronger, of two antagonistic powers, when some Russian experts expressed concern that better relations with China might ruin those with the Soviet Union at an earlier NSC meeting in May.[67] The administration ended up excluding the option of siding with the Soviet Union and focused on only two options: "impartiality" and "shading" toward China. An NSC memo concluded that trying to be "even-handed and impartial or neutral" when China was attacked would be "tantamount to supporting the USSR." However, an open partiality toward China might cause dramatic reaction from the Soviet Union and hurt the arms reduction talks. So the memo recommended that Washington maintain public impartiality and at the same time give a strong signal that it would not encourage a Soviet nuclear attack on China.[68]

Interestingly, a story in *Newsweek* on August 18 expressed a position similar to Nixon's as it argued that if the Russians won the war against China, it would dramatically change "the international balance of power" to the disadvantage of the United States and would cause deeper suspicion and animosity in Soviet-American relations than those that prevailed during the worst of the Cold War.[69] It seems that Nixon faced much more favorable international and domestic environments for improving relations with China.

In a speech at the sixty-fifth annual meeting of the American Political Science Association in Baltimore on September 5, Under Secretary of State Elliot Richardson made what was considered Washington's first official statement on the Sino-Soviet conflict. After explaining the U.S. position of not siding with either side against the other, he said: "We are not going to let Communist Chinese invective deter us from seeking agreements with the Soviet Union. Conversely, we are not going to let the Soviet apprehensions prevent us from attempting to bring China out of its angry, alienated shell."[70] The next day, the *Times* featured the headline "Nixon Aide Affirms U.S. Will Press for China Ties," which only published the statement "we are not going to let the Soviet apprehensions prevent us from attempting to bring China out of its angry, alienated shell," omitting his remarks about Washington seeking agreements with the Soviet Union. Essentially it rendered what appeared to be a neutral statement of the government into an official bias toward China. The *Post* headline, in contrast, used the title "Keep Peace, U.S. Cautions China, Soviet." which claimed that Richardson's statement was the "first high level public admonition to the Soviet Union and China not to breach the peace of the world."[71] The *Post* gave the impression that the United States was assuming the moral high ground over the Sino-Soviet conflicts and adopting a tough policy toward both of them. The agenda of improving relations with either of them was underplayed. For some reason, the newsweeklies and the nightly newscasts ignored Richardson's statement.

Kissinger argues that Richardson's statement was a "revolutionary step" for the U.S. government when it publicly warned against a threat to China, a country that had been hostile to the United States and with which it had had no communication since Nixon took office. In his memo to Kissinger on October 8, NSC staffer John Holdridge suggested calling the attention of the Chinese to Richardson's statement as part of the U.S. overtures.[72] Actually, *Reference News* reprinted the full text of Richardson's statement,[73] which might have impressed leaders in Beijing.

While fears of a full-scale war between China and the Soviet Union were increasing, Soviet premier Alexei Kosygin suddenly stopped at the Beijing airport on September 11 to meet with Zhou Enlai on his way back from the funeral of Ho Chi Minh. After the meeting, the Russian news agency TASS declared, "The two sides openly explained their positions and held a conversation useful for both sides." *People's Daily* published a terse statement, declaring that the two premiers had met and engaged in a "frank" conversation.[74] According to Gao Wenqian, in drafting the announcement of the Zhou-Kosygin meeting, Moscow had used several positive adjectives such as "comradely" and "friendly" to create the impression that the Sino-Soviet tensions had been relieved. However, Zhou Enlai crossed them out when he received the Soviet draft and retained only the word "frank."[75] The word "frank" could be interpreted either as a sign of distrust or coldness, but it could still leave the door open for the Nixon administration to approach China.

The U.S. media expressed great "astonishment" upon learning of the Zhou-Kosygin meeting. All three networks made the news one of their lead stories. NBC used "enigmatic" in describing the behavior of the Chinese and the Russians.[76] Both the *Times* and the *Post* read the Russian use of the word "useful" and the Chinese use of the word "frank" as signs that no substantial progress was achieved at the talk. In their editorial pages, the *Post* was skeptical that the Sino-Soviet war had been avoided, whereas the *Times* took the opposite position, interpreting the meeting as a sign that "the tension had been eased" and suggesting that those observers who had been predicting an imminent war should "take another look."[77]

Even though the Kosygin-Zhou meeting relaxed the "extreme tension" between China and the Soviet Union, it did not relieve Beijing's suspicion of a Soviet surprise attack.[78] The pressure from Moscow had the potential of pushing Beijing further toward Washington. On September 17, the four marshals, who had read reports of Nixon's recent initiatives and the minutes of the Zhou-Kosygin meeting, submitted another report. They proposed that China use negotiation as a tactic and wage "a tit-for-tat struggle" against Moscow and Washington since they were both trying to exploit the other two parties in the triangle with China in order to gain strategic advantages. Besides agreeing on the Soviet requests for negotiation on border issues, they suggested responding "positively" to the Amer-

ican request for resuming the Warsaw Talks when the "timing is proper."
Marshal Chen Yi, the foreign minister who had lost his actual power, submitted a separate report to present his "wild" thoughts about how to pursue a "breakthrough" in the Sino-American relations. He recommended
that at Warsaw China should take the initiative to propose talks at the
ministerial level or even higher without raising prerequisites and that the
Taiwan question could be gradually solved by talks at higher levels.[79] Nobody can tell for certain whether Mao followed the suggestions of the marshals. At least they provided perspectives and some legitimacy for Mao if
he was thinking about moving in the same direction. More importantly,
the articulation of Sino-American rapprochement by the four marshals itself shows that this concept was no longer taboo among the top leadership.
When Sino-American talks were renewed in early 1970, things developed
just as Marshal Chen had proposed.

The Zhou-Kosygin meeting did not eliminate Beijing's worry. There
was worry in Beijing that Kosygin's China trip might be a smokescreen for
a Soviet surprise attack. On September 17, *People's Daily* published twenty-
nine slogans for the National Day celebration. The twenty-second slogan
called on the people of the world to "oppose the invasion started by any
imperialist or socialist imperialist powers, especially nuclear wars" and
asked the people to "be prepared right now." The next day, it ran an editorial pointing out that the twenty-second slogan was a "great order of
mobilization with profound strategic significance."[80]

After the publication of the "great order of mobilization," there were
more significant developments in *People's Daily*. On September 21, it published Mao and Lin's order to honor ten soldiers in the Zhenbao battle
as "war heroes." In an October Day joint editorial, Beijing expressed its
desire to "use negotiation" to solve border disputes between countries. At
the same time, it called on the Chinese people to be "highly alert" against
the enemy's "surprise attack" and to be prepared to defend China's "sov-
ereign frontier." In an address to foreign dignitaries at the National Day
reception, Zhou Enlai reiterated the principle that China would never attack any country unless attacked first and the Chinese determination to
"fight to the very end until victory" if anyone imposed a war of aggression
on China. In order to raise the morale of the Chinese people, the official
organ on October 5 reported a story that China had been successful in ex-

ploding another H-bomb and in its first underground atomic test a week earlier. It claimed that these new achievements delivered a "severe blow to the nuclear hegemony of the American as well as socialist imperialists."[81] These calls for war preparation against the socialist imperialists—the Soviet Union—revealed the intensity of war nervousness in Beijing. *Reference News* also emphasized the atmosphere of war preparation when it reprinted foreign news agencies' response to the editorials and speeches of Chinese leaders.[82]

On October 7, China took a major step to defuse tensions with the Soviet Union by announcing its decision to start border negotiations at the level of vice foreign minister. Beijing's statement went: "The Chinese government has never covered up the fact that there exist irreconcilable differences of principle between China and the Soviet Union and that the struggle of principle between them will continue for a long period of time. But this should not prevent China and the Soviet Union from maintaining normal state relations on the basis of the five principles of peaceful coexistence." The next day, it published Beijing's "five-point proposal" calling for mutual troop withdrawal from the disputed areas. What was noticeable was that it even carried the congratulatory letter from the Soviet Union on the twentieth anniversary of the People's Republic.[83] It was an effort to show the reduced tensions between the two governments.

Beijing's decision to sit down and talk with Moscow was watched with great interest in Washington. In a memo to Kissinger, John H. Holdridge wrote that he found the thesis of "normal relations on the basis of the five principles of peaceful coexistence" in the Chinese statement particularly interesting because it reminded him of the Chinese call for the renewal of Warsaw Talks a year earlier and that it could apply to the United States as well. Holdridge also pointed out "concrete evidence" of Beijing's reduced hostility toward Washington. For example, he mentioned the Norwegian ambassador who had talked about the "even-handed" discussions he had with Chinese officials about Sino-American relations. As the French ambassador related, Zhou Enlai did not reject resuming the talks in Warsaw, but he said that the "situation was complicated," apparently referring to the situation in Beijing. He also referred to Zhou's statement that the American attitude in the Sino-Soviet conflict was "ambiguous." Based on these indicators, along with the "apprehensive tone" he saw in the Chinese statement, Holdridge suggested it might be an "opportune moment" for a move toward Beijing.[84]

Interestingly, Holdridge's report was leaked in a *Times* story, "U.S. Aides Discern Signs That Peking Is Easing Enmity."[85] This resulted in widespread attention when reporters tried to verify its contents with the State Department. CBS reported that the State Department had denied the "rumor" through an "unspecified channel" that China had become "soft" on the United States, citing the Chinese cancellation of the Warsaw Talks as evidence.[86] The *Times* article even attracted the attention of the Chinese media. *Reference News* carried a front-page article in which State Department spokesman Carl Bartch stated, when he was asked about the article, that Washington had always hoped to improve relations with Beijing.[87]

The *Post* noticed the "unusual display of candor" in Beijing's statement, which it interpreted as a sign that China had emerged from "three years of rigidity" to a period of "relative realism." However, its headline "Fear Drives China to Talk to Russia" emphasized Chinese fear when it claimed that Beijing's move toward a détente with Washington suggested a lesson that "nothing has a greater impact on Peking than the menace of force." In an editorial entitled "A Momentous Sino-Soviet Breakthrough?" the *Post* maintained that the United States had a "compelling interest in cooling off of the dispute." That is, if Moscow could get the China border issue in hand, the Soviet-American missile talks would "soon" begin.[88] An editorial of the *Times,* in contrast, suggested a different lesson, which was that "Chinese leaders were not mad, but rational men able to weigh the costs and advantages of alternative policies."[89] Here, the *Post* editorial seemed to be more interested in the Soviet Union, whereas the *Times* was more focused on China.

Beijing's effort to relax tensions with the Soviet Union not only reduced the terror of war but also meant that the Chinese need for improved relations with the United States was no longer especially urgent. In a way, it became a test of intentions for the Nixon administration. In order to obtain a diplomatic advantage, it was better for Washington to establish contact with Beijing before it reached any settlement with Moscow. ABC showed Washington's eagerness when it reported the State Department's statement that the United States was ready to talk with China "anywhere" and "as soon as possible."[90] The story appeared only one day after Beijing's announcement of border talks with Moscow.

Meeting Again after the "Unusual Encounter"

In order to contact Beijing as soon as possible, the Nixon administration tried different channels. On October 27, 1969, the U.S. consul-general in Hong Kong, Edwin W. Martin, wrote Liu Xingyuan, chairman of the Provincial Revolutionary Committee of Guangdong, and inquired about the whereabouts of two Americans who had been imprisoned in China since February. At Zhou Enlai's personal instruction, the Foreign Ministry reported the inquiry to the Central Committee on November 7 with a note: "This is obviously a new act on the part of the U.S. government to test our response. We suggest that we take over the matter and have the two released at the right moment."[91]

On November 16, the Nixon administration sent another friendly signal to China by decreasing its naval patrol in the Taiwan Strait by two destroyers attached to the Seventh Fleet on account of "budget reasons." Earlier that month Pakistani president Yahya had called the Chinese ambassador to inform him of his impressions of the talk with Nixon in August and the U.S. intention to withdraw the destroyers.[92] Interestingly, the story about the removal of destroyers did not show up in the U.S. media until Christmas, and it came through a Japanese news agency claiming that the United States had informed Japan of its decision. Neither the *Times* nor the *Post* made a big deal about the issue, and they merely ran short stories in interior pages.[93] In the case of naval patrol withdrawal, the U.S. government may have tried hard to keep it under the radar. It is also possibly due to the unwitting cooperation of the U.S. media, which did not prioritize it, that Nixon avoided serious opposition from conservatives at home.

As early as September during the height of the war scare, Nixon and Kissinger had urged Ambassador Stoessel to get in touch with his Chinese counterpart as soon as possible. It was not until December 3 that he finally had a chance to approach a Chinese diplomat at a Yugoslavian fashion show at Warsaw's Palace of Culture. Without clear instructions from Beijing, the Chinese diplomat did not know how to handle the situation. As a result, he tried to flee the scene as the U.S. ambassador ran after him. Stoessel managed to catch a Chinese interpreter and told him that he had an important message for the Chinese government.[94]

When the American ambassador's "unusual behavior" was reported to Zhou Enlai, he immediately relayed this "encounter" to Mao and said, "The opportunity is coming; we now have a brick in our hands to knock at the door [of the Americans.]" Zhou Enlai at once instructed the Chinese embassy in Warsaw to let the Americans know of Beijing's interest in reopening communications. Moreover, with Mao's approval, on December 7 Zhou Enlai ordered the release of the two Americans about whom the U.S. consulate in Hong Kong had inquired.[95] In order to make sure the American side received this signal, Zhou suggested that the release should be announced in the press and that the Chinese ambassador to Poland be informed of it.[96] As the Chinese leadership hoped, the release of the two Americans duly appeared on the front pages of the *Times* and the *Post*.[97] After *People's Daily* announced the release of the two Americans, *Reference News* noted on its front page the "surprise" of the State Department, whose spokesman stated that they had learned of the news from the Xinhua News Agency.[98] The release of Americans was a clear signal of friendliness. Beijing wanted the message to be delivered to Washington quickly and accurately. Announcement in the Chinese media could achieve both. The incident at the Yugoslavian fashion show thus became a turning point, after which Beijing became much more active in reciprocating the initiatives from Washington.

On December 11, the Chinese embassy took the initiative by calling the American embassy and inviting U.S. representatives to have a meeting at the Chinese embassy the next day.[99] When State Department spokesman Robert McCloskey announced the meeting the next day, it was placed among the lead stories of the television programs and the headlines of the two elite newspapers. Both the *Times* and the *Post* called it an important "breakthrough" in Sino-American relations after two years of "diplomatic silence." As an editorial of the *Times* pointed out, the importance of the meeting could be shown by the speed at which China responded to Stoessel's informal initiative a week earlier and from the fact that he was invited to the Chinese embassy. The *Post*, by taking into account the

Soviet-American strategic arms limitation talks in Helsinki, the renewal of Sino-American contact in Warsaw, as well as the Sino-Soviet border negotiation in Beijing, concluded that the formation of the "Washington-Moscow-Peking triangle" by the end of 1969 had become a "historic event in international affairs."[100]

Conclusion

This chapter shows that the Chinese and U.S. media, in their distinctive ways, provided a foundation for possible policy change with the normalization of China's domestic politics as well as diplomatic activities and the eruption of Sino-Soviet border clashes in 1969. They responded positively to the Nixon administration's forthcoming public signaling to China of its interest in improved relations, so that both Chinese Party officials and U.S. public opinion were well prepared for policy change.

In covering the CCP's Ninth Congress and Beijing's handling of the Sino-Soviet border negotiations, the U.S. media presented a rational China that was potentially more responsive to U.S. overtures. On the Sino-Soviet conflict, the U.S. media not only pictured the Soviet Union as more aggressive than China but also called attention to the Soviet fear of possible Sino-American reconciliation. The U.S. media were earlier than Nixon in viewing the border clashes as an opportunity for a U.S. opening to China. When the Nixon administration was moving in that direction, news stories and editorials in the media provided an impetus for the more cautious White House to believe that a changed China policy would be well received inside the United States. While Washington maintained a public posture of neutrality, the U.S. media were not worried about upsetting Moscow as they discussed at length the benefits of improving relations with Beijing. They helped the government cultivate the public by elaborating on something it might want to do but was otherwise unable to state explicitly. Essentially, the U.S. media prepared the public opinion for the Nixon administration to take more active steps in approaching China and justified this policy change.

On the other hand, the Chinese media showed aloofness as well as reception to the U.S. overtures. Even though *People's Daily* sustained its public attacks on the United States, it revealed signs of flexibility, especially in the treatment of Nixon's inaugural address and his first press conference. In the context of Sino-Soviet crises, the Chinese media's attack on Soviet-American "collusion" not only served to mobilize the domestic solidarity against foreign invasion but also revealed Beijing's concern about this possibility.

During this period, *Reference News* played a crucial role in passing on American intentions to the Chinese cadres. While carrying explicit commentaries that the Soviet Union posed the greatest threat to China's security, it also featured stories about U.S. support for China in the Sino-Soviet border clashes and about U.S. signals of interest in improved relations. Essentially, it objectively reported Washington's overtures that might have impressed the Chinese. Through stories in the open media and internal communications, the Chinese government effectively left open the option of reconciliation with Washington when their leaders were deliberating on their own options.

Interactions between the media in the two countries are also important. The Nixon administration's high-profile announcement of the relaxation of embargos on China and Beijing's public announcement that it was releasing imprisoned Americans were both overtures that did not require any response from the other side. In both cases, the media became a useful channel to send out signals before the genuine intentions of the other side could be confirmed because direct contacts between the two governments had yet to be reestablished. When it comes to these key events between the two countries, the coverage of one government's announcement or move in its own media would always appear in the media of the other country. As such, the media of the two countries seemed to move in tandem.

The war nerves in the Chinese media from September through the Chinese National Day on October 1, 1969 shows that Beijing was truly worried about a Soviet surprise attack. This worry was decisive in pushing China toward the United States. Ultimately, "the unusual encounter" at the Yugoslavian fashion show in Warsaw convinced Chinese leaders to stop hesitating and to become more active players in the Sino-American reconciliation.

4

From Warsaw to Beijing

THE "INTRICATE MINUET" OF SIGNALS, 1970-1971

U.S. ambassador to Poland Walter Stoessel Jr.'s dramatic pursuit of Chinese diplomats at the Yugoslavian fashion show in Warsaw in December 1969 was a turning point in moving Beijing closer to Washington because it not only reassured Chinese leaders of Nixon's sincere desire to improve relations, but it also satisfied the Chinese national pride. Mao and Zhou later repeatedly told other Chinese leaders, "It is the Americans who need something from us, not the other way around."[1] In announcing the renewal of the Warsaw Talks, *People's Daily* also particularly emphasized that the initial meeting at the Chinese embassy was held "at the request of the American ambassador."[2]

After the encounter at the fashion show, China became a much more active player in advancing Sino-American rapprochement. As Henry Kissinger claimed, between November 1969 and June 1970, there were at least ten instances where U.S. officials exchanged words with Chinese officials at diplomatic functions, and on at least four occasions the Chinese initiated the contact. However, twenty years of hostility without direct contact had made Sino-American relations so delicate that leaders of both countries had to be extremely cautious in communicating their intentions in order to avoid a backlash at home. Kissinger described the diplomacy between Beijing and Washington as "an intricate minuet" that was "so delicately arranged that both sides could always maintain that they were not in contact, so stylized that neither side needed to bear the onus of an initiative, so elliptical that existing relationships on both sides were not jeopardized."[3]

Since the two governments had limited channels of communications at the time, the media of the two countries played important roles in the "intricate minuet" between them. This chapter focuses on the media performance in the two countries from the renewal of the Sino-American Warsaw Talks in early 1970 to Kissinger's secret visit to Beijing in July 1971. Besides examining how the two governments sent signals of goodwill to each other through the media, this chapter also analyzes the process of transmission and particularly whether those signals were delivered successfully. In order to look at how Beijing shrewdly employed the media to advance better relations between the two countries, this chapter will shed new light on Edgar Snow's visit to China in 1970 with a more in-depth analysis of his interview with Mao and of the stories behind the publication of Snow's photo with Mao on Tiananmen Square. Moreover, in addition to newspapers and magazines, new resources from television footage are included in the analysis of the media's unique role in Ping-Pong Diplomacy.

Publicizing the Triangular Politics

The Warsaw Talks had a totally different atmosphere when they were officially reopened in early 1970. Beijing took the initiative to propose that the meetings be held alternatively at the Chinese and U.S. embassies instead of the venue provided by the Polish government. This arrangement could avoid eavesdropping because Poland was a close ally of the Soviet Union. The Nixon administration seemed to understand Beijing's concern and stopped the previous administrations' "standard practice" of briefing the Russians with the records of the Warsaw Talks. This policy signified an important change in Washington's attitude toward the Soviets and the Chinese. In proposing the policy shift to Nixon, Kissinger argued that he saw no point in giving the Russians the opportunity to "gloat" to the Chinese that they were kept informed, which he thought would heighten Chinese suspicions from the start.[4]

The Chinese approach to the meetings also witnessed an obvious change. In contrast to its aloofness and secretiveness during the Cultural Revolution, Beijing emphasized publicity this time. On December 11, 1969, Chinese chargé d'affaires Lei Yang called Stoessel and invited him to talk at the Chinese embassy. When Stoessel said he would be happy to arrive "discreetly at the rear door," Lei told him that the main entrance was "eminently suitable."[5] Lei's visit to the American embassy a few days later, as described by both the *Post* and the *Times,* was quite an "impressive" scene. Crowds of passersby reportedly watched "the largest and longest black limousine in Poland, sporting silk red-and-gold starred flags on its fenders and curious tail lights, shaped like Chinese lanterns," drive up to the American embassy.[6] When the two sides decided on the date of the next formal U.S.-China ambassadorial talk, Lei Yang immediately proposed making the plan public. Lei Yang's "flamboyant" arrival at the American embassy and his proposal to announce the meeting, as Kissinger correctly observed in his memo to Nixon, indicated Beijing's intention to show the "*appearance*" of its ability to deal with the United States—primarily for "Soviet consumption."[7]

On January 8, 1970, when the United States and China announced simultaneously that the Warsaw Talks would resume on January 20, the State Department used the term "People's Republic of China" (PRC) for the first time. In their front-page articles, both the *New York Times* and the *Washington Post* called attention to the change.[8] An editorial in the *Times* and a column by Harrison Salisbury instantly used the term. Actually, that was not the first time for the newspaper. It had used that term several times a year earlier, though not in prominent places.[9]

The U.S. signal was instantly caught by *Reference News,* which reprinted on its front page the full text of the U.S. announcement in which "PRC" was used several times. It also ran a piece pointing out that the Chinese ambassador's visit to the U.S. embassy was the first by a senior Chinese diplomat and that the meeting signified "a progress the Nixon administration had achieved in its attempt to improve relations with Beijing," also emphasizing the American initiative. On the same page, *Reference News* also had two articles about the lack of significant progress in the Sino-Soviet border negotiations and the possibility of increased Soviet pressure on China.[10] The contrast, on the same page, between the reports of progress in Sino-American talks and the fruitlessness in Sino-Soviet negotiations made clear for the reader the changed relations among the three countries.

In covering the resumption of the Warsaw Talks, *Washington Post,* as usual, seemed more cool-headed than the optimistic *New York Times.* On their front pages, while the *Times* interpreted the renewal of the Warsaw

Talks as the "fruition of a year-long effort by the Nixon administration" to engage China, the *Post* viewed it as China's "formal entrance into a triangular relation" with its two main adversaries. Whereas the *Times* editorial was optimistic about a "good beginning" toward better Sino-American relations, the *Post* argued that Beijing only wanted to use Washington as a "counterweight" against the Soviet threat, and it expressed doubt as to whether there would be genuine progress in Sino-American relations because Mao had been believed to be the "most opposed to doing business with the United States." The *Post* even claimed that Mao's absence and the resumption of the Warsaw Talks suggested something "unusual" in China.[11] Instead of looking at the latest developments as positive signs for better relations, the *Post* still viewed the Chinese leadership with distrust. It also reflected the positions of the realistic elements in American society.

In their coverage of the triangular politics, the U.S. media did not forget about the Soviet factor, and they paid close attention to its response to the development in Sino-American relations. The day after the Sino-American joint announcement, both the *Times* and the *Post* reported on their front pages the fierce attacks on Beijing in the Soviet media. The *Post* noticed that Sino-Soviet polemics had resumed a week earlier after several months of quietness since the Sino-Soviet border talks began. The *Times* claimed that Moscow appeared to link the scheduled resumption of talks with Beijing's "military psychosis" against the Soviet Union. It referred to Soviet officials who drew attention to the resumption of the talks in early December, which was at about the same time the Sino-Soviet talks reached a deadlock.[12]

The newsmagazines also made references to the Soviet Union in their analyses of the Sino-American talks. Both *Newsweek* and *Time* took note of the violent attack on Beijing by the Soviet Army newspaper *Krasnaya Zvezda* (Red Star). Whereas *Newsweek* argued that the Soviet reaction would benefit Washington in its strategic arms limitation talks with Moscow, *Time* claimed to have found signs of Soviet fear of attacks from its newly released maps, which had modified the location of many cities close to the Chinese border.[13] By highlighting the uneasiness of the Soviet Union, the elite media could possibly make the readers aware of the potential benefits of Sino-American rapprochement.

When the Warsaw Talks restarted in early 1970, the U.S. media responded with different levels of confidence in the improvement of Sino-American relations. One thing they had in common, however, was the presentation of a new development in international relations—the involvement of China in the triangular politics. The high-profile approach of Chinese delegates in handling the Warsaw Talks shows that the Chinese leadership was well aware of the importance of their meetings with the Americans in enhancing China's own international standing and particularly their impact on the Soviet Union. By taking advantage of the media, Beijing was becoming an active participant in the triangular politics.

The Cambodia Incursion

In early 1970, Beijing and Washington were on the verge of a breakthrough. At the 135th meeting of the Warsaw Talks, Lei Yang expressed Beijing's offer to talk through "higher-level discussions or any other channel that both sides might agree upon." At the 136th meeting in February, he made an unusually conciliatory statement and accepted the U.S. proposal to send an emissary to Beijing.[14] Actually, U.S. emissary Henry Kissinger had to wait for a year and half before making his historic trip to China. During this one and a half years, the two governments had to face several challenges at home and abroad as they moved slowly toward each other.

One of the challenges came from the Vietnam War. On March 18, 1970, when Prince Norodom Sihanouk of Cambodia visited Moscow seeking Soviet support in dealing with Hanoi, the National Assembly deposed him from power and installed the pro-U.S. general Lon Nol as the head of the government. With the tacit agreement of Lon Nol, Nixon authorized U.S. forces to move into Cambodia to clear Viet Cong sanctuaries on April 30. The timing was inconvenient because two days earlier the Chinese side had informed the U.S. embassy that they were ready to meet in Warsaw on May 20.[15] Since China had been a traditional supporter of Sihanouk in Cambodia, U.S. military operations put the Chinese government in a dilemma.

Beijing's response to the Cambodian incursion was mild at the beginning. On May 4, it issued a statement warning the United States against its "flagrant provocation." Even though it declared that 700 million Chinese would provide strong backing for the three Indochinese peoples, what it offered was merely Mao's quotations that the United States was just a "paper tiger" and that they would definitely defeat the American "imperialists" if they worked together and persisted in fighting. Even Kissinger could see the toothlessness of the statement when he told Nixon, "The Chinese have issued a statement, in effect saying they wouldn't do anything."[16]

In addition to the Cambodian scenario, Beijing had to consider Vietnam. On May 11, the first secretary of the North Vietnamese Party, Le Duan, arrived in China for a visit. The Chinese media extended prominent coverage to his visit. In *People's Daily,* stories of his arrival at the airport, his meeting with Mao, Lin Biao, and Zhou Enlai the next day, and his meeting with Sihanouk later were all placed on the front page with photos.[17] In the middle of this propaganda campaign to show support for the Indochinese people against "American imperialists," Chinese meetings with the Americans would look awkward. On May 16, Zhou Enlai presided over a meeting in the Foreign Ministry that came up with three decisions: (1) the Sino-American meeting in Warsaw should be put off; (2) Mao would issue a brief statement showing support for the Indochinese people and Sihanouk's government; and (3) Mao and Lin Biao would attend a rally where Sihanouk was to make a speech.[18]

On May 19, Beijing announced its decision to put off the scheduled Warsaw Talks. In a terse statement, the Foreign Ministry declared, "In view of the increasingly grave situation caused by the United States, which has brazenly sent troops to invade Cambodia and expanded the war in Indochina, the Chinese government deemed it no longer suitable for the 137th meeting of the Sino-U.S. ambassadorial talks to be held on May 20 as originally scheduled." Beijing probably picked that day to make the announcement as a gesture intended to show support for Vietnam because it was the birthday of the late Ho Chi Minh, who had died a year earlier. While the announcement was buried on page five, the front page of *People's Daily* prominently featured a letter from the Chinese Communist Party (CCP) to the Vietnamese Workers' Party memorializing Ho Chi Minh's birthday.[19] Placement of the two stories shows that meeting with the Americans had to take a back seat to the revolution in Indochina.

On May 20, the scheduled day of the Warsaw meeting, Mao issued his famous pronouncement entitled "People All over the World, Unite and Defeat the American Aggressors and Their Running Dogs." In this statement, Mao not only showed his support for the Indochinese people but also targeted the Soviet Union when he highlighted that more than twenty countries had recognized Sihanouk's Cambodia within ten days of its establishment and that the Soviet Union was not on that list. In reality, when Sihanouk established his government-in-exile in Beijing on May 5, 1970, the Chinese government was the first to recognize it. Moscow did not recognize the Sihanouk government until June 23, but it still retained diplomatic relations with the Lon Nol government in Phnom Penh.[20] Envisioning himself as the leader of world revolutions, Mao had to display China's "clear position" when a fraternal third-world country was invaded by the United Sates. His personal attendance at the rally could display the seriousness of the Chinese support even though it was mainly symbolic. Portraying the Soviet Union as a traitor of world revolutions on this important occasion served both his own personal agenda and China's image.

As planned earlier, the day after his pronouncement, Mao and his heir apparent, Lin Biao, attended a rally of a half million people at Tiananmen Square with Sihanouk. In reporting the rally, *People's Daily* front-page article did not focus on the statement. It instead listed the names of almost everyone on the Tiananmen rostrum, especially representatives from Communist parties in India, Burma, Cambodia, Vietnam, North Korea, Romania, Albania, Pakistan, and Japan. Interestingly, while it placed most of the foreign dignitaries at the front of the guest list, it consigned the names of the Soviet representatives to the very bottom of the article to display its slight of Moscow.[21]

Despite Beijing's cancellation of the talk on May 20, it did not shut the door of communication. While the official statement said that the date of the next meeting would be "decided upon later through consultation by the liaison personnel of the two sides,"[22] in private the Chinese side offered to meet again on June 20.[23] Then, on June 16, a CCP Politburo meeting decided that the official Warsaw Talks should be further postponed "in view of the current situation," but it decided that liaisons of the two governments would still meet on the day.[24] Even though Beijing once again postponed the official talks, it announced the meeting between the liaisons. The announcement in *People's Daily* was noticeably milder in tone than the one a month earlier. Without blaming Washington for the postponement, it stated that the current situation was "clearly understood by both sides" and that the date of the next meeting would be discussed "at a proper time."[25] Beijing's mild announcement not only signaled to Washington its interests in continued contact but also had the effect of unsettling Moscow. Judging from their high profile in early 1970, the Chinese government did not want to give the impression that the Sino-American talks had totally died down.

Information in *Reference News* was much clearer. In covering the "regret" of the U.S. government in response to China's cancellation of the Warsaw Talks, it used the subtitle "American Side Says the Resumption of Talks Serves the Interests of Both Sides." The article stated that "Beijing has for sure left the door open for a future meeting in Warsaw." It even cited American officials who expressed hope that "the talks would be resumed once the situation in Cambodia cooled down."[26] For the Chinese cadres, this story clarified the policy intent of their own government.

After the U.S. withdrawal from Cambodia in late June, Beijing made a friendly move on July 10 by suddenly releasing James Walsh, a seventy-nine-year-old Roman Catholic bishop who had been detained in China for twelve years on charges of espionage.[27] Unlike the statement announcing the release of two American yachtsmen on December 8, 1969, Beijing offered detailed information about the prisoner's name, age, and hometown. The justification for his release was that "the bishop had confessed his crime upon education from the Chinese authority. Considering his senior age, our authority decided to release him ahead of schedule on the proletarian principle of 'leniency to those who confess and severity to those who resist.'"[28] By prioritizing the release of the bishop on page two and providing his detailed information, the Chinese government was probably hoping it would attract more attention and be interpreted as a signal of friendliness by the American people.

As the Chinese government hoped, the bishop's release made headlines in the U.S. media. Both elite newspapers related the timing of his release to the exit of U.S. forces from Cambodia. The *Post* commented that by doing so Beijing sought to "take the edge off some of its recent sharp verbal attacks on the United States." In addition to the front-page piece, the *Times* ran an editorial titled ". . . and a Signal from China," which argued that his release was not accidental and that it was "the most important signal since the Chinese People's Republic agreed to resume the Warsaw talks."[29]

With its vivid images and the ability to reach a larger audience, television could have greater influence than newspapers. The three networks showed images of the bishop crossing the border into Hong Kong and his press conference afterward. ABC and CBS rushed to interview Walsh's sister and brother, both of whom said his release was a "miracle."[30] When the bishop showed up in a wheelchair at the press conference, he was described as "alert." Even though he claimed that he had been forced to sign the confession and that he found it hard to justify the severity of the sentence "meted out" to him, overall he received "good treatment" in prison and that he "could not feel angry toward any Chinese" because he just "loved the Chinese people."[31] Instead of a condemnation of the Chinese government, the message from the press conference was more about the gratitude people felt about Walsh's release and thus was positive in tone. The bishop's experience stood in sharp contrast to the brutal scene when the eight expelled nuns crossed the border into Hong Kong at the peak of the Cultural Revolution in 1966.[32] Through the media's prominent coverage, Beijing showed to the U.S. government as well as its people that China had become much more rational and that it was taking steps to reduce the tension between the two countries.

Signals through Edgar Snow

The most important overture from Beijing in 1970 came through Edgar Snow, an "old friend" of the Chinese Communists since the mid-1930s, when he visited their headquarters in Yan'an. Snow's greatly acclaimed book *Red Star over China*, published in 1939, provided a favorable description of the Chinese Communist revolution to readers within China and without.[33] The Chinese government sent the invitation to Snow in the name of Mao in June. When Snow entered China on August 14, 1970, he became the first American journalist to visit China after the Cultural Revolution.[34] Snow's first public appearance was at an exhibition match between the Chinese and North Korean Ping-Pong teams. On its front page, *People's Daily* placed him among dignitaries from Communist parties around the world and featured a separate photo story about Zhou Enlai's meeting with him.[35]

One of the highest moments during Snow's visit to China occurred on October Day, when Zhou Enlai deliberately arranged for him to stand next to Mao on the Tiananmen rostrum in reviewing the parade and a photo of Snow with Mao was taken.[36] Interestingly, *People's Daily* did not publish the photo immediately. On its front page the next day, the photos of Mao with the guests at Tiananmen Square were mostly those taken from the distance, and Snow could barely be recognized in them.[37] Mao's photo with Snow was not published in *People's Daily* until Christmas 1970 under a prominent headline "Chairman Mao Zedong Meets with American Friend Edgar Snow" on the front page. Since the beginning of the Cultural Revolution, all Chinese newspapers carried a quotation of Mao in the small box at the upper right-hand corner of every front page. The Mao quotation for that day was, "People of the world, including the American people, are our friends." When they met in January 1965, *People's Daily* also published a photo, but it called Snow "an American writer, the author of *Red Star over China*."[38] When the two countries were locked in hostility, Snow was treated as a private citizen without any hint of friendship. He was not even treated as a journalist because Beijing did not want to establish a precedent for receiving any "American journalist." The different treatments Snow received in the official organ illustrated the change in Sino-American relations. In 1970, he had become a representative of the American people whom Beijing wanted to befriend.

It is worth noting that Lin Biao was standing next to Mao in the photo published on Christmas, but he was omitted in the headline and only mentioned in the footnote, in a much smaller font, that read "Chairman Mao and Vice Chairman Lin with Snow on Tiananmen Rostrum on October 1st " The highest leaders of China standing next to an American during an important event was indeed striking in the Chinese media. Scholars agree that the photo was an important message to Washington. Several of them, however, have neglected the three-month delay before its publication.[39] Chen Jian refers to secondary sources claiming that Zhou Enlai had overseen its publication in late December for other major Chinese newspapers to follow,[40] but he fails to explain the cause of the delay. What happened during those months might have changed Mao's attitude to Sino-American rapprochement.

On October 12, Zhou Enlai wrote a note on a Foreign Ministry report to Mao, suggesting that he conduct the interview with Snow before October 15 because the American journalist would have left Beijing by then. Mao wrote: "All right. [I am] planning to listen to his views about international affairs."[41] Though Mao agreed to meet with Snow, he deferred it until mid-December. From his note to Zhou, Mao seemed to be more interested in consulting with Snow than in delivering the message in October. Xia Yafeng and Yang Kuisong argue that Mao had been vacillating between revolution and reconciliation even in 1970 and that he might not have been "psychologically ready" for reconciliation at the time.[42]

Xiong Xianghui, Zhou Enlai's aide who had assisted the four marshals in their study of international conditions in 1969, claimed that Mao's decision to conduct the interview with Snow had to do with Zhou Enlai's earlier interview with him. The interview first appeared in the Italian magazine *Epoca* on December 13 and was translated in the internal publication *Reference Materials,* which reprinted along with the article several stories about how Zhou's interview had impressed Western news agencies. Xiong thought that Mao must have read them and responded favorably. From the "minutes of the Mao-Snow conversation" later distributed among Chinese leaders, moreover, he found that not long after the interview started, Mao took the initiative to talk about the *Epoca* article, saying that it was "pretty good." Finally, Snow wrote in *The Long Revolution* that he was summoned to meet with Mao without advance notice and that Mao had a slight cold when they met. Based on these observations, Xiong argued that the *Epoca* article must have triggered Mao, who then decided to meet with him immediately even though he was not feeling well.[43] Yang and Xia claim that it was the line "China was building a broader anti-imperialist united front not excluding the Americans" in the interview with Zhou that had enlightened Mao.[44]

As Xiong, Xia, and Yang point out, Zhou Enlai's interview with Snow might have reminded Mao to use the media to send signals. One thing they all have failed to consider, however, is the larger context that might have given Mao increased confidence in handling the Nixon administration on a public basis.

During these three months, Nixon himself sent more signals to Beijing through public and private channels. In his interview with *Time* magazine published on October 5, 1970, Nixon said: "If there is anything I want to do before I die, it is to go to China. If I don't, I want my children to."[45] Nixon's willingness to visit China did not stand out in the article entitled "I Did Not Want the Hot Words of TV," which was mostly about his general view of the world. It was literally ignored in the U.S. media at the time. The *Times* did not pay attention to the interview. The *Post* reported the interview, but it ignored Nixon's remarks about visiting China.[46] Maybe the newspapers did not want to credit their magazine competitor with a scoop.

On October 26, in Nixon's toast to Romanian president Nicolae Ceausescu at a White House banquet, he sent another signal to Beijing by stating that he was in a rather unique position because "he heads a government which is one of the few in the world which has good relations with the United States, good relations with the Soviet Union, and good relations with the People's Republic of China." That was the first time an American president addressed China with its proper name on an official occasion. Even though the *Times* and the *Post* both made references to China in reporting the meeting, they failed to catch the nuance in the president's message. The *Times* quoted Nixon's toast on the jump page without commenting on its significance. The *Post* did not pay attention to the toast, to say nothing of Nixon's signal.[47] While the U.S. media missed the significance of Nixon's new posture, *Reference News* was quick to understand the nuance of the "historical" toast and reprinted its full text.[48]

Moreover, Mao might have gained confidence from the elevation in China's international standing when it established diplomatic relations with Canada and Italy in October and November. In negotiating with these two countries, Beijing became more flexible and no longer insisted that they acknowledge its sovereignty over Taiwan as a precondition for diplomatic recognition. When Beijing and Ottawa issued the joint communiqué on October 13, its most important lines were: "The Canadian government recognizes the People's Republic of China as the sole legal Government of China. . . . The Chinese government reaffirms that Formosa is an inalienable part of the territory of the People's Republic of China. The Canadian government takes note of this position of the Chinese government." Both the *Times* and the *Post* picked up the Chinese concession on Taiwan when they interpreted the phrase "takes note of" as not accepting.[49] With the formula provided by the Canadian recognition, the Italian government quickly concluded the treaty with Beijing and issued the joint communiqué on November 6, 1970.

Beijing's recognition by two major Western powers had a great impact on the General Assembly voting on China's UN membership. On November 20, the PRC won 51 percent of the votes supporting its admission into the UN and the expulsion of Taiwan, a simple majority for the first time. Even though it was not admitted because of the American insistence on a two-thirds majority, American journalists viewed it as a "setback" for the United States and a sign that Beijing would enter the UN very soon.[50] Washington had changed its rhetoric even before the voting. In his speech to the General Assembly on November 12, Christopher H. Philips, the deputy permanent representative of the United States, said, "The United States is as interested as any in this room to see the People's Republic of China play a constructive role among the family of nations." He also went out of his way to compliment "the industry, talents, and achievements of the great people who live in that ancient cradle of civilization." Before and after the voting, the two newspapers noted that Washington had refrained from saying anything that might be interpreted as opposition to China's entrance into the world body.[51] The media's depictions of Washington's change in position on China's UN membership were another friendly signal to Beijing. At the same time, the flexibility Beijing demonstrated in the recent recognition negotiations, as the U.S. media pointed out, was also a positive sign, which, along with the substantial progress in China's UN status, brought great hope that China would rejoin the international community.

Besides public signals from Washington, Mao might also have been encouraged by the message from Nixon through the secret channel. In his meeting with Pakistani president Yahya Khan in the White House on October 25, Nixon asked him to convey two key points to Beijing: that Washington would "make no condominium against China whatever may be put out" and that his government would like to send emissaries to Beijing for the establishment of secret link. Yahya visited China from November 10 to 15. However, the Chinese reply did not come until December 9 through Pakistani ambassador Agha Hilaly from Zhou Enlai, a more than three-week delay. Kissinger speculated that Beijing might have deliberately wanted Yahya to postpone the message until then.[52] Again, Beijing seemed to have been waiting for something before sending out messages to Washington. The condition seemed to be more favorable in December.

Mao's interview with Snow happened on December 18, and it reveals a lot about Mao's latest thoughts on Sino-American relations. Because of the Chinese censorship, the "minutes of Snow-Mao Talk" that later circulated among Chinese officials contained more details than Snow's *Life* magazine article in April 1971.[53] In his interview with Snow, Mao "casually" said that Nixon would be welcome to visit China because the current problems between China and the United States had to be solved by the American president and that he would be happy to talk with Nixon "either as a president or as a tourist." This remark was later published and known to the outside world as Mao's invitation to Nixon. Actually, Mao sent more messages. In the "minutes," Mao said that Nixon had expressed his desire to talk with Chinese leaders in Beijing or Washington under extreme secrecy without even the knowledge of the Foreign Ministry or the State Department. Mao said: "If he really wants to come to Beijing, you can take a message to him. Tell him not to sneak in. He can just come in a plane." When Snow asked Mao, "Since I don't know Nixon, but if I meet him, Can I . . . ?" Before he finished the sentence, Mao said, "You can just say [that I think] he is a good person, the world's top good person. Brezhnev is not good. Brandt is not good either."[54] It seems that Mao was expecting Snow to tell Nixon that he had learned of his intention of visit China, and he was also probably hoping Snow could pass on his "invitation" to Nixon. Mao's interview with Snow indicates that by December 1970 he was in a much more comfortable position to deal with high-level American officials on a public basis. Having the photo published a week after the interview was in line with his state of mind at the time. The photo also looked like a Christmas gift to the Nixon administration.

Despite Mao's efforts, the signals through Snow did not produce the expected effects. When the *Times* and *Post* received a copy of Zhou's conversation with Snow in *Epoca*, they paid attention only to his remark that "China was still threatened with war by the superpowers with some one million men as well as rocket troops to the north and west; and with the United States in alliance with a remilitarizing Japan on the east." They interpreted this line as evidence of Beijing's inflexibility and refused to buy Snow's argument that "Zhou Enlai's willingness to have serious conversations with an American writer after the Cultural Revolution was itself meaningful.[55] The magazines and networks simply ignored the article. Even though *Beijing Review,* the only China-published English magazine targeting the Western audience, published Mao's photo with Snow in the first issue of 1971, American journalists did not pay much attention. C. L. Sulzberger of the *Times* did mention it in his "Foreign Affairs" column entitled "The Tea Leaves Change," but it was published in late January and buried deep.[56] Obviously it did not catch the attention of the Nixon team.

Other U.S. media were not impressed by Mao's high-profile appearance with Snow, probably because of their natural suspicion of leftists, especially those with a pro-Communist record. During the Cultural Revolution, Robert F. Williams, author of *Negroes with Guns* published in 1962 and a black power activist hounded into exile by the U.S. government over criminal charges, had been treated as a head of state when he joined Mao on the Tiananmen rostrum with the honor of making a speech to the crowd for China's National Day celebration.[57] Williams's experience in China had received very little coverage in the U.S. media.

Nor could Snow deliver Mao's message at an earlier date. His interview with Mao was not published in *Life* until April 30, 1971, in the same issue that called attention to Nixon's remark to *Time* that he would like to visit China.[58] By that time, these stories could only stand in the shadow of the "aftershock" caused by Ping-Pong Diplomacy. According to Snow, after every interview with Zhou Enlai and Mao, he had to submit to the Chinese for correction a long dispatch based on his notes. When the clearance came a week later, the official version omitted things not publishable. Huang Hua, a senior diplomat who would become the first Chinese ambassador to the UN and the foreign minister, also said that when Snow's wife left China before Christmas 1970, he had to wait for the interview draft.[59] The Chinese arrangements made it difficult for Snow to publish the interview at an earlier date.

Seymour Topping, foreign editor of the *Times,* claimed that, after leaving China in February 1971, Snow sent his newspaper a lengthy article based on a series of interviews with Zhou Enlai. Unfortunately, executive editor Abe Rosenthal, who was strongly anti-Communist due to his experience as a reporter in Poland, felt uneasy about giving too much space to a piece written by a journalist known for his strong sympathy for the Chinese Communists. He insisted on drastic cuts, arguing that the article was too long and "propagandistic." When Snow refused to make the cut, Rosenthal "summarily" rejected his article, not knowing that it actually reflected Mao's attitude that had been conveyed to Snow in "off-the-record remarks" and that it contained important information that Beijing was ready to "do business with the Nixon administration."[60] The *Times* thus missed a great opportunity to pass on the important signal to the Nixon administration and also a scoop. The suspicion of Communist sympathizers in the U.S. media, to some extent, had prevented Mao from delivering his message through Snow at an earlier date.

Kissinger's explanation was that the State Department probably could not have obtained a full text of Snow's talk with Mao because a memo to him on April 1, 1971, did not mention the element of an invitation to Nixon. It instead reported that Snow had gained the impression from his meetings with Chinese leaders that "there was no immediate prospect of improving Sino-American relations because of the war in Indochina."[61] Richard Nixon claimed in his memoir that he learned of Mao's statement to Snow within a few days after their conversation.[62] He was probably bragging or simply lying because nobody else could verify his claim. Nor has he produced any evidence about how he obtained it.[63]

The missed signals between Nixon and Mao well exemplified the delicate nature of the "intricate minuet" between Beijing and Washington. These signals through public media had the danger of being delayed or even totally lost. The Snow scenario also reflects the different roles of Zhou and Mao in handling Sino-American rapprochement. While Zhou's job was to deal with specifics such as arranging the photo op, Mao had the final say on when and how to deliver the message. According to Gao Wenqian, after the Ninth Congress, Zhou often picked important international developments and commentaries as briefing materials for Mao to read, thus to subtly influence Mao's thinking on foreign policies.[64] Without Mao's approval, Zhou Enlai was extremely cautious in the signals he sent out. It explains the mixture of restrained optimism and tough rhetoric in his interview with Snow in November. It is probably why the two U.S. elite newspapers did not read any significant change from the interview published in *Epoca*. The difference in their importance was also illustrated by the fact that Zhou Enlai's photo with Snow in August as well as his interview with Snow caused much less sensation and were interpreted with much less symbolic meaning than were Mao's interactions with Snow. Another evidence of their difference is that only Mao's conversation with Snow was later distributed as a Party document.

Breakthrough via Secret Diplomacy

While signals through the public media did not produce timely effects, the two governments achieved a breakthrough by communicating through the third party. The 137th Warsaw Talk ended up never occurring after the break-off in February 1970. After that, Nixon and Kissinger tried to reestablish contact with Beijing through different channels. At first, they tried Lieutenant General Vernon A. Walters, the military attaché in Paris. Between July and September, Walters tried several times to tell his Chinese contact that he had an important message from Washington to Beijing. However, the Chinese official said only that he would inform his government that Walters had a message without making any further response.[65] The Paris channel did not produce any result.

It was mainly through the Pakistani channel that Washington and Beijing achieved a breakthrough. As mentioned earlier, on October 25, Nixon had asked Pakistani president Yahya Khan to take his message to Zhou Enlai. Yahya visited China from November 10 to 15. On December 9, the Pakistani ambassador, Agha Hilaly, met with Kissinger and dictated Zhou's "authoritative personal message" to Nixon. Acknowledging Washington's past messages from different sources, Zhou emphasized that it was "the first time a proposal has come from a Head through a Head, to a Head" and that he spoke not only for himself but also for Chairman Mao and Lin Biao. He also expressed his willingness to receive a special envoy of Nixon in Beijing to talk about the Taiwan issue.[66]

On December 16, Kissinger summoned Hilaly and asked him to tell the Chinese that Washington was "prepared to attend a preliminary meeting at an early date" to make arrangements for sending a U.S. delegation to Beijing for higher-level talks. He stated that the talks would not be "confined to the question of Taiwan" but would address all issues concerning the improvement of relations between the two governments. He also said that the Chinese request for withdrawing U.S. forces from Taiwan was not hard to comply with because there were no military forces there except "advisory and training missions."[67]

Zhou Enlai's reply came through Romanian ambassador Corneliu Bogdan on January 11, 1971. Even though he insisted that the U.S. "occupation" of Taiwan was the only "outstanding issue" between the two governments, Zhou wrote that Beijing was ready to receive a U.S. special envoy if the United States had a "desire to settle the issue" and a "proposal for its solution." More importantly, he added, since President Nixon had visited Bucharest and Belgrade, he would also be welcome to visit Beijing. It was the first time Zhou formally expressed Beijing's willingness to receive the American president in China. Unfortunately, Nixon and Kissinger interpreted his message as China's insistence that the U.S. government agree to the Chinese principle on Taiwan as a prerequisite for negotiations. Nixon wrote a note on Kissinger's memo: "I believe we may appear too eager. Let's cool it. Wait for them to respond to our initiative."[68] As the two sides were bargaining over the agenda through intermediaries, South Vietnamese forces invaded Laos with the air cover of the United States in February 1971. The operation in Laos again put the Sino-American secret negotiations on a temporary hold.

The Laos Incursion

The Chinese response to the Laos incursion was even milder than its response to the Cambodian invasion a year earlier. This time, Mao did not attend any rallies or make any pronouncements attacking the United States. What *People's Daily* offered was his words, "So long as the peoples of Indochina work closely with each other and persist in a prolonged people's war, they will definitely overcome whatever difficulties and win the final victory." When the Party newspaper covered a half-million-person demonstration against the United States in Beijing ten days later, it did not mention any Chinese leader being present.[69] The Chinese response was more like a slap on the wrist.

According to Kissinger, on the day of the editorial attack on the Laos incursion in *People's Daily*, Qiao Guanhua, the Chinese deputy foreign minister and an old associate of Zhou Enlai, told Ole Aalgard, the Norwegian ambassador to China, that his government was aware of a new trend in American policy and he particularly expressed a desire to meet with Kissinger. Washington noted the message and reassured Beijing of its limited purposes in Laos. In a press conference on February 17, Nixon declared that the operation in Laos was not directed against China.[70]

Because part of the area invaded by the Saigon forces was close to the Chinese border, the response from Beijing was worth attention. Both the *Times* and the *Post* read from the Chinese statement that it would not resort to military counterattack in response. Under a *Times* headline, there was a small subheading, "Peking Issues a Warning on Incursion—Ziegler Says It Is No Threat to China." The juxtaposition of the two made the Chinese warning look much less threatening. When Xuan Thuy, the chief North Vietnamese negotiator in Paris, made the front page of the *Times* by declaring that the Laos incursion posed a threat to China, his statement was followed by the comments of the administration's China specialists, who expressed confidence that China would not intervene when the United States was withdrawing troops from the region.[71] Similarly, when Laotian premier Souvanna Phouma reportedly claimed that Chinese volunteers might enter Laos, the *Post* ran an article entitled "Peking Silent about 'Volunteers.'"[72] These articles fostered the impression of congeniality between Beijing and Washington, who would not fight over the Laos incursion.

Chinese cadres also understood the American intentions on Laos incursion from the internal *Reference News*. In a story entitled "Chinese Official Statement Is Indignant" on February 14, it featured the White House statement that the American action in Laos "did not constitute any threat to China" and people's belief that the American statement was intended to prevent Beijing from escalating its anti-American propaganda and not to provoke the "People's Republic which the United States was pursuing reconciliation with." What is more remarkable is that on February 20, it reprinted on its front page the transcripts of Nixon's remarks at the Oval Office and of McCloskey at a press conference. The byline of the McCloskey press conference story was, "The US Is Preparing for the Resumption of Warsaw Talks. . . . Reiterating That the Laos Invasion Was Not a Threat to China. . . . Saying China Will Not Send in Troops."[73] Just like its handling of the Cambodian invasion a year earlier, *Reference News* clearly revealed to Chinese cadres the limited goal of American operations in Laos and particularly its hope that the incursion would not block its pursuit of reconciliation with China.

In the middle of the Laos incursion, Nixon sent another signal by addressing China with its official name in his State of the World Message to Congress on February 25, 1971. The most notable line was, "I wish to make it clear that the United States is prepared to see the People's Republic of China play a constructive role in the family of nations." On its front-page article entitled "Highlights of the Message," the *Times* called attention to Nixon's "subtle compliment" of China, "the first of its kind by an American President." Even though the *Post* still used "Communist China" in commenting on Nixon's desire to "establish a dialogue" with Beijing, it reprinted the section where he talked about the problems of Indochina and China.[74]

The *Post*'s overlooking of Nixon's nuance might have to do with its preoccupation with the Vietnam War. As Kissinger stated, no matter how hard Nixon tried to make his annual State of the World Message a statement of the basic philosophy of American foreign policy, each year the press would focus on the section on Indochina. Instead of a debate over the U.S. purpose in the world, it "invariably generated a discussion in Vietnam."[75] In reporting Nixon's State of the World Message, the *Times* headline was, "Nixon Sees Risk of Isolationism if Disengagement Is Too Swift," and the *Post* used, "President Sees No Early End to War in Asia." The networks also gave prominence to Indochina and the China policy in their coverage of Nixon's report.[76]

Reference News was quick to catch Nixon's signal. It carried an article that called attention to the fact that Nixon had used "PRC" "seven times" in his foreign-policy report and that it was the first time an American president had done so in an official document. What was unusual was that when it reprinted on its front page the section of Nixon's message about China the next day, the source was not any foreign press agency but "this newspaper."[77] This arrangement seemed to tell readers that the article with Nixon's message was not selected by accident, but by the order of the central government.

In contrast to *Reference News'* undistorted presentation of Nixon's message, *People's Daily* attacked his administration for its determination to "occupy" Taiwan" and its "criminal trick" of creating "two Chinas."[78] By displaying China's "firm" position on Taiwan, the article helped Beijing retain its public image as a revolutionary power. Nevertheless, the secondary placement of the comments showed a reduced level of hostility to Washington. Sophisticated readers who read both newspapers could see the change in Beijing's attitude toward the United States.

Ping-Pong Diplomacy

In late March 1971, the operation in Laos ended in a fiasco, eliminating an irritant between China and the United States. In April, Beijing made a bold initiative that greatly accelerated Sino-American rapprochement, a move that amazed the whole world. Between March 28 and April 7, 1971, the thirty-first World Table Tennis Championships was held in Nagoya, Japan. From the beginning, Beijing regarded whether to send a team as a "political" issue because it would have been the first time a Chinese sports team appeared in a major international event since the Cultural Revolution. According to Chen Jian, the Foreign Ministry and the National Commission on Sports were opposed to the idea at first because they were worried that Chinese players might have to deal with players from "puppet regimes" in South Vietnam and Cambodia. However, Mao and Zhou, who were well aware of the public relations value of the Chinese players in displaying the "new outlook" of the Chinese people to the world, decided to send the Chinese team.[79]

During the championships, *People's Daily* devoted considerable space to the Chinese team's activities besides reporting the game results. It repeatedly mentioned the theme of "friendship" in covering the interactions between Chinese players and those from other countries. In reporting the opening ceremony, it featured an article entitled "Transmitting Friendship through the Silver Ball—Chinese Ping-Pong Team in Nagoya." In an article called "Friendship First, Competition Second," *People's Daily* called on the Chinese players to "use politics to guide skills and friendship to direct matches."[80]

The Chinese players performed excellently in fulfilling their "political" task and showed extraordinary courtesy when they encountered American players on several occasions. On March 27, they talked with a few American players at the opening reception. On April 4, Glenn Cowan, a nineteen-year-old American player from Santa Monica College in California, boarded a bus carrying Chinese players "by accident," as Chen Jian states. In the bus, three-time world champion Zhuang Zedong approached him and offered an embroidered scarf as a gift. When Cowan and the Chinese players got off the bus, they ran into a crowd of waiting journalists. The next day, Cowen returned the favor by giving Zhuang a Beatles T-shirt. Their exchange was again caught by journalists and cameras.[81]

In reality, Cowan got into the bus not by accident but by the invitation of Chinese players. According to Xiong Xianghui, the story that *Reference Materials* reprinted from the Kyodo News Service went as follows: Cowan was hurriedly walking to the gym wearing a U.S. team jacket. When he passed by the bus for the Chinese players, they waved to him and said, "Are you going to the gym? Hop in." Cowan was surprised, but he got in.[82] Without clear encouragement from the government in advance, Chinese players probably would not have been so eager to invite him in. If it were during the Cultural Revolution, doing so might have caused the players themselves serious trouble.

What happened between Zhuang and Cowan might have encouraged the Chinese leaders to make bolder moves. According to Mao's head nurse, Wu Xujun, Mao, who was intrigued upon learning of the story of Zhuang and Cowan from *Reference Materials,* praised Zhuang for his "diplomatic adroitness" and "political smartness." During the tournament, leaders of the American delegation had inquired repeatedly whether they could visit China when they met their Chinese counterparts. They became especially eager upon learning that Beijing had invited teams from England and Canada. When the American request was reported to Beijing, Zhou Enlai's position was positive. Mao was undecided at the beginning. On April 6, when the tournament was about to end, he suddenly made the decision to invite the American team.[83]

On April 11, Beijing allowed three U.S. newsmen, John Roderick from the Associated Press along with John Rich and Jack Reynolds from NBC, to travel with the American team. Roderick and Rich had reported from the mainland during the Chinese Civil War. In addition to them, there were two Japanese technicians working for NBC and two non-U.S. reporters working for *Life* magazine. On April 16, Tillman Durdin, head of the *Times'* Hong Kong bureau and a prominent China watcher, was given a one-month visa, the first of this kind issued to an American journalist for regular news coverage since 1949.[84] The selection of the *New York Times* was not an accident. Chinese leaders must have noticed its efforts in promoting better Sino-American relations and known that it was the most influential U.S. newspaper.

During the week in China, the American Ping-Pong team toured universities, factories, as well as farms, watched a revolutionary ballet, and played exhibition matches with the Chinese players in front of a large audience. Besides Beijing, they toured Shanghai and Guangzhou (Canton). *People's Daily* devoted substantial space to their activities, even their departure from China. The matches between Chinese and American players received live coverage on Chinese television and radio. The Chinese television anchor's comments that "for a long time, friendship has existed between the Chinese and American peoples" and that "the visit by the American table-tennis team will enhance such friendship" had been carefully examined and revised by Zhou Enlai.[85]

The high moment of the visit came on April 14, when Zhou Enlai met with the American team in the Hall of the People, where he said, "Your visit has opened a new page for more friendly relations between the two peoples." *People's Daily* placed Zhou's pictures with them in prominent places. The quotation of Mao for that day was: "People all over the world support each other in their just fight. Our friends are all over the world."[86] Obviously these friends included the Americans.

Ping-Pong Diplomacy displayed Beijing's use of "people-to-people" diplomacy before the establishment of the official relationship with Washington. Zhou Enlai's welcoming speech as well as the Chinese media carefully separated the "aggressive and imperialistic" American government from the "heroic" American people.[87] When the game in Japan was over, *People's Daily* featured an article entitled "Our Friends Are All over the World." It claimed that Chinese player Zhuang Zedong had reportedly told an American couple: "Even though the U.S. government is hostile to China, Chinese people and American people are friends. We differentiate the American government from the American people." After the American team's visit to China, *People's Daily* ran an editorial entitled "Salute to the Courageously Fighting American People."[88]

The U.S. media were much more excited than their Chinese counterparts. When the Nixon administration completely lifted travel restrictions to China three weeks before the Chinese invitation, the *Times* and the *Post* did not attach too much importance to the move.[89] Beijing's invitation to the first sizable group of Americans and its granting of visas to U.S. reporters thrilled American newspeople indeed. Walter Cronkite of CBS called the invitation a "consolation prize" for the U.S. team and "unexpected good news." The *Post* headline was, "Surprise Served at Table Tennis Match: U.S. Team Invited to Peking."[90] Harrison Salisbury, in his *Times* column, claimed that the invitation was "not only a gesture of friendship, but also one of national honor" considering the importance of Ping-Pong as China's "paramount international sport." With the phrase "Major Policy Change" in its headline, the *Times* interpreted Beijing's granting of visas to American newsmen as "more significant" than the invitation to the Ping-Pong team because it symbolized China's discarding of the policy of "self-isolation." It referred to the two moves as Beijing's "first positive response" to American overtures.[91] For American newsmen who had been denied access to China for a long time, the opportunity to report from China was truly exiting. Here the media themselves became part of the story they were covering.

For two weeks, Ping-Pong Diplomacy dominated the front pages of the two elite U.S. newspapers. For example, the *Post* pictured that "the smile on the face of the dragon was dazzling" as the American team received "first class treatment, warm welcomes and speeches of friendship." The *Times* reported Zhou's meeting with the American team with a headline "Chou, 73, and 'Team Hippie' Hit It Off."[92] Due to the special privileges the Chinese government granted to the *Times,* readers might have noticed that it featured several firsthand accounts by its own journalists of their experiences in the field. In contrast, a lot of stories in the *Post* were dispatches sent by Norman Webster of the *Toronto Globe and Mail.*[93]

Ping-Pong Diplomacy also made the cover stories and picture stories of newsmagazines. The cover of *Newsweek* was a big cartoon depicting Mao and Nixon playing Ping-Pong with the caption "A New Game Begins." The featured story pointed out that the Chinese Ping-Pong players appeared in Japan with "no small little red book, no chanting of quotations, no speech making and no singing." Instead, they were "profusely" polite when socializing with their Ping-Pong rivals and the local people.

Also, it put the "cleanness" of Guangzhou (Canton) in sharp contrast to the "litter-strewn shanty towns of Hong Kong" and claimed that everything, including the Chinese guards and officials, had been "freshly scrubbed."[94]

Time magazine featured several large pictures of the American team's activities in China. In an article based on the eyewitness accounts of *Life*'s two reporters, it described China as "a nation that was unified and organized—with a level of poverty, but absolutely no misery"—and the people as "healthy and self-confident. Moreover, it described Zhou Enlai as "smooth, very handsome, and quite witty." In 1954, when Zhou Enlai led the Chinese delegation to the Geneva Convention, *Life* called him "a political thug," "a ruthless intriguer, a conscienceless liar and a saber-toothed political assassin."[95] In the brand-new atmosphere, newspapers and magazines also ran articles tracing the development of Sino-American relations. Some of them dated the "traditional friendship" between the two countries back to the American Revolution.[96] Some of these stories might contain elements of exaggeration or wishful thinking, but the media's willingness to present China in a positive light told the American people that the overall relationship between the two countries had greatly changed.

Television had obvious advantages in covering Ping-Pong Diplomacy. For the first time the networks had the chance to show films provided by the Chinese official news agency. As the only network with reporters in China, NBC sent more than ten thousand feet of color film and thirty-odd voice-casts back to the United States through telephone relay without being censored by the Chinese.[97] In the NBC video, there were smiling Chinese children holding Mao's red books and a large crowd waving to the Americans when they toured the Summer Palace. During the exhibition match between the Chinese and the American teams, eighteen thousand audience members were shown clapping for the American team. The most impressive scene of the game came at the closing ceremony, when players of the two countries marched into the gym in pairs holding each other's hands. In the end, the reporter stated, "In sports at least, the Chinese and the Americans have found a common meeting ground."[98]

ABC had its own way of illustrating the new relationship. While the anchor was talking in the studio, the background changed from the Communist "hammer and sickle" into two crossing Ping-Pong bats, each bearing the Chinese and American flags.[99] Through the Canadian Broadcast Company, CBS ran a video of American players visiting the elite Qinghua University, where Chinese students produced tractors. Under the influence of the Cultural Revolution, it claimed, students would not be trained as an intellectual class but as workers with their own hands.[100]

Ping-Pong Diplomacy excited Nixon so much that a few hours after Zhou Enlai's meeting with the American team, he announced the plan to remove the trade embargo with China over nonstrategic goods. White House Press Secretary Ron Ziegler deliberately linked it with Ping-Pong Diplomacy by telling the media that Nixon had made the decision two weeks earlier, but the timing was greatly "influenced" by the Chinese decision to invite the American Ping-Pong team and Zhou Enlai's remarks about a "new page" in U.S.-China relations.[101]

Reference News fully documented the positive response to Ping-Pong Diplomacy. It reprinted stories about how the American team was warmly received at the White House upon its return home, and Nixon's hope to receive the Chinese Ping-Pong team as Zhou Enlai had the American team. It even reported that Nixon had started practicing Ping-Pong to prepare for the meeting with Chinese players. As always, it also reported the worries of Brezhnev and the Nationalists on Taiwan, and their concern about the possibility that Japan might follow the example of the United States.[102]

Most observers might expect that the venues visited by American players and journalists in China would have been carefully screened and stage-managed. What matters, nonetheless, was that the overwhelmingly positive report on China by American journalists helped create an image of stability and rationality, which stood in sharp contrast to the chaos during the Cultural Revolution. They displayed to the world that the Chinese government felt confident enough to receive journalists from other countries, especially the United States. The film of Chinese and American players holding hands must have had a strong impact on American audiences considering the long period of hostility between the two governments. The Chinese government was well aware of the media's role in propagating the impact of Ping-Pong Diplomacy when it invited the American journalists to travel with their Ping-Pong team. It is fair to say that the Chinese government successfully used American media to improve the chances for rapprochement.

One of the few to express dissent about Ping-Pong Diplomacy in the Nixon administration was Vice President Spiro Agnew, and he was particularly unhappy with the media. While attending the spring Republican Governors Conference in Williamsburg, Virginia, on April 19, Agnew told journalists that he had misgivings about Nixon's policy of easing relations with Beijing because it might undermine Taiwan's position. He especially disliked the media's overwhelming positive coverage of China, for example, their stories about the "contented and productive" lives of workers who lived in tiny apartments in Beijing. He argued that it helped the Chinese government achieve a "propaganda triumph" over the United States. Agnew's attitude reflects the response from some of the conservative elements in the American society. It also shows how secretive Nixon was in conducting the communications with China. Obviously, Agnew had been kept in complete darkness about the progress Nixon had made with China up to that point. Agnew's remarks were so shocking that it made the headlines in newspapers and the networks. In order to clear up the impression of a policy rift within the Nixon administration, Ziegler summoned the media the next day and declared that there was "no disagreement" between the president and the vice president and that Mr. Agnew "fully" supported Nixon's initiatives to improve relations with China.[103] While most media accepted Zielgler's assertion, CBS speculated that Nixon might have "orchestrated" Agnew's statement to appease conservatives.[104] According to Nixon's memoir, he had no such intention at all. He called Agnew a "bull" that "inadvertently careened into this diplomatic China shop."[105]

The U.S. media's coverage of Ping-Pong Diplomacy most likely played an important role in changing public opinion about China. In its wake, a Gallup Poll in May found that for the first time, people supporting the admission of China into the UN exceeded those who were against it by 45 percent to 37 percent. The poll also indicated that for the first time, the number of Republican respondents who favored China's UN membership exceeded that of their Democratic counterparts.[106] This was great progress considering the Republicans' traditional support for Taiwan. It should be noted that this change happened before the July announcement of Kissinger's secret trip to Beijing and Nixon's coming visit to China. In reporting the poll results, while the *Times* used an article entitled "Gallup Poll Reports a Plurality Favors Entry of Peking in U.N," which suggested favorable public opinion, the *Post* used the title "Peking U.N. Seat Favored by 45%."[107] Whether the *Post* editor was deliberate in choosing such a headline or not, readers with no knowledge about past poll results could hardly read from it any significant progress or any sign of promising change in public opinion because it was below 50 percent, even though the supporters outnumbered the opponents.

no analysis

Kissinger's Secret Trip to Beijing

Ping-Pong Diplomacy, which turned out to be a great success, greatly encouraged the leaders of the two governments to move toward a common ground. Soon after the U.S. Ping-Pong team left China, Zhou Enlai sent a message through Yahya to Nixon explaining that it had not been possible to reply earlier to his message "owing to the situation of the time." Zhou selected his wording very carefully this time: "As the relations between China and the U.S.A. are to be restored fundamentally, a solution to this crucial question can be found only through direct discussions between high-level responsible persons of the two countries." The focus of negotiation had changed from solving the Taiwan issue, which had stalled the previous communications, to the restoration of Sino-American relations. Moreover, Zhou again included Nixon on the list of people invited to visit China.[108]

Beijing's concession cleared the last obstacle in the way of the American president's accepting the invitation. In his reply to Zhou Enlai on May 10, Nixon said that Kissinger was to visit Beijing in advance to discuss arrangements for a presidential visit and that he hoped the first meeting between Kissinger and Chinese officials would be kept "strictly secret." At first, Zhou was not too pleased with the suggestion about secrecy. After Yahya explained that Nixon wanted to handle these negotiations entirely by himself to prevent any politicians from disrupting his efforts until a "government-to-government channel" was established, Zhou Enlai accepted the American suggestion. When Washington and Moscow were about to reach an agreement on arms limitation, Nixon sent a special message to Zhou Enlai on May 20, reassuring him that the agreement was not "directed against the People's Republic of China." Finally, on June 4, Nixon informed Zhou Enlai that in order to make arrangements for the presidential visit to China, Kissinger would visit Beijing between July 9 and 11, 1971.[109]

On June 10, the Nixon administration announced the relaxation of China trade, which went much further than the previous step announced during Ping-Pong Diplomacy. He authorized the export of a wide range of "nonstrategic items" and lifted all controls on imports from China. Though trade with China was still limited to "nonstrategic items," the *Times* and the *Post* both regarded the policy as a move to "end the 21-year trade embargo against trade with China." The *Times* regarded this announcement as "the most important milestone" in a two-year series of diplomatic efforts by Nixon to improve relations with China—the White House turned it into a "major political occasion" when it issued the list of items that could be exported to China without special licensing. The *Post* viewed the Nixon measure as a "prelude" to the ending of U.S. opposition to China's UN seat later in the year.[110] Among the three networks, ABC commented that the biggest reaction to the U.S.-China trade announcement might occur in the Soviet Union. NBC interpreted it as a "resumption of direct trade" with China without considering the response of the Chinese government.[111] Considering the insubstantial volume of trade between China and the United States at the time, the resumption of "direct trade" had more symbolic meaning than substance. Whereas the Chinese media were not impressed by this gesture because trade was not the top priority of Mao, the U.S. media treated it with great prominence. Therefore, it had a larger impact on American audiences.

Three days before Kissinger set out on his secret trip to Asia, the *Times* worried him by speculating that he might go to China in a story about possible new ambassadorial assignments in the Far East. As the article stated, the White House had "refused to confirm—and pointedly declined to deny—repeated reports" that Nixon had asked some months earlier that he or his representative Henry Kissinger be invited to China in early 1972. While William Rogers thought it was "funny," Kissinger regarded it as a possible State Department leak to get him away from Washington.[112] The context of that article was its claim that there was "a race to be the first prominent American official" to visit Beijing between Nixon and his Democratic competitors Senators George McGovern (D-SD) and Edward Kennedy (D-MA).[113] Ping-Pong Diplomacy had brought about a favorable change in American opinion. After that celebrated event, Beijing invited several nonofficial U.S. delegations to visit China, which made American officials jealous. Politicians of both parties were eager to reap the benefits of visiting China, especially those interested in their own Party's presidential nomination.

On July 1, Kissinger started his visit to South Vietnam, Thailand, India, and Pakistan. At the beginning of the trip, he made it look as "boring" as possible to reduce media interest. Upon his arrival in Pakistan, the last leg of his tour, Kissinger started complaining about an upset stomach. As a result, all his appointments were canceled, and word was put out that he would recuperate at Pakistani president Yahya Khan's rest house in Murree, a hill station not far from Islamabad. At 3:30 a.m. on July 9, Kissinger boarded a Pakistan International Boeing 707, a civil flight with regular service to Beijing, and started his adventure into China.[114]

The talks between Kissinger and Zhou Enlai went well. Before the trip, Nixon had told Kissinger to secure reassurances from Beijing that no other American political figure would be invited before his visit. Zhou said that he had a great pile of letters from American politicians asking for invitations, but he had not answered them. Zhou also told Kissinger that he had placed James Reston, vice president of the *Times,* on a slow train so that he would not arrive in Beijing until Kissinger had left.[115]

Before the meeting was over, one last thing they could not agree upon was how to announce Kissinger's secret trip and Nixon's forthcoming visit to China. The Chinese wanted to make it appear that the U.S. president had asked for the invitation. Kissinger, who did not want to give the impression that the United States was playing the role of supplicant, reminded Beijing that it was the Chinese who had proposed such a visit. Finally, under Mao's instructions, the Chinese side agreed to the wording that suggested the initiative came from both sides. The final version was: "Knowing of President Nixon's expressed desire to visit the People's Republic of China, Premier Zhou Enlai on behalf of the People's Republic of China has extended an invitation to President Nixon to visit China at an appropriate time before May 1972. President Nixon had accepted the invitation with pleasure."[116] With their final agreement on the agenda of Nixon's trip, the next step for Beijing and Washington was to make the announcement that shocked the world.

While Beijing and Washington were reaching agreements on Nixon's visit to China, he dropped hints in this direction on several public occasions. Unfortunately, these hints impressed the Chinese more than the U.S. media. Besides his interview with *Time* published in October 1970, Nixon explicitly talked about his intention to visit China on at least two occasions in April 1971. The first was on April 16, when he spoke to the convention of the American Society of Newspaper Editors, two days after Zhou Enlai's meeting with the American Ping-Pong team. Nixon said he had suggested that his two daughters consider visiting China for their honeymoons. He also said: "I hope they do, as a matter of fact, I hope sometime I do. I am not sure that it is going to happen while I am in office." Neither the *Times* nor the *Post* was impressed by his remark to mention it in their front-page stories the next day. The second occasion occurred at the end of a news conference on April 29, the day before *Life* published Snow's article containing Mao's signal to him. Nixon said: "I would finally suggest—I know this question may come up if I don't answer it now—I hope, and as a matter of fact, I expect to visit mainland China sometime in some capacity—I don't know what capacity. But that indicates what I hope for the long run." Nixon gloated in his memoir that "even the most rigorous monitors and analysts of Nixon rhetoric" could not pick up his hints.[117] In both cases, "tricky Dick" deliberately left the date of the China trip open, which made the comment seem less serious. However, *Reference News* faithfully reprinted his remarks in prominent places.[118] The Chinese newspaper understood well his signals.

On another occasion, when addressing a large group of midwestern media executives in Kansas City on July 6, 1971, Nixon spent considerable time talking about the potential of China and the importance of improving relations with it. Again it attracted more attention in Beijing than in the United States.[119] Actually, when Zhou Enlai mentioned Nixon's speech in Kansas City to Kissinger during their talk, Kissinger was embarrassed that he knew nothing about it. Later, he had to borrow a copy of the speech from Zhou Enlai.[120] Having known about the secret from the top, the official Chinese media were probably more alert to Nixon's signals than independent U.S. newspapers.

Another reason for the failure of American newspeople to take seriously Nixon's remarks about visiting China was because they had seen such comments before. During Nixon's 1960 presidential campaign against John F. Kennedy, the *Post* carried articles speculating on the possibility of his using a China trip as a "gimmick" to enhance his own reputation. They thought he might want to repeat the personal triumph he had achieved while confronting Soviet premier Nikita Khrushchev in the famous "Kitchen Debate" a year earlier.[121] Since none of those stories had turned into reality, the media probably did not think he was serious this time either.

Moreover, Nixon and Kissinger had been very successful keeping their communications with Beijing secret. Even Secretary of State Rogers did not learn of Kissinger's secret trip to Beijing until July 8, when Nixon told him that it was a "last-minute decision" in response to an invitation received while Kissinger was in Pakistan.[122] Before the two countries established diplomatic relations, no one could imagine Nixon meeting Mao, regardless of what he said.[123] By comparing the U.S. media with *Reference News*, it seemed that more Chinese than Americans picked up on Nixon's hints about visiting China before Kissinger's secret trip to China was announced.

Conclusion

The time between the renewal of the Warsaw contact in December 1969 and Kissinger's secret trip to Beijing in July 1971 witnessed the most important breakthroughs in Sino-American reconciliation. During this period, Beijing became a much more active participant in the "intricate minuet" in which leaders of the two governments communicated their desire to improve relations through sophisticated means. Again, when there was no direct contact between them, the media in both countries functioned as important message carriers.

As the U.S. media correctly pointed out, Beijing's entrance into talks with Washington marked the beginning of the triangular politics with the two superpowers. The Chinese eagerness to publicize the meetings with the Americans was mainly used to increase the Soviets' uneasiness. Besides displaying to the world China's support for the Indochinese people, the anti-U.S. campaign in the Chinese media was also intended to embarrass Moscow for not providing them with enough support. Though Beijing broke off the Warsaw Talks in response to the U.S. invasion of Cambodia and Laos, it was tough in words but flexible in deeds, leaving the door open for further contact with Washington. Through stories in the internal *Reference News,* Chinese cadres could clearly understand the intentions of the Nixon administration on the invasions, such as its unwillingness to threaten China and particularly its eagerness to prevent them from undermining its pursuit of reconciliation with China.

As stated in the previous chapter, a key feature of the "intricate minuet" was that many of the signals emanating from the two capitals were unilateral steps that did not require reciprocity. Therefore, several of these signals might not reach the intended audience. While articles reprinted in *Reference News* show that the Chinese side understood most of the signals from the Nixon administration, Mao's signals through Edgar Snow were too nuanced for the U.S. media or the White House to comprehend. Moreover, Nixon's signals of addressing China with its proper name at the reception for Ceausescu and his remarks about visiting China did not attract enough attention in the U.S. media. The Chinese media were more impressed with these signals because they were clearer than their American counterparts about the progress in Sino-American relations. American officials' public compliments to China also showed the cadres that China had earned its "rightful" place on the world stage.

Another difference is that the U.S. media seemed to be more interested than their Chinese counterparts in Nixon's initiatives of releasing trade and travel restrictions. Between 1969 and 1971, the Nixon administration shrewdly coordinated the timing of these announcements with important political events, such as Nixon's Asia trip in July 1969, the renewal of Warsaw contacts in December 1969, and Ping-Pong Diplomacy in April 1971. The prominent coverage and positive response from the U.S. media helped reinforce the effect of these initiatives. Though the U.S. media were free from government control, they acted as the unwitting "cooperative partners" of the government in promoting Sino-American rapprochement.[124]

By inviting American Ping-Pong players to China and allowing U.S. reporters to cover their activities, Beijing achieved a great public-relations success. As a landmark in Sino-American relations, Ping-Pong Diplomacy made great contributions to preparing the two peoples for a change in relations. For the audiences in both countries, it was the first time they had seen friendly exchanges between the two peoples since the establishment of the PRC. The headlines, pictures, and videos had a profound impact on their perception of the relations. More importantly, the U.S. media's overwhelmingly positive coverage of China changed its image in the United States from a militant, irrational revolutionary power into a more stable country that was rational and possible to deal with. In this sense, the media functioned not only as observers but also as crucial participants in U.S.-China rapprochement.

5

Setting the Stage for the Show in Beijing, 1971–1972

After the announcement of Kissinger's secret trip to Beijing in July 1971, both Washington and Beijing faced problems at home. Nixon needed to deal with the formidable challenges from conservatives who stood up for Taiwan. He would counter their opposition with a well-calculated public-relations project to maximize media coverage of his China trip, especially through television. In an election year, this would appeal to the majority of Americans, who could understand the benefits to be gained through the dramatic diplomatic breakthrough.

On the other hand, Beijing used different channels, especially its media, to accustom its people to the fact that their government had forged a new relationship with the United States, formerly its archenemy. Nixon's trip turned out to be a great success for both his own administration and China. Massive media coverage contributed to and became part of this success story. This chapter studies how the two governments prepared for the Beijing summit through their respective media and then how the media covered the visit itself.

Impact of the Announcement

At 7:30 p.m. on July 15, 1971, in the NBC studio in Burbank, California, President Nixon announced that Henry Kissinger had paid a secret visit to Beijing and met with Chinese premier Zhou Enlai during his recent Asian tour and that Nixon had accepted Zhou's invitation to visit China sometime before May 1972.[1] Eager to be part of the "historic moment," Nixon had requested airtime so that his "major policy statement" would receive live broadcasting on national radio and television.

As Nixon hoped, his photo as well as the "surprising" news became the main headlines in the two elite newspapers as well as the cover story of the newsmagazines. The *Times* described his acceptance of the visit as "simply astounding" and a "dizzying performance." The *Post* compared the China trip to a "moon landing" and called the news "mind-blowing." It went as far as predicting a "possible end of the Cold War." *Time* was amazed by the "extraordinary Nixon-Kissinger diplomatic adventure." Calling Nixon's move a "political masterstroke," *Newsweek* argued that his "awesome power" in conducting foreign affairs had "shattered two decades of hallowed American policy" in just three and half minutes.[2] In the case of Kissinger's secret trip, the media seemed to support Nixon's use of executive power in conducting secret diplomacy for the sake of good ends.

In response to the Nixon announcement, congressional leaders including Senate majority leader Mike Mansfield (D-MT), House Republican leader Gerald Ford (R-MI), and Senate Republican leader Hugh Scott (R-PA), in addition to Senator George McGovern (D-SD), who was the only announced Democratic presidential candidate, responded favorably. Two conservative Republicans, Senators James Buckley (R-NY) and John Tower (R-TX), expressed their opposition. In evaluating the overall response, the *Times* claimed that Nixon had won "bipartisan support" and that the conservative Republicans constituted only "a handful." The *Post* described it as "universally favorable." *Time* mentioned conservatives who compared Nixon's move to going to Berlin to "wine and dine with Adolf Hitler." Noting the irony that Nixon's announcement came during the "Free China Week" designed by supporters of Taiwan, it admitted that Nixon's anti-Communist credentials made him far less vulnerable than a liberal Democratic president. In an article "A Setback for the Democrats," *Newsweek* similarly noted how Nixon could easily get away with such a bold move when the conservative outcry was "surprisingly slight."[3]

Though Nixon said in the announcement that his decision was not made "at the expense of old friends," journalists noted its ramifications for Taiwan. The front pages of the *Times* and the *Post* published photos not only of Nixon, Zhou Enlai, and Kissinger but also those of the Nationalist ambassador to the United States, James Shen, and Premier C. K. Yen. They predicted that Nixon's visit to China would increase the chance of China's entrance into the UN and Taiwan's expulsion from it.[4] A cartoon in *Time* featured Uncle Sam leading Mao to the door of the UN with a subtitle "Tell 'em Sam sent you." *Newsweek* ran a picture of the Nationalist leader Jiang Jieshi (Chiang Kai-shek) looking afar with a telescope. The subtitle was "Chiang: A Bleak Prospect."[5] Though journalists offered generally favorable reviews of the Nixon visit, their expressed worry about Taiwan served as a restraint on Nixon's approach to Taiwan.

In contrast to Nixon's dramatic announcement of his trip, the Chinese media assigned the news a much lower profile. *People's Daily* placed the joint announcement on the front page, but in the lower right corner. While other articles were arranged horizontally and easier to read, the font of the announcement was smaller and the text was arranged vertically, which made it harder to read.[6] This arrangement shows the complex mentality of the Chinese leadership. On one hand, they knew that the visit to China by the head of a former enemy was important news. On the other, its secondary position on the front page displayed the detachment of the Chinese government, which did not want to appear too excited about Nixon's visit.

After the announcement, *People's Daily* refrained from making any commentaries on the Nixon trip. The only one it published was an editorial entitled "The Tide of History Is Irresistible," reprinted from North Korea's *Rodong Sinmun* (Newspaper of the Workers). Buried on the last page, this editorial claimed that Nixon's planned visit to China signified the failure of the United States in "isolating and containing China" and that it was "a great victory of the Chinese people as well as the revolutionary people of the world."[7] Beijing apparently suggested that the North Korean article represented the position of all "revolutionary" people of the world.

While *People's Daily* refrained from commenting on Nixon's visit, *Reference News* devoted considerable space to the shock and positive response of the international community. For example, it reprinted Agence France-Presse (AFP)'s claim that Nixon had exploded the "most shocking bomb of diplomacy" and Reuters's comments that the "warming between Washington and Beijing will have incalculable impact on the world situation, especially the Vietnam War and the general election the next year." It even reprinted a story about how Nixon had spent "the happiest night" by having a dinner of "crab legs and wine" before making the historic announcement. For a diplomatic payoff, it reported how the Greek government declared that Nixon's move would accelerate its negotiations with China over normalization of relations.[8] The positive world response described in *Reference News* vindicated to the Chinese people the correctness of the government decision to host Nixon.

The articles selected by *Reference News* also highlighted a theme that the Chinese government had been consistent in its position on Sino-American relations whereas the United States had changed its policy. It reprinted a comment from an Egyptian newspaper that claimed, "The American Giant Had Been Beaten by the Asian Giant" and Zbigniew Brzezinski's *Newsweek* article arguing that Nixon's action symbolized a "kowtow" to Beijing.[9] In an article entitled "Why Did Mao Agree to Let Nixon Come to Beijing?" Zhou Enlai told several foreign visitors that it was the United States, not China, that had taken the initiative, and that he did not think of the new contact between the two governments as something of a "miracle." By comparing a growing China with a declining United States plagued with all kinds of problems, Beijing wanted to show the world it was the United States that was eager to seek reconciliation. These commentaries also reduced the threat of the United States before the Chinese audience and made their own country appear superior.

Nixon's Media Campaign

In order to guarantee the success of his trip, Nixon started his own media campaign. First, he had to deal with unrealistic illusions about it. In briefing congressional leaders on July 19, he cautioned against tying it to the solution in Vietnam. Press Secretary Ron Ziegler made similar comments in his news briefing afterward.[10]

Moreover, Nixon asked Kissinger to explain the rationale of the new development in communicating with the media. After his return from Asia, Kissinger held several news briefings hosted by the White House or in the presidential jet flying from California to Washington. In those briefings, he made very positive comments about his China experience and Zhou Enlai in particular.[11] In a memo, Nixon asked Kissinger to tell the press how he himself was "uniquely prepared" for the meeting and how, "ironically," he was similar to Zhou Enlai in terms of personality and background in coming up through "adversity."[12]

Nixon also changed his discourse on China. In a press conference on August 4, 1971, he claimed that China could potentially become the "most powerful nation in the world" and that there could be no world peace without communication between the "two great superpowers, the People's Republic of China and the United States."[13] By elevating China to the status of a "superpower," Nixon wanted to magnify the impact of his trip. Granting China such an equal status could also unsettle the Soviet Union in the triangular relationship.

Nixon's dramatic announcement of his China trip encouraged other countries to seek diplomatic relations with Beijing, which directly affected the balance in the UN vote on China's membership. In fact, since the UN vote a year earlier, when China's entry won a simple majority for the first time, the Nixon administration had envisioned that it would not be able to stop the inevitable. The State Department proposed "dual representation," which meant a shift from stopping the entry of Beijing to fighting against Taiwan's expulsion. Due to his concern for the conservatives, Nixon still felt leery about announcing the policy shift. According to Kissinger, Nixon prevented Rogers from announcing the policy in January, April, and June 1971. When Kissinger met with Zhou Enlai in July, he got the impression that the UN seat was not Beijing's utmost concern and that it could continue to wait if conditions to enter were not favorable. Seeing the positive response to his announcement of the China trip, Nixon became convinced that "the price was manageable." He then authorized Rogers to declare on August 2 that in the coming fall at the General Assembly the United States would support the seating of China, but it would oppose the expulsion of Taiwan.[14] In a conversation on September 30, 1971, Nixon and Kissinger told U.S. ambassador George Bush to "fight hard" to keep Taiwan in the UN. At the same time, Nixon told Rogers that he did not want any "personal involvement" in the UN issue, particularly when Washington was "working on" Beijing.[15] Besides his consideration of the ongoing Sino-American reconciliation, Nixon was taking steps to disassociate himself from a possible defeat.

The most important part of Nixon's preparatory work was with the media. The *Washington Post*'s White House correspondent Carroll Kilpatrick said that Nixon "understood the press better than Johnson did and he knew how to make news."[16] Early in his political career, Nixon had learned about the power of the media in the Alger Hiss case, which not only brought him national prominence but also made him the enemy of eastern liberals and particularly the elite media.[17] Though Nixon despised most journalists and believed that they hated him in return, as a shrewd politician, he was well aware of the importance of their favorable coverage of his trip, which he knew would place him in a unique position in history and would help him in his reelection.[18] Among different forms of the media, Nixon was particularly suspicious of the print press. Living in an era when television had become widely available to ordinary Americans, he knew well that television could help him reach a larger number of people with far less physical effort.[19] In his "farewell" to the journalists in 1962, he declared, "Thank God for television and radio for keeping the newspapers a little more honest."[20] After he became president, Nixon chose to deliver his key messages through television speeches. As he told the press, "I think the American people are entitled to see the President and to hear his views directly and not to see him through the press."[21] Kissinger said, "Television in front of the President is like alcohol in front of an alcoholic."[22] Nixon's hatred of the newspapers is not completely baseless because of their ability to put a spin to his meaning by highlighting parts of it while leaving out others or interpreting him in ways that he did not like. Through television, he wanted his messages to go to the American public unfiltered by any forms of editing or interpretation.

John Ehrlichman, Nixon's assistant for domestic affairs, described him as "usually capable of a passionless and penetrating analysis of his press opportunities" and that he thought "like an editor."[23] With his China trip, Nixon believed that "people" contact was more important in terms of public relations than meetings. Before Kissinger's interim trip in October, Nixon asked him to raise the question of Pat Nixon's going since he wanted her to act as a "prop" for "good people pictures." Nixon also thought it was a good opportunity to convey to the American audience the "human side of the Chinese." He told his chief of staff, H. R. Haldeman, "On TV the American President received by a million Chinese is worth a hundred times the effect of a communiqué."[24]

As a successful advertising man in Los Angeles and a tireless worker, Haldeman was not only Nixon's chief of staff but also his chief "stage manager." He shared Nixon's suspicions of the media and his consciousness of their role in public relations. Knowing well how to sell an image, Haldeman wanted to make sure that Nixon "shone" as a great leader and statesman in China.[25] According to Kissinger, in the cabinet meeting upon his return from the secret trip to China, what concerned Haldeman most was the "size of the press contingent." He was "disdainful" upon learning that Kissinger had not settled the issue with Zhou Enlai, especially when Kissinger said that forty was enough, which was even less than the number of secret service people. As he said, "Haldeman saw no sense in making history if television was not there to broadcast."[26]

In order to guarantee the success of the TV coverage, the White House worked, in the words of the *Post* columnist Don Oberdorfer, "hand-in-glove" for several months to bring it about. According to him, four days after Nixon's TV announcement of his China trip, the Washington bureau chiefs of the three networks met with Press Secretary Ron Ziegler to talk about coverage. The networks put forward three plans: (1) film cameras only with footage to be flown out of China and transmitted to the American audience via satellite from Tokyo, Seoul, or Hong Kong; (2) film cameras only with footage transmitted directly from China via satellite through a ground station in China; and (3) live coverage with electronic cameras transmitting images directly from a ground station in China. They pushed hard without hope of success for the third choice: live coverage.[27]

During Kissinger's trip to Beijing in October, he secured from Zhou Enlai permission to build ground stations in China. Zhou said he understood the equipment would be used to "manage the whole show."[28] In early January, when General Alexander Haig, Kissinger's deputy, and Ziegler led the advance team of eighteen into China, seven network executives and engineers went along. Their job was to install the ground stations to be used for communication and live transmission through satellites. During his talks with the Chinese, Haig emphasized the importance of making Nixon's trip a "visible success." Traveling to Beijing, Shanghai, and Hangzhou, the advance group literally traced every place Nixon planned to visit, paced every step he might take, and worked on every camera angle.[29]

The White House also gave extraordinary privileges to networks in allocating the seats of correspondents who would travel to China. On the list of eighty-seven newsmen Ziegler announced on February 7, 1972, only fifteen independent newspapers were invited, and six went to the two wire services. Three went to columnists Richard Wilson; William Buckley, whom Ziegler described as a "conservative"; and Joseph Kraft, whom he depicted as a "nonconservative."[30] Six slots went to magazines including *Reader's Digest,* which did not normally cover the White House but was friendly to Nixon.[31] Each of the three networks could send four correspondents. In addition to the eight seats for cameramen and seventeen for television technicians, they received thirty-seven in total. This did not include the sixty television technicians who had arrived in China earlier in the month. In the end, the networks each had twenty-one seats while newspapers, magazines, and non-network broadcast organizations had only one seat each—if they were lucky. In order to attend the festivities, many TV executives and producers disguised themselves as "television technicians," bumping real engineers.[32]

Max Frankel, the only *Times* correspondent lucky to be on the press plane, wrote about the "massive competition" he faced when he arrived in China. As he noted, "From the moment we landed, I saw myself outgunned by cameras, so I labored to paint verbal pictures into interpretive commentaries in ways that television could not match."[33] Frankel won a Pulitzer Prize in 1973 for his reporting of Nixon's epochal trip. The three networks also "scooped" the print media when *TV Guide* reported a week in advance many details of Nixon's plans, inciting the envy of the newspapers. Without any other options, they had to give credit to *TV Guide* in their own reports.[34]

To deal with conservative fears of the betrayal of Taiwan, on February 9, a week before his departure for China, Nixon reiterated in his State of the World Message that the United States would maintain its "friendship, diplomatic ties, and defense commitment" with Taiwan.[35] Three days before his departure, he ordered a further easing of trade restrictions with China whose effect, as Ziegler told the media, would place China on an equal footing with the Soviet Union and Eastern European countries. Though Ziegler denied that the timing of the new trade action was connected to Nixon's forthcoming trip, his statement that "we would hope that the People's Republic of China will be receptive to this step" was interpreted by both the *Times* and the *Post* on their front pages as a move to "improve the political atmosphere" for the visit. In the press briefing, Ziegler also brought up Nixon's recent meeting with André Malraux, the celebrated French author who had known Mao and Zhou since the 1930s and had kept in intermittent contact with them through the years. Nixon had recommended his book *Anti-Memoirs* to the journalists in his press conference on February 10, 1972. When he honored Malraux with a small working dinner with many officials, Nixon invited ABC commentator Howard Smith to be present.[36] By showing the media how "diligently" he was preparing for the China trip, Nixon was building the crescendo of his "show."

Preparing the Chinese People for the New Relations

When Chinese leaders made the decision to reconcile with its former number-one enemy, they had to take steps to educate the Chinese people, who had been taught to hate the American "imperialists," about a new relationship. Beijing's education was done at three different levels: the internal channel of the Party institution, the semi-internal channel through *Reference News,* and its main propaganda machine—*People's Daily.*

In order to reduce the shock to the Chinese people before the announcement of Kissinger's secret trip and Nixon's visit to China, the decision was first passed on to the top leadership in the Party, the government, and the military. On May 26, 1971, at Mao's instruction, Zhou Enlai explained to the CCP Politburo the rationale of Sino-American rapprochement. Stressing that the decline of the United States and its desire to leave Vietnam had caused it to seek reconciliation with China and that an improvement in Sino-American relations would be beneficial to the struggle against "imperialist expansion and hegemonism," to peace in Asia as well as the world, and to China's security and the solution to its "unification problem" in a peaceful way, Zhou pointed out that a successful opening might accelerate the "competition between the two superpowers" and benefit China.[37]

Between May 27 and 31, the central government convened a national conference on foreign affairs, where Zhou Enlai suggested that the attendees should adapt to the new situation when China renewed its contact with the world and received people from "the left, the center, and the right."[38] The "right" refers to anti-Communist politicians like Richard Nixon. On May 31, the Central Committee, with Mao's approval, ordered the distribution of the minutes of Mao's interview with Edgar Snow to the Party's lower branches with the instruction that it be "verbally related to every party member." It also ordered that "the study of the interview should be carefully organized so that the spirit of the chairman's words will be correctly comprehended."[39] On June 4, Zhou Enlai read the "Report of the CCP's Politburo on Sino-American Talks" at a working conference attended by 225 officials from different levels.[40] After the joint announcement of Nixon's visit, the CCP on July 21 issued a confidential document to local Party branches, explaining that the chairman himself had invited Nixon and that it was "another tactic in the struggle against imperialism."[41] In order to ensure that CCP members from top to bottom would go along with Mao's decision, messages in these Party instructions were clear and straightforward.

The second level of education was through the internal newspaper *Reference News*, which was the only source for most Chinese cadres and intellectuals to learn about foreign affairs, especially the status of the Sino-American reconciliation. In July 1970, before Snow started visiting China, Mao had ordered the most dramatic expansion in the circulation of *Reference News* so that it could be read by all local Party branches in factory workshops, village production teams, PLA companies, and college students. He even suggested putting *Reference News* on public bulletin boards so that everyone could read it. As a result, its circulation increased from four hundred thousand in 1964 to around five million in 1970.[42] At the working conference on foreign affairs in May 1971, Zhou Enlai said: "After his meeting with Chairman Mao, Snow published articles, which have been read all over the world. We should reprint their excepts in *Reference News*. If the current circulation of four to five million is not enough, we can add a million more copies." His point was that every local Party branch should have *Reference News*, from which the cadres could learn about the chairman's assessment of the international situation.[43] The arrangement greatly enlarged the impact of *Reference News*. More importantly, it exposed more people to the new developments in international affairs and particularly the progress in rapprochement with the United States.

On June 19, *Reference News* made an unusual gesture by running a special notice that read, "From June 17, this newspaper publishes American friend Edgar Snow's articles about his China trip one piece every other day. Readers, please pay attention." This notification is important because it represents the position of the editorial board, suggesting the endorsement of the government. It also reprinted an article from *Life* magazine carrying Nixon's remark to *Time* that he would like to visit China.[44] The publication of these inside stories in *Reference News* attracted so much attention in China that the readers' demand could still not be met even though many of its local offices printed copies far above the quota. As it turned out, instead of the one million additional copies required by Zhou, two and a half million were printed.[45] Though messages in *Reference News* were not as direct as those in the Party instructions, simply by seeing stories that Nixon wanted to visit China and that Mao was ready to meet with him, millions of Chinese could have felt the great change in Sino-American relations. It is worth pointing out that these stories appeared even before Kissinger's secret visit in July 1971. Therefore, it is also safe to conclude that more Chinese than Americans were aware of the forthcoming thaw.[46] The Chinese government's preparation for public opinion was far ahead of that of the United States.

At the third level, *People's Daily* played an important role in cultivating the largest number of Chinese about the new relations with the United States. One method was to bring up the "united front" policy, which the CCP had employed effectively in their fighting against the Japanese and the Nationalists in the 1940s. On August 17, 1971, for example, it published a front-page article entitled "A Powerful Weapon to Unite the People and Defeat the Enemy—On Policy." The article called for a study of Mao's 1940 article "On Policy," which argued for cooperating with the Nationalists in fighting the Japanese. The "united-front" policy can be used to justify the policy of reconciliating with a previous opponent to deal with the more threatening enemy at the time.

The other function of *People's Daily*, which is more important, was its coverage of the "people-to-people" diplomacy between the two countries. It was based on a separation between the "heroic" or "revolutionary" American people and the "imperialistic" or "oppressive" American government, a distinction Mao first proposed in 1965 when he met with a

Japanese delegation. He was especially supportive of American civil-rights fighters who opposed their own government.[47] By displaying American visitors to the Chinese people through public ceremonies, banquets, and the intensive coverage of the Chinese media, especially *People's Daily,* the Chinese government promoted the friendship between the two peoples.

Beijing's "people-to-people" diplomacy started with Edgar Snow. During his stay in China, Snow felt like "a symbol to be paraded" by the Chinese, who arranged for him to attend so many banquets and ceremonies that he had no real chance to talk to people long enough to learn anything.[48] During his interview with Snow on December 18, 1970, Mao questioned the policy of not allowing Americans to visit China and said that the Foreign Ministry should study the issue of inviting Americans from the "left, middle, and right." On February 17, 1971, when the Foreign Ministry's report reached his desk, Mao approved it.[49]

After the celebrated Ping-Pong Diplomacy, Beijing invited several American delegations to China. Though *People's Daily* claimed that the Chinese People's Association for Friendship with Foreign Countries, a nongovernmental organization, made these invitations, its official connections were not hard to discern. Moreover, its head, Wang Guoquan, had served as the former Chinese ambassador to Poland during the Johnson administration.[50] Given Wang's experience as a diplomat in dealing with American officials in Warsaw, he should have been very clear about the importance of his job of hosting American visitors for the improvement in the Sino-American relations during that special period.

In covering their trip in China, *People's Daily* provided no information on the identity or the occupation of these visitors and simply identified them as "American friends" or "American visitors of goodwill." A closer look, however, reveals that many of these people were either leftists who had been victims during the McCarthy era or activists of the civil rights movement. For example, there were John Service and Koji Ariyoshi, both of whom were members of the Dixie Mission, a group of State Department officials who had worked with the Communists at their headquarter in Yan'an in the 1940s, and William Hinton, a Marxist journalist and vocal China sympathizer, and his wife. Botanist and bioethicist Arthur W. Galston and MIT biologist Ethan Signer, who had just visited North Vietnam before their arrival in China, became the first two American scientists to visit China.[51] There were also Max and Grace Granich, who had published a pro-CCP newsletter when they worked for the Comintern in Shanghai in the 1930s and, more importantly, had taken the Chinese side in the Sino-Soviet split.[52] There were also members of the Committee of Concerned Asian Scholars and radical students who supported the Cultural Revolution in China. Beijing invited as well African American delegations whose "revolutionary struggle" had been applauded in the Chinese media, for example, the Black Workers Congress, the Black Panthers, and prominent Communist activists like Bill Epton. The Hintons, the Granichs, and the three leaders of the Black Panthers were treated as state leaders when they were invited to attend the National Day reception hosted by Zhou Enlai in 1971.[53] Admitting Americans who had been "friendly" to China was good for Beijing because these people were more likely to write positively about China when they returned home.

People's Daily's coverage of these American delegations had a common pattern. Neither revealing the contents of the meetings nor elaborating on their significance, it focused on apolitical news such as their tour itineraries. For every American delegation, there were separate news entries covering how they had been received and seen off by Chinese officials at the airport or train station. Though these delegations were nongovernmental in nature, Zhou Enlai would meet with almost every one of them irrespective of their numbers. Stories of Zhou's meeting with the American visitors, usually with photos taken, were placed in prominent places in People's Daily. The frequency of coverage was also increased by the fact that Zhou Enlai met with several Americans repeatedly when they were grouped under different names. For example, William Hinton and his wife stayed in China for seven months, during which Zhou Enalai met with them five times in total, and all meetings were reported on the front pages of People's Daily. As a result of this intensive coverage, there was news about American visitors in China in People's Daily every few days, especially during the second half of 1971. At one time during September and October, there were three or four such entries in a single issue. The intensive coverage of so many American visitors in the official newspaper cultivated among the Chinese a sense of a friendly atmosphere between the two peoples. Readers of the Party organ could have seen the departure from the past.

Beijing's people-to-people diplomacy also included its working on the U.S. media when it allowed U.S. journalists into China after Ping-Pong Diplomacy. According to Seymour Topping, managing editor of the *New York Times,* when he, along with William Attwood of *Newsday* and Robert Keatley of the *Wall Street Journal,* attended a dinner hosted by Zhou Enlai in June 1971, the Chinese premier expressed his belief that American journalists could help to "mobilize their fellow countrymen to bring about the withdrawal of American forces from Taiwan and Indochina." Topping perceived that Beijing's "courting" of American public opinion was an effort to achieve its foreign-policy goals.[54]

After China opened the door to American journalists in April 1971, it granted the *New York Times* special privileges. As stated in the previous chapter, chief of the Hong Kong Bureau Tillman Durbin had been the first American newsman to receive a visa to report in China. Both Durdin and Topping were old China hands who had reported extensively from the country before the Communist victory in 1949.[55] Max Frankel claimed that the reputation of the *Times* had been established because Topping married Audrey Ronning, whose father, Chester Ronning, had been the chargé d'affaires of the Canadian embassy in China between 1949 and 1951 and an "old friend" of Zhou Enlai.[56] When talking about foreign-news coverage of China, *Reference News* especially noted that the number of China stories in the *Times* had increased fivefold since Ping-Pong Diplomacy.[57] Beijing must have been impressed by the influence of the *Times* and especially its generally favorable coverage of China.

In May 1971, James Reston became the third *Times* journalist to receive a visa to enter China. Upon his entrance from Hong Kong, *Reference News* ran a special entry introducing him as "an influential figure in the American journalistic as well as the political circles" with "close connections" to the U.S. government.[58] When he arrived in Beijing, Reston developed acute appendicitis and had to undergo surgery in the Anti-Imperialist Hospital. As soon as he recovered, Reston published an article on the front page of the *Times* elaborating on how well he had been treated as Zhou Enlai had sent eleven leading medical experts to work on his case, which was not a major surgery. Reston also catered to the imagination of Americans by writing at length about how the Chinese doctor treated his pain with acupuncture, a traditional Chinese therapy that many Americans considered mysterious.[59]

Reston also received the honor of an official interview with Zhou Enlai on August 9, 1971. In the interview, Zhou expressed his admiration for the *Times* because it criticized Nixon's invasion of Cambodia a year earlier. Reston was proud of the position of his newspaper. When Zhou Enlai praised Nixon's courage to visit China, Reston did not give him much acknowledgment. While admitting that Nixon's trend of thought on Vietnam and China was "bold and even right," Reston criticized the lack of "clarity and definition and boldness" in his plan to cut the killing in Indochina and to normalize relations with China. When Zhou expressed his desire to see the solution to the Indochina conflict before that of the Taiwan issue, Reston was very flattering to China as he said, "We cannot resolve the problems in the world without China . . . but we can resolve the problems of the world without Taiwan." Reston also commented on Nixon's personality as a Californian and his ambition to get reelected so that he could "preside over the 200th anniversary of the Declaration of Independence." He described the "Nixon turnaround" as simply a "personal redemption" by which he attempted to repair the damage he had done to Sino-American relations as the alleged chief "red-baiter." After publishing the interview transcripts, the *Times* optimistically ran an article entitled "Chou's Views Encouraged U.S. Aides."[60] Haldeman, however, claimed in his diaries that Nixon viewed the interview as evidence that the *Times* was attempting to "sabotage" his trip. According to him, Nixon became so furious that he wanted every White House official to enforce his rule not to talk to the *Times* people, and he even threatened not to take them on his China trip.[61] Reston's case demonstrated the uneasy relationship between Nixon and the influential *Times* despite the newspaper's approval of the president's tactics on China. It also shows Nixon's extreme sensitivity to the evaluation of his foreign policy by the elite newspaper.

During his three-week stay in China, Reston wrote several columns and commentaries that presented favorable impressions of China. In one of his "Letters from China" series, Reston vividly described the atmosphere after Ping-Pong Diplomacy: "The routine of life for an American visitor in China these days is full of paradox. For example, you live in an atmosphere of vicious and persistent anti-American propaganda, but are treated with unfailing personal courtesy and are free to cable your impressions without censorship from the lobby of your hotel."[62] Reston's stories of China were so positive that *Reference News* reprinted many of them.[63] Zhou Enlai's effort in winning over prominent U.S. opinion shapers like James Reston and his newspaper seemed to have paid off.

The Lin Biao Incident and Kissinger's Interim Trip

While the two countries were preparing for Nixon's China trip, a political drama—the Lin Biao Incident—occurred, and at one point it seemed to call the Beijing summit into question. What happened on the night of September 13, 1971, whether Lin Biao had fled after plotting Mao's assassination or he had been ignorant of the plot but was simply forced to leave by his wife and son, remains a mystery. One certain thing was that after their plane took off, it crashed in Mongolia with no survivors. The death of Lin Biao caused an earthquake in Chinese politics. That very night, Zhou Enlai ordered the grounding of all planes in China for three days. Lin Biao's closest four generals, Huang Yongsheng, Wu Faxian, Li Zuopeng, Qiu Huizuo—who occupied the most important posts in the Chinese military and were members of the Politburo—were all arrested. Ye Jianying, one of the four respected marshals who had studied the international situation during the Sino-Soviet border clashes of 1969, became the new head of the Chinese military. Lin Biao's death also dealt a severe psychological and physical blow to Mao, who was bedridden for a long time thereafter. As a result, the Chinese government decided to cancel the National Day parade at Tiananmen Square for that year.[64]

The U.S. media watched the developments in China closely. On September 22, both the *Times* and the *Post* reported on their front pages that the Chinese government had just informed the foreign embassies in Beijing of the parade's cancellation. They sensed that a major political crisis might be occurring in China judging from the unusual military movements, the disappearance of so many top members of the Politburo from public view, and particularly Beijing's unprecedented cancellation of the parade.[65] On the National Day of China, the *Post* ran a story in TASS that nine people with unspecified identities had been killed in a Chinese jet crash well inside Mongolia on the night of September 12–13. As the *Post* correctly indicated, Moscow knew more about the incident from its closest ally Mongolia, and the TASS story on the eve of the Chinese National

Day was highly embarrassing to the Chinese government.[66] The TASS story added further mystery to the situation in China. Around that time, American journalists offered all sorts of speculations. There were rumors that Mao might have been dead or dying and that a power struggle over his succession was going on in Beijing. There was also the possibility that China and Moscow were on the verge of war and even a story that State Chairman Liu Shaoqi might have escaped.[67]

The mystery around the Lin Biao Incident raised the question of China's stability. The U.S. media began to worry whether Nixon's China trip could still materialize. Concerns of the *Post* can be shown in headlines like "China Uncertainty Clouds Nixon Visit Plans" and "China Events Raise U.S. Concern," as well as Joseph Kraft's column entitled "Portents from China."[68] A *Times* editorial speculated that the political crisis in Beijing could have been precipitated by the invitation to Nixon, and it worried whether the moderate forces led by Zhou Enlai could prevail over the radical forces if there was indeed a power struggle.[69] On October 2, Secretary of State Rogers told the media that he hoped what occurred in China did not "signal any change in the possibility of the President's visit." His use of the word "possibility" raised further uncertainties. Both the *Times* and the *Post* regarded his statement as Washington's first official expression of concern. The *Times* interpreted it as an indication that "political changes in Peking could make it impossible for President Nixon to carry out his planned visit." U.S. officials later explained that Rogers's use of the word "possibility" had no special significance.[70]

Despite the concern of American newspeople, communications between Beijing and Washington on Nixon's visit continued. Kissinger also thought that the political crisis might have been caused by the sharp turn in China's policy toward the United States, but he pointed out that Chinese officials never mentioned Lin Biao and U.S. officials never asked.[71] During Kissinger's secret visit to Beijing, the two sides had agreed to set up direct communications in Paris through U.S. military attaché Lieutenant-General Vernon Walters and Ambassador Huang Chen. On important matters, Kissinger would personally go to Paris to meet with Huang under the cover of negotiating with representatives from Hanoi. He met with Huang three times between July and September. In their meeting on September 13, Kissinger said he preferred to announce the date of his interim trip on September 21 because it was before Soviet foreign minister Andrei Gromyko's planned visit to Washington, during which they would probably decide on a date for Nixon's visit to Moscow. He did not want the announcement of his trip to China to look like a reaction to Gromyko's visit.[72]

On September 23, Huang informed Walters that the Chinese government could not agree on the date because of Bush's submission of a "two-China" proposal to the UN one day earlier. However, he agreed to announce the trip on October 5. What was remarkable, as Walters pointed out, was that Huang put his arm around his shoulder when saying goodbye.[73] The rapport between officials of the two governments in Paris showed that the Lin Biao Incident did not change Beijing's decision about rapprochement. To some extent, the incident intensified Beijing's feeling of vulnerability. It did not want other powers, particularly the Soviet Union, to take advantage of it. Therefore, the continuation of the Sino-American accommodation served Beijing's interests.

On October 5, Kissinger personally showed up with Press Secretary Ron Ziegler when the latter announced his interim trip. His appearance not only added weight to the announcement but also reassured worried newspeople. Both the *Times* and the *Post* ran headlines and editorials to elaborate on the steady relationship between Beijing and Washington. The *Times* was so relieved that "the party line now is that there was never any uncertainty." Stanley Karnow, the *Post*'s chief China watcher, wrote in a column entitled "Kissinger Trip Reflects Accord.[74]

When Kissinger went to Beijing in late October, he was deeply impressed by Beijing's commitment to improving relations. On his arrival, he noticed several anti-American slogans on the city walls. When he asked Zhou Enlai about those slogans, Zhou said that was just "firing empty cannon." On the day that he left Beijing, Kissinger noticed that many of the anti-American slogans had disappeared or had been freshly painted over.[75]

The other thing that impressed Kissinger was Beijing's effort to get its people "accustomed to" the idea that their government was dealing with a senior U.S. official in a friendly manner. He noticed that about five hundred officials were present when his party watched a "revolutionary" performance of the Beijing Opera and that crowds of Chinese spectators looked on when he toured the historical sites in Beijing. His impression was that Marshall Ye and Acting Foreign Minister Ji Pengfei "saw to it"

that they could be "properly displayed together" before the Chinese people. One of the most remarkable scenarios happened when they were having tea together aboard a boat in the lake of the Summer Palace "in plain
view of literally hundreds of Chinese spectators." As Kissinger wrote: "The
fact that a strong, cold wind was blowing (on an otherwise perfect day)
did not deter our hosts; they clearly wanted this boatride to take place and
only a hurricane could have prevented it. When I waved to the crowds of
people on the shore, they clapped loudly."[76]

Kissinger's second trip to Beijing was indeed given much publicity in
the Chinese media. Besides prominent coverage of his arrival and departure, *People's Daily* also published large photos of his meetings with Chinese officials. In reporting Kissinger's departure, it even mentioned that
he had visited tourist sites and watched theatrical shows amid the negotiations. Upon his departure, the two governments issued a joint communiqué, which especially emphasized that preparations for Nixon's trip had
been "proceeding exceedingly well."[77] Beijing wanted to show the world
how its normal diplomatic activities, especially the Sino-American rapprochement, had not been disrupted despite worldwide speculation about
its internal politics.

Another thing worth noting was how Marshal Ye Jiangying figured
prominently in *People's Daily*'s coverage of Kissinger's trip. Ye not only
led the party that received and saw off Kissinger at the airport but also
attended all meetings between Kissinger and Zhou Enlai. In the published
group photo, Ye stood on one side of Kissinger while Zhou Enlai stood on
the other.[78] As Snow pointed out, "Nothing the Chinese leaders publicly do
is without purpose."[79] John Holdridge, Kissinger's aide who accompanied
him on both his China trips in 1971, argued that the public appearance of
Marshal Ye with Kissinger informed the Chinese audience that the PLA
supported Sino-American rapprochement.[80]

The publication of Kissinger's photos with Chinese officials in *People's Daily* attracted the attention of the U.S. media. Both NBC and the
Times displayed the photos in their news stories. As the *Post* claimed, even
though the Chinese audience had grown "accustomed in recent months
to seeing their leaders pose with groups of visiting Americans," it was the
first time the Chinese official press published photos of American officials
with the Chinese. The *Times* correctly pointed out that their publication in

People's Daily meant they would also appear in newspapers all over China, which showed that Beijing wanted its people to know about the positive developments in Sino-American relations.[81]

China's Admission into the UN

Before Kissinger's return from China, the United States had suffered what the *Times* called a "crushing defeat" in the United Nations on October 25. After the American proposal to make Taiwan's expulsion an "important matter" was defeated 59 to 55, an Albanian resolution that called for China's admission and Taiwan's expulsion won by the large margin of 76 to 35. All NATO members except Greece, Portugal and Luxembourg voted against the United States.[82]

The U.S. media sympathized with Taiwan. In the ABC story, Nationalist representatives received applause of sympathy when they walked out of the General Assembly before the vote on their expulsion. NBC played the last speech of the Nationalist ambassador to the UN. All three networks featured the wild reception from representatives from countries that supported China. In a nice touch, they also showed pictures of vacant seats and the flag post waiting for Chinese representatives.[83] On the front page of the *Times,* a photo of China supporters clapping hands over their victory was contrasted with a photo of Nationalist representatives walking out of the General Assembly. The *Post* had a picture of Taiwan's foreign minister, Chou Shu-kai, listening to the debate with a stern face. Both newspapers also reported that Senator James L. Buckley (R-NY), who reacted sharply by proposing in Congress "a major reduction" in the American financial contribution to the UN. Both of them deplored the "injustice" to Taiwan and the dangerous precedent of expelling a "member state" in their editorials. Interestingly, both newsweeklies used the line "The Chinese Are Coming" in their coverage of the UN votes. While *Time* featured a big sketch of Zhou Enlai on its cover with the line, *Newsweek* used it as the title of an article featuring a crowd applauding for the victory for China.[84]

Though the Nixon administration felt obliged to address the domestic sentiment over Taiwan's expulsion, it did not want to create an anti-China impression. In their public statements, administration officials reiterated how the government had tried hard to keep Taiwan in the UN, but their condemnation mainly focused on the expulsion and the behavior of small states, instead of the vote. In an official response on TV, Secretary of State William Rogers accepted "the will of majority" and welcomed the admission of China, but he emphasized that Washington and its cosponsors had made "an all-out effort" to keep Taiwan in the UN. In order to appeal to conservatives, he said that the administration was not opposed to a reduction in UN allocations because it might be spending too much and "living beyond its resources."[85] In a press briefings two days after the UN vote, Ron Ziegler told reporters that the president condemned the joyful response of the delegates after the UN vote as a "shocking demonstration" and "undisguised glee" and "personal animosity" toward American policy. Calling it "offensive and undignified," he said the president felt that it "could very seriously impair support for the United Nations in the country and in Congress." Nixon's condemnation of the "glee" made headlines in the *Times* and the *Post*.[86] At least he could show the American public his moral support for Taiwan.

In their editorials, both the *Times* and the *Post* criticized the Nixon administration for playing to the irrationality of conservatives and called on the country to move ahead with the Beijing dialogues. The *Post* called retaliation against the UN "petty and vindictive" and criticized Rogers for "hardly discouraging" those in Congress who were bent on reducing the U.S. contribution. It argued that the consensus should be "that it was past time to begin pursuing a policy of realistic accommodation with Peking—a policy whose most intense advocate these days is the U.S." Similarly, the *Times* argued that since the issue had been finally settled, it was the "height of folly" to retaliate against the UN and that the solution of China's UN membership problem might "not be unhealthy in the long run" because it might give Washington a chance to improve its relations with its friends and allies. James Reston claimed that Nixon had "more flexibility" on the world stage than he had before.[87]

The two newspapers also seemed to have seen through Nixon's tricks. The *Post* pointed out that the White House had left Rogers to make explanations "in an apparent effort to keep the President's personal prestige separated from the voting setback." In an editorial entitled "Crushing Defeat . . . or a Blessing in Disguise," the *Times* maintained that Nixon had "put on a calculated display of anger—however genuine his anger may have been—with the primary object of deflecting from himself the sense of outrage in Congress and on the right." It also pointed out that, after all, Nixon still had his major "political assets intact" on his road to Beijing and the 1972 election.[88] When U.S. publications condemned the UN for expelling Taiwan, they never mentioned the fact that the Nationalists did not accept the two-China idea either, which means the admission of mainland China would have caused the departure of Taiwan anyway, despite the efforts of some members in the UN to convince it to stay.

Another measure the Nixon administration took to deflate criticism was to coordinate Kissinger's second trip. In order to avoid the impression that his success in Beijing had caused the American defeat in the UN, Kissinger not only asked Bush to deliver his UN speech after his departure for Beijing but also delayed his return at the request of Nixon so that he could arrive home after the UN vote.[89] In the press briefing upon his return, Kissinger described the timing of the UN vote during his stay in China as a "painful experience." Emphasizing that the visit had been planned during his last trip, he especially reiterated that it "did not affect the outcome of the U.N. decision."[90]

Nixon's tactic of delaying Kissinger's return from China seemed to pay off. On the same front page where Nixon's denunciation of the delegates' "glee" was reported, large photos of Kissinger with Zhou Enlai appeared in the two newspapers, which were thrilled because that was the first time when officials of the United States and China had posed together for a photo shoot. In an article entitled "China: A Stinging Victory," *Time* placed a picture of the Nationalist ambassador walking out of the UN together with the one featuring Zhou Enlai and Kissinger.[91] The agenda quickly shifted from the UN to the Sino-American dialogue.

After Kissinger's October trip to Beijing, the two governments worked on a communiqué announcing the exact date of Nixon's visit. On November 18, Ambassador Huang Chen told Walters that his government wanted to change the date of announcement from November 23 to 30 because it was not "opportune" to make such an announcement when "the chief of government from a neighboring state" was visiting China. When Walters offered to guess that it was North Vietnam, Huang slapped him on the back and said, "You guessed right for the first time." In his memo, Walters wrote, "All of the foregoing was washed down with jasmine tea and accompanied by the now usual friendly pats on the arm and back."[92] The rapport between officials in Paris suggested that the Chinese leadership no longer regarded the United States as its archenemy.

When North Vietnamese premier Pham Von Dong visited China between November 20 and 27, 1971, Beijing launched an enormous propaganda campaign to highlight the "solidarity" between the two Communist "comrades and brothers." *People's Daily* devoted extensive and prominent coverage to Vietnam with front-page stories, pictures, and editorials and published an unusually long communiqué between the two governments at the end of Pham's visit. Three days after Pham left, *People's Daily* announced Nixon's visit with only one sentence placed at the very bottom of the front page: "The governments of the People's Republic and China and the United States of America have agreed that President Nixon's visit to China would start on February 21, 1972."[93] Beijing's public enthusiasm for the visit of the North Vietnamese and the "low profile" it gave to the communiqué showed its effort to hold together its ideological friends who were hostile to the United States.

On February 15, 1972, a week before Nixon started his China tour, Edgar Snow died of cancer in Switzerland. *People's Daily* made a big deal of the death of "a friend of the Chinese people" by publishing on its front page official condolences from Mao and his wife, Jiang Qing, Zhou Enlai and his wife, Deng Yingchao, and Madam Sun Yat-sun, who was the vice state chairman. It also featured a story that Zhou Enlai and Jiang Qing had attended a memorial service for Snow in Beijing, a ceremony reflecting the tribute usually paid to the head of a state. In his published cablegram of condolence to Mrs. Snow, Zhou called Snow a "witness" of good friendship between the two peoples and expressed his strong belief that "the friendship that Snow had dedicated his whole life to would definitely grow."[94] Even though Snow probably would not have gotten along with Nixon if they had met, the Chinese government's high-profile treatment of his death in the media created an atmosphere that suggested a close bond between the two peoples, which would benefit Nixon's coming trip. This was another effort for Beijing to prepare the Chinese people.

American newspapers and networks also gave Snow's death prominent attention. All three networks covered the story. Both the *Times* and the *Post* ran Snow's photos with Mao on their front pages and called attention to the "unique tribute" Chinese leaders paid to him in their official media. The *Times* pointed out that Zhou Enlai had sent a medical team of three doctors and a nurse to attend to Snow when he failed to "rally from" the surgery on his spleen. Moreover, it posted a special editorial that praised Snow as a "first-class journalist" who had played an important role in maintaining the "tenuous link" between the Chinese leaders and the United States.[95] Beijing's treatment of Snow's death even impressed the elite U.S. media, who by now had discarded their bias against the pro-Communist journalist and joined the Chinese in praising his role in cultivating the friendship between the two countries.

The Show in Beijing

After several months of preparation, Nixon set out for China on February 17, 1972. All three networks stopped their regular programming to live-broadcast his farewell ceremony on the South Lawn of the White House. The front pages of the *Times* and the *Post* both featured pictures of Nixon and his wife waving good-bye in front of their helicopter.[96] After stopping in Hawaii and Guam for two days, Nixon's party set off for Shanghai, where they made a brief stop, picking up Chinese navigators, and flew to Beijing. On February 20, Nixon's plane, the *Spirit of 76*, landed at the Beijing airport. In the middle of cameras and spotlights, Nixon disembarked from the plane and stepped forward to shake Zhou Enlai's waiting hand. This moment became the main story in the media around the world the next day. According to Kissinger, Nixon and Haldeman wanted to make sure the president would be alone for the television cameras in his first encounter with Zhou Enlai. He and Rogers had been instructed several times that they were to stay on the plane until the historic handshake between Nixon and Zhou had been accomplished. Notwithstanding the instructions, Haldeman did not want to leave anything to chance. A burly aide blocked the aisle of the presidential plane when the moment came.[97]

To the dismay of U.S. reporters, only a few dozen Chinese officials and five hundred honor guards showed up at the airport. When CBS's Charles Collingwood in New York asked Walter Cronkite whether there was an air of excitement in Beijing, Cronkite said he did not think so. NBC's Barbara

Walters found an "air of disappointment." NBC's Edwin Newman commented that Zhou Enlai's handshake with Nixon "did seem to be a cordial" one.[98] James Thomson Jr., a China hand in the Kennedy and Johnson administrations and a Harvard professor who worked as ABC's commentator on the Nixon trip, said the receiving ceremony was "low key, but very, very serious." Harry Reasoner, the ABC anchor in Beijing, did not think Beijing tried to downplay its importance, considering the presence of a number of high-level Chinese officials and the involvement of the PLA at the reception. The *Times* reported that Nixon received a "quiet greeting," which was "studiously correct but minimally official." It speculated that it was probably because the two governments had no diplomatic relations yet. The *Post* also pointed out the "lack of fanfare" when it contrasted to the receptions accorded to other foreign visitors, such as Emperor Haile Selassie of Ethiopia, who was greeted by three hundred thousand Chinese citizens when he arrived a year earlier.[99]

Despite the low profile of the reception, the images at the airport were still powerful. For example, when the People's Liberation Army band played "The Star-Spangled Banner," James Thomson Jr. noted that it had been a while since it was last played in China. Reasoner echoed Thomson and said that it was a "startling moment." Talking about the Zhou-Nixon handshake, Thomson referred to the Geneva Conference in 1954 when John Foster Dulles refused to shake hands with Zhou. Interestingly, when Howard K. Smith criticized China because of its troop maneuvers in the capital, the rumor that China shipped luxurious cars from Hong Kong to prepare for Nixon's visit, and the three Americans still imprisoned in China, Thomson brushed aside those negative comments and expressed high hopes for the coming summit. Thomson also keenly noted that the appearance of Marshal Ye Jianying behind Zhou Enlai in receiving Nixon showed that the military and the civilian branches were still "holding together."[100] Thomson shared an Emmy award with the ABC news team for his ten-day service as a television commentator during Nixon's visit.[101]

The Chinese government did not set up the exact date when Nixon would meet with Mao. As soon as Nixon arrived at his residence, Mao became so excited that he told Zhou he wanted to meet with the president right away. Winston Lord, Kissinger's aide who attended the meeting, thought the arrangement was a "typical Chinese example" where the emperor kept visitors on edge. Nevertheless, Nixon was so thrilled that he rushed to the meeting with Kissinger and Lord without bringing along William Rogers, who, as the secretary of state, should have been present at the summit but in whom the president had little confidence. The one-hour meeting happened behind closed doors. Only the Xinhua News Agency was allowed in briefly for photo shooting. Before the Chinese media released photos of the meeting, Kissinger asked them to cut off the much lower-ranking Lord in order not to embarrass Rogers.[102] Nixon later told Haldeman how he was impressed during the meeting when "at one point Mao reached over, talking, and grabbed my hand and held it for more than a minute while he made his point." Feeling that scene was significant, Nixon was especially happy that the Chinese film crew captured it.[103] After the Nixon-Mao meeting, Ron Ziegler announced it to the journalists. Though he simply said that the conversation was "frank and serious" when asked for details, the photos and black-and-white film of Nixon with Mao became major stories in the United States. Under a big picture of the Mao-Nixon meeting on its front page, the *Post* described it as "Mao's apparent endorsement of an eventual improvement in Sino-American ties."[104] This statement would have pleased Nixon because it would silence conservatives who were worried that Nixon might be slighted in China.

On the night of Nixon's arrival, Zhou Enlai hosted a state banquet. On television, American audiences could see how Nixon clinked cups with Zhou Enlai and other Chinese officials with the national flags of the two countries on display together and the PLA band playing "Home on the Range" and "America the Beautiful" in the background. As Nixon was delivering his toast, the CBS camera offered a long close-up of the Chinese premier so that the American audience could have a better look at him.[105] Nixon's remark "Let us start a 'Long March' together" was widely quoted in the media.[106] When he reviewed the news summaries with Haldeman before going to bed that night, Nixon was extremely pleased with the coverage and especially happy because they got all the images he wanted, such as his use of chopsticks and the toasts as well as glass-clinking between him and Zhou Enlai. Nixon also told Haldeman that when he clinked Zhou's glass, the Chinese premier said he had the band play "America the Beautiful" because it was played at Nixon's first inaugural. Assuming that was one of his favorite songs, Zhou offered it to Nixon as a toast to his next inaugural.[107]

As Ron Ziegler told a UPI correspondent, Nixon's trip was indeed a "picture story." There were no regular news briefings, and the correspondents had no important news to cover except when the Nixons went sightseeing or Pat Nixon visited Chinese citizens and their families at a model farm, in a kitchen, kindergarten, or factory. While Nixon's closed-door conversations with Zhou Enlai were totally kept from the media, the Chinese arranged image-makers and photo opportunities so that they would be transmitted home via satellite and played at "prime-time viewing hours."[108] For an entire week from February 18, the front pages of newspapers ran photos following Nixon's itinerary until his return to Washington. The magazines, though published after his return, both used the trip as their cover stories and similarly offered many photographs.[109] Nixon's trip commanded live broadcasting, often in prime time, and the lion's share of the evening news during that week.

The Chinese media expressed qualified enthusiasm for Nixon's visit. The day after his arrival, *People's Daily* featured several large photos of Nixon's meeting with Mao and Zhou Enlai on its front page. Several U.S. news agencies, newspapers and networks included, picked this front page as a highlight in their stories. As they reported, *People's Daily* had caused a "sensation" in Beijing and was sold out within a few hours when throngs of people crowded the newsstands.[110] They were deeply impressed by Beijing's effort to publicize Nixon's visit.

Beijing might have felt that the "unusual" coverage of Nixon's first day in China had caused too much excitement. In the days that followed, readers of *People's Daily* witnessed a subtle change. Photos of Nixon's activities remained on the front pages, but they became smaller and were placed in less prominent places below stories of domestic matters. Interestingly, whereas the U.S. media ran pictures showing the warm interpersonal relations between the leaders, such as the Nixon-Zhou toast, Nixon's handshake with ordinary Chinese in Hangzhou, and especially his offer to help the Chinese premier with his coat,[111] *People's Daily* coverage was more official and ceremonial in nature, ignoring the "personal" dimensions in the exchanges. As Kissinger said, Beijing faced "a philosophical crisis, torn between the imperatives of Realpolitik and the dictates of ideology."[112]

Reference News provided more insights than *People's Daily*. It covered the world response to Nixon's planned trip and the China craze it caused in the United States, U.S. preparatory work including advance-team activities in China and media allocation, how Americans watched Nixon's tour on TV, and their response to the Shanghai Communiqué. It also reprinted many stories about how Nixon was "diligently" studying the history and culture of China. More importantly, it reprinted the full text of many of Nixon's statements on TV and radio. Whereas *People's Daily* covered Nixon's tour with pictures and brief introductions to the itinerary, *Reference News* printed in detail his talks with the press when he visited tourist sites. It also mentioned the picture that showed Nixon helping Zhou with his coat.[113] Beijing wanted its cadres to know more about Nixon and his China policy. These details in *Reference News* revealed how the Chinese government valued the trip.

In covering the opponents to Nixon's visit, *Reference News* seemed in some respects to be more objective or comprehensive than the two elite U.S. newspapers. In January and February 1972, for example, it reported twice on Carl McIntire, a minister in the Bible Presbyterian Church sympathetic to Taiwan, who announced his plan to organize demonstrations in eighteen American cities to protest Nixon's toast with "murders and slave owners."[114] Interestingly, neither the *Times* nor the *Post* covered the activities of the reverend during that period, perhaps because he was an obscure critic on the right fringe. Another interesting thing was that when Henry Winston and Gus Hall, the secretary and chairman of the Communist Party of the United States, attacked Nixon's China trip as a "cover" for his Vietnam War, *Reference News* branded them as "revisionists."[115] Obviously, Beijing did not regard the American Communists' attack on the Nixon trip as friendly actions, considering that the Party was a Soviet appendage. The newspaper seemed to be trying to find opposition to show how difficult the demarche was for Nixon.

The Shanghai Communiqué

Nixon's visit to China concluded with a joint communiqué announced in Shanghai on February 27. During Kissinger's visit in October 1971, the two sides had decided that the communiqué would state their agreements to move toward the normalization of relations and to reduce the danger of military conflict, as well as their commitment not to seek hegemony in the Asia-Pacific regions and to oppose other countries that might try to establish such "hegemony," which had become the new code word for "Soviet expansionism." With regard to issues with ideological differences such as Indochina, Korea, Japan, and the Indian-Pakistan conflict, they agreed that each side would state their own positions. While Beijing would express its commitment to support "revolutions and national liberation movements" around the world, Washington would reiterate its support for people around the world in their "pursuit of personal freedom and social progress free from outside interference." However, Taiwan remained a "thorny" problem because it involved principles on both sides. While Washington had to deal with a strong domestic sentiment for the island and a commitment expressed in the mutual security treaty of 1955, Beijing regarded Taiwan and its unification with the mainland as an issue of sovereignty. When Nixon arrived in Beijing, the two sides still differed on the wording about Taiwan. The Chinese side wanted the U.S. acknowledgment that Taiwan was a "province" of China and its promise to withdraw all forces from the island unconditionally. Washington could go no further than to describe the withdrawal as an "objective" and needed conditions attached to it.[116]

When the Nixons went sightseeing, Kissinger was still bargaining with Chinese deputy foreign minister Qiao Guanhua. At one time the negotiation reached a deadlock, and even Zhou Enlai joined it temporarily. Kissinger explained to him that Washington could not made "unconditional commitments" and that the communiqué had to be "explicable" or "defensible" to the American public. His proposal was to link the "final withdrawal from Taiwan" to the "premise of peaceful settlement," and to tie the "progressive reduction of forces" to the "gradual diminution of tension in the area," because the United States had an interest in the peaceful resolution of the Taiwan issue, and the conflicts in Indochina would end in time. The Chinese side promised to consider his proposal, but they preferred the "prospect" of a peaceful settlement rather than "premise," arguing that it had a "more active and more bilateral connotation." Finally, on February 25, less than forty-eight hours before Nixon's scheduled departure from China, the Chinese accepted the American formulations. Kissinger claims that he even managed to secure the Chinese consent to the wording that Taiwan was a "part" rather than a "province" of China, thus avoiding a suggestion of subordination. Though the real American security role on Taiwan was defined by the mutual defense treaty, neither side mentioned it in the communiqué.[117]

In the final version of the communiqué, the U.S. position on Taiwan was stated as follows:

> The United States acknowledges that all Chinese on either side of the Taiwan Strait maintain there is but one China and that Taiwan is a part of China. The United States government does not challenge that position. It reaffirms its interest in a peaceful settlement of the Taiwan question by the Chinese themselves. With this prospect in mind, it affirms the ultimate objective of the withdrawal of all U.S. forces and military installations from Taiwan. In the meantime, it will progressively reduce its forces and military installations on Taiwan as the tension in the area diminishes.[118]

As the communiqué came out, the U.S. media ignored all other issues and jumped on the U.S. pledge to "withdraw gradually from Taiwan," terming it a "major concession." The *Post* headline was "Nixon Pledges Pullout of Forces on Taiwan." Under a photo in which Nixon and Zhou Enlai stood below a giant statute of Mao, there was an article entitled "China Trip: Limited Results." The *Times* ran the headline "Taipei Is Bitter: Paper Reflecting View of Regime Assails U.S. 'Cowardice'"[119]

Responses from the networks were more favorable. They presented Senators Mike Mansfield (D-MT), Hugh Scott (R-PA), Edward Kennedy (D-MA), George McGovern (D-SD), and Representative Paul McCloskey Jr. (R-CA), who praised the communiqué as a forward-looking document, in front of Senators James Buckley (R-NY) and John Tower (R-TX), and Representatives John Ashbrook (R-OH) and Hubert Humphrey (D-MN), who expressed either concern or shock at the American position on Taiwan. The overall response, as described by Howard K. Smith of ABC, was "cautiously favorable for most part, although there were dissenters."[120]

During the flight from Shanghai to Alaska, Haldeman noted that their press reports did not include the networks. Even though he tried hard to convince Nixon that the general press was not that negative, the president was still worried about "dealing with a bad story." He then instructed his aides to work in haste on the plane, adding points that could clarify his position in the return message.[121] After a long layover in Anchorage scheduled by White House television specialist Mark Goode, Nixon's plane arrived in Washington during prime TV time.[122] Surrounded by a large, welcoming crowd, Nixon delivered to the cameras his triumphant return address in which he highlighted what he considered the "heart of the communiqué"—the agreement of both governments to renounce the use of force in dispute settlement and their commitment to prevent the domination of Asia by any power. In terms of Taiwan, he emphasized that the gradual withdrawal of forces was based on the easing of tensions and that the United States would not relinquish its commitment.[123]

The *Post* changed its tone after Nixon's speech. Its headline the next day was "Nixon Back from China Trip, 15,000 Welcome President." The front page featured another article entitled "U.S. Communiqué Is Praised by Both Parties on Hill." In an editorial entitled "Sellout' of Taiwan?" the *Post* argued that the charge of Nixon's abandonment of Taiwan was "insupportable." Calling the communiqué an "agreement to disagree," the *Times* argued that it offered "no dramatic surprises," but contained "no major disappointments." It praised the "renunciation of force in favor of diplomacy" and highlighted the agreement on exchanges in trade, science, technology, culture, sports and news reporting as a "concrete achievement."[124] The communiqué did not change the status of Taiwan. People may ask what, if anything, Nixon had brought back from Beijing. The answer from *Time* magazine was "the event itself, the fact that it took place." As far as the gains of the Nixon's administration, *Newsweek* pointed out its success in securing the agreement from the Chinese not to include in the communiqué its usual propaganda tirade that the American defense treaty with Taiwan was "null and void" and the Chinese agreement to resolve the Taiwan issue by "peaceful means." Similar to *Time,* it argued that the China trip was not a "great leap forward," but it was at least an "important first step," which brought a much better chance of peace in Asia.[125] Overall, after Nixon's clarifications upon his return, the elite media supported the Shanghai Communiqué and reviewed the significance of his China trip more favorably.

In China, one noticeable development was that when Zhou Enlai returned to Beijing from Shanghai, where he saw Nixon off, he received an extraordinarily warm welcome at the airport. *People's Daily* ran a headline

"Resolutely Support and Carry Out the Revolutionary Diplomatic Line of Chairman Mao: Premier Zhou Was Warmly Received by Five Thousand People at the Airport upon His Return to Beijing from Shanghai" with three big photos of the greeting party. Among the party, the article listed several key members of the Politburo, leaders of the PLA and the government, and even Mao's wife, who was the head of the radicals who might have doubts on the reconciliation.[126] As the crowd was much bigger than Zhou normally received when he returned from somewhere within China, the *Times* argued that the "triumphant welcome" Zhou received marked Beijing's "satisfaction with the outcome of Nixon's visit as contained in the joint communiqué."[127] Publicizing the ceremony at the Beijing airport not only showed the consensus among the Chinese leadership in supporting the outcome of the Nixon visit. It also sent a positive signal to the United States.

The "TV Spectacle" as Part of the Story

David Broder, a prominent columnist for the *Washington Post*, wrote that television, with its strength in images, creates a "communication loop" that makes the TV coverage "part of the story it is covering."[128] In covering Nixon's China trip, television, or the "TV spectacle," did become a hot topic. Largely feeling at a disadvantage in the competition or due to their envy, the print media pointed out many problems with their electronic rivals to critique Nixon's overdoing of the TV drama. In its editorial entitled "Spectacle and Substance," the *Times* described Nixon's departure ceremony as a "genuine drama" with an "elaborately staged fanfare." It warned of the danger that the spectacle Nixon had "assiduously" created might obscure the differences between the two governments and foster "illusions" about Sino-American relations.[129] The *Post* similarly maintained that the audience had to tell "show business" from "diplomatic business." Stanley Karnow, the *Post*'s correspondent in Beijing, called Nixon's visit an exercise of "TV Diplomacy," arguing that TV not only helped him maximize public attention but also helped the Chinese irritate Japan, Southeast Asia, and the Soviet Union. He also surmised that the Chinese leadership might use TV as a "lever" to build up the American expectations that Nixon might return home with some kind of "arrangement" by inflating his image.[130]

Time described Nixon's trip as an excellent opportunity for "a presidential candidate seeking re-election to make a television appearance."[131] It maintained that all was "elaborate scrollwork, hiding content." In its cartoon, Nixon and Mao stood in the middle of TV cameras and spotlights with a row of saluting guns firing in the background. The caption read, "Just think, all this will have gone to waste if you're not re-elected!"[132] In an article "TV: An Eyeful of China, A Thimbleful of Insight," *Newsweek* showed CBS journalists "huddled together" in the Beijing press room, "bemoaning" their isolation and the lack of "hard" news. As it indicated, CBS president Richard S. Salant decided to cancel live broadcasts on Thursday, saying "we'd had enough picture postcards" from the Great Wall one day earlier. It also mocked the lack of in-depth reporting in television coverage because the networks all sent their most experienced anchors who "made up standard news teams to cover a spectacular in standard American terms," while their sinologists, who were better equipped to uncover information from sources in China, were sitting in New York studios "7000 miles from the scene."[133]

As pointed out in a *Post* editorial, Nixon in his "Man of the Year" interview with *Time* had confidently said, "Where you need a lot of rhetoric, a lot of jazz, a lot of flamboyance, is where you don't have much to sell." Using Nixon's own words, it argued that his effort to "embellish" his trip with "rhetoric and flamboyance and jazz" encouraged the suspicion that he "did not have all that much to sell."[134] When television coverage was used to this frothy extreme, the media themselves began to question what Nixon could bring back from Beijing.

Conclusion

Ever since the Chinese government made the decision to reconcile with the United States, it faced a great task in accustoming the Chinese people to the change in relations. Beijing gradually transmitted Mao and Zhou's decision from the central leadership at the top to ordinary Chinese people. Through the internal channel of the Party infrastructure on the first level, it informed leaders at higher levels to mobilize their support for the departure in China's foreign policies. On the second level, the insightful news stories and analyses in *Reference News* kept the Communist cadres as well as ordinary Party members updated about international developments. It was also through this internal newspaper that the Chinese audience learned about Nixon's wish to visit China, Mao's desire to meet with him, and the favorable international response to the visit. On the third level, Beijing promoted the friendship between the two peoples through *People's Daily* in the form of people-to-people diplomacy. By displaying Americans such as Edgar Snow, the Ping-Pong team, the "friendly" visitors, and Henry Kissinger before Chinese crowds as well as in the official media, Beijing prepared its people for the new relationship with the United States.

Though the U.S. government did not have too much work getting its people used to the change in relations since debates about this topic had been going on in the media increasingly frequently since the early 1960s, it faced a challenge from conservatives, especially when it came to the Taiwan issue. On UN membership, Washington slowly changed its position from banning China's entry to preventing Taiwan's expulsion. Besides disassociating himself from a possible failure, Nixon asked his aides to tell the media that his administration was fighting hard to keep the Nationalists in the UN. By focusing on the progress and longtime benefits of the coming rapprochement with China, the media helped Nixon fend off the challenges from conservatives.

Being well aware of the role of the media in promoting his own position in history, Nixon was very sophisticated in using them, particularly television, in order to guarantee the success of the "show" in Beijing. The White House granted the TV networks extraordinary privileges, not only by giving them more seats in the media plane but also by joining their advance team in tracking every spot Nixon planned to visit so that they got the best camera angles. As Nixon hoped, his one-week trip turned out to be a "TV spectacle," which not only helped him score a public-relations success but also aroused the media's criticisms about the lack of "substance" under the fanfare.

As a *Post* editorial pointed out, although "Nixon overdid the TV bit badly," television "helped educate the American people," showing them that China was not a monster but a nation "to be dealt with as best one can."[135] Zhou Enlai must have known what it meant when he agreed to allow an American press corps of 150 into China, especially when he agreed to their proposal of live television coverage. He knew they would be volunteer promoters of China's image to the world. Although Nixon's visit did not formally normalize relations between the two countries, as journalists and Nixon said during several occasions during that historic week, his presence in China signified a new relationship between two countries that had been separated for more than two decades. The start of exchanges in trade, education, culture, and news reporting seemed not as significant as the summit. However, the reopening of dialogue through these channels provided a means by which the two peoples could engage and learn about each other before the formal normalization of relations in 1979.

Conclusion

This book does not ask *why* the Sino-American rapprochement could happen. Instead, it evaluates *how* it occurred in the media of both countries between 1963 and 1972 and what role they played in the evolution of relations. In the Sino-American rapprochement, media in the United States and China made different contributions because of their distinctive relationships with their own governments. Nevertheless, as means of communication, they were similar in their roles in message sending and preparing the people for the change in relations.

The U.S. Media

On the relationship between the American media and the government in terms of foreign policy, scholars of communications have developed several theories. One school of thought, widely known as the "hegemony" school, claims that government manipulates the media when officials "stage events, leak selective information, cover up facts behind a wall of secrecy, overwhelm the media with barrages of press releases," and of course, lie occasionally to the point that the media become "putty in the hands of the president and his legion of media managers." A fundamental argument of the hegemony theory is that the media make "no independent contribution" to the foreign-policy debate. A contrary school portrays the media as participants in the foreign-policy process. For members of this school, the media play the role of the "fourth estate" in politics, exerting unique influence on government policy. The problem with the hegemony theory is that it perceives the media as too subservient to the government.[1] The "fourth estate" school, on the other hand, tends to exaggerate the role of the media in the policy-making process of the government.

In my study of the elite U.S. media's coverage of Sino-American relations, I find that they did make an "independent contribution" to the reconciliation between the two countries. They played important roles as transmitters of diplomatic signals and active participants. They also cultivated the American people about the progress and significance of Sino-American reconciliation.

As transmitters of political information, the U.S. media functioned as a "diplomatic signaling system" between the two governments, especially when direct communications did not exist.[2] When Nixon and other U.S. officials addressed China by its proper name or emphasized its importance in world affairs, they expected the media to deliver these gestures of friendliness to the American public as well as the leadership in Beijing. However, there were times when the messages did not get across. For example, Beijing's signals through Edgar Snow were not delivered to Nixon at an earlier time because of the media's suspicion of Communist sympathizers and the inability of American officials to pick up the nuances in the Chinese media. Moreover, when Nixon "casually" talked about his intention to visit China, his remarks attracted more media attention in China than in the United States. In both cases, the media's intentional or unintentional underestimation of the signals' importance caused the failure of message transmission. To some extent, they reflect the independence of the media in passing on the political information because of their ability to "select" what they want to cover.

By participants, Robert M. Batscha means that the media acted as an "advocate" of policy and "representative of the people" in foreign relations.[3] The U.S. media's advocacy of foreign-policy options caused them to endorse or to criticize government policies. During the Johnson administration, newspapers and newsmagazines acted as vocal critics of the government's inflexible China policy, especially after the escalation of the Vietnam War and the Chinese nuclear test in 1964. Besides calling on the government to make initiatives to reduce tensions with China and to incorporate it into the international community, they criticized officials who evoked the "China threat" as an excuse for the American involvement in Vietnam. In both the Johnson and Nixon administrations, journalists urged the White House to be more creative on the issue of China's UN membership and to move toward a "two-China" solution sooner to prevent the expulsion of Taiwan before it was too late. In these cases, the media ran ahead of public opinion and the government in pushing for policy reform.

As the relations between the two countries began to unfreeze, especially after Ping-Pong Diplomacy in April 1971, Beijing admitted members of the U.S. media into China, granting them extraordinary privileges and displaying them to the Chinese people. By winning over prominent opinion influencers such as James Reston and his *New York Times,* Beijing promoted the positive image of China among the American people. These journalists not only wrote generally favorable stories about China but also acted as participants, or "cultural diplomats," between the two peoples when official contacts were scarce.

The participatory role of the media can also be shown when they became part of the stories they covered. During Ping-Pong Diplomacy, for example, Vice President Spiro Agnew accused the U.S. media of helping the Chinese government win a "propaganda triumph" over the United States because he was aware of their power in influencing public opinion. The use of live television to cover Nixon's visit was unprecedented in history. While it helped him achieve a public-relations success, the media also criticized Nixon for arousing unrealistic expectations through his overuse of television. By talking about the distinction between "content" and "form," they questioned how much the president could bring home. Both cases highlight the importance of the media as historical players.

The media also educated the American people about China policy by providing forums for public deliberation. The best example was the Fulbright Hearings in 1966, when their prominent and intensive coverage magnified critical voices in the academic community and Congress. It contributed to the relaxation of public hostility toward China. Moreover, when Washington announced new initiatives to China, the media illuminated their significance with phrases such as "the most significant" or "a major step." These positive responses helped the government win public support. If the flexibility and understanding of the American people was an important factor in Nixon's willingness to make bolder moves toward China upon taking office, the media made a great contribution in cultivating them.

Because the media did not have to worry about political restrictions as the U.S. government did, they had more freedom to elaborate on ideas that Washington could not openly talk about. The concept of "containment without isolation" had existed in the U.S. media long before the Johnson administration acknowledged it. During the Cultural Revolution, the Johnson team refrained from making comments on Chinese domestic politics to avoid provoking China or undermining the moderate forces in China. In contrast, the U.S. media reported widely on the violence in China. Some even reported on the U.S. interests in the victory of Mao's faction. After the eruption of the Sino-Soviet border clashes in March 1969, the Nixon administration assumed a posture of impartiality in order to avoid provoking the Soviet Union (even though in private it tilted toward China), whereas the U.S. media were not worried about upsetting Moscow when they openly delineated the benefits of closer ties with Beijing. Similarly, while the media offered various sensational speculations in response to the Lin Biao affair, Washington neither inquired about it with Beijing nor made comment, in order to avoid sabotaging Nixon's China trip. In these cases, the media did have independent voices and could and often did express opinions that differed from the official positions of the U.S. government.

Despite my argument that the U.S. media made independent contributions to Sino-American rapprochement, they were far from being completely independent players. They relied heavily on the government as their main source in reporting on foreign affairs. Kissinger's secret trip to China is a good example where the government totally denied the media access to the political process. Moreover, there were ample examples in which the U.S. government turned a deaf ear to prominent news agencies' call to admit China into the UN. On the other hand, even though the government initiated policies, the media's ability to set the agenda of political debates and to influence public opinion makes them a restraining force that the government could not manipulate at will or simply ignore. For example, whereas Nixon wanted to illustrate his comprehensive approach to the world situation in his annual foreign policy report, the U.S. media, including the *Times* and the *Post*, tended to focus on Vietnam in their headlines. In another example, whereas Nixon wanted to demonstrate the historic significance of his China trip, several journalists focused on his "betrayal" of Taiwan in the Shanghai Communiqué.

The extensive comparison between different media agencies in the United States has yielded interesting observations. Between the two elite American newspapers under study, the *New York Times* appeared much more forthcoming than the *Washington Post* in promoting an improvement in Sino-American relations. During the Cultural Revolution, the *Post* was more graphic in describing the chaos in China and Red Guard brutalities. On Sino-Soviet conflicts in 1969, while the *Times* editorials promoted closer ties with Beijing, the *Post* editorials appeared more detached and paid more attention to American interests. When the Warsaw Talks were renewed in 1970, the *Times* was more optimistic about the prospect of better relations than the *Post,* which showed more suspicion of Beijing's intention.[4] Essentially, in approaching US-Chinese relations, the *Times* showed more liberalism, which promotes more international cooperation, and the *Post* demonstrated more realism, which emphasized American national interests. Between the two magazines, *Time* was more hostile to China before the death of its founder, Henry Luce, whereas *Newsweek* was more balanced in presenting different perspectives.

In comparison to the print media, the three television networks devoted less coverage to news analysis and were generally more neutral in their brief "headline" reporting. As a visual medium with a much larger audience, television had a larger impact, especially when it provided live coverage of the events. The networks made tremendous contributions to the success of Ping-Pong Diplomacy in 1971 and Nixon's visit in 1972. The large number of videos they provided about China and the friendly exchanges between the two peoples were truly refreshing to the American audience after two decades of alienation between the two countries.

The Chinese Media

Unlike the independent U.S. media, the Chinese media have been controlled by the Communist Party to serve its own political interests. *People's Daily* and *Reference News* represented the two levels of information transmission in China: public and internal. During the period under study, *Peo-*

ple's Daily mainly worked to propagate China's image as a fighter against "imperialists" and "revisionists." The anti-American and anti-Soviet articles aimed not only to mobilize Mao's struggle against his political enemies at home but also to display Beijing's support for the revolutionary struggles around the world, especially those in Indochina. By attacking the Soviet Union as the "number-one accomplice" of the American "imperialists," Beijing assumed a moral high ground in its ideological competitions with Moscow.

The propaganda in *People's Daily* had nuances. On the conflicts in Indochina, for example, Beijing was radical in words but cautious in deeds. Even though it repeatedly warned against the American "war provocations" and expressed the Chinese determination to support peoples in these areas with all means, readers could see its lack of commitment as it did not specify when and how it would intervene. Its anti-American rhetoric was mainly used to hold together its ideological friends, particularly those opposed to the United States. When Hanoi decided to negotiate with Washington in 1968, Beijing displayed its unhappiness by remaining silent and lowering the place of Hanoi on its list of "friends" in the media. During the Cultural Revolution, despite Beijing's fierce attacks on the Soviet Union, *People's Daily* was silent on the Sino-Soviet conflicts on the border. The contrast shows that Beijing did not want to start a real war with the Soviet Union. When it started to report the border clashes after the Soviet invasion of Czechoslovakia in 1968, its wording of "socialist-imperialist" shows that, in Beijing's view, Moscow had changed from an ideological opponent to a strategic threat.

Besides its propaganda function, *People's Daily* was an important channel through which Beijing sent diplomatic signals to Washington. It publicized Beijing's "four points" when the Vietnam conflicts were dramatically escalated. When Beijing decided to move closer to Washington, it publicized the release of American prisoners and the photos of Chinese leaders with the "friendly American" Edgar Snow as signals of a new posture. By 1970, even its anti-American tirades in response to incursions into Cambodia and Laos became relatively toothless.

People's Daily also played an important role when Beijing felt the need to reorient the public's attitude toward the United States. By maintaining the distinction between the "imperialistic American government" and the "heroic American people," it promoted the friendship between the two peoples. Moreover, by giving prominent and intensive coverage to the activities of "American friends" in China after Ping-Pong Diplomacy, Beijing tried to get its people used to the fact that their government was dealing with Americans.

As an internal newspaper, *Reference News* targeted only a limited number of Chinese Communist cadres as well as loyal intellectuals and constituted the only legal way for them to learn about the outside world. Being less propagandistic, it reprinted foreign news agencies' objective reports about China's diplomatic problems with North Korea, Cambodia, and even North Vietnam during the Cultural Revolution. More importantly, it transmitted friendly signals from Washington in their original form, usually with commentaries on their significance for Sino-American relations. When Beijing decided to reconcile with Washington, it reported Chinese signals to the United States such as Mao's stated intention to meet with Nixon in his interview with Snow.

With the dramatic expansion of its circulation in August 1970, *Reference News* played a particularly important role in preparing Party members and intellectuals for a change in Sino-American relations. Its reproduction of foreign news agencies' insightful analyses of the benefits of Sino-American rapprochement, especially by alluding to the impact on the Soviet Union, Japan, and Taiwan, and the favorable world response, provided useful perspectives for the Chinese audience to consider. A comparison between *People's Daily* and *Reference News* shows that, under its cover of anti-American invective, the Chinese government had started preparing cadres for the reconciliation with its former number-one enemy long before it became evident.

For all the differences between the U.S. and Chinese media in terms of their freedom of action and mechanisms of news reporting, they were similar in their roles as deliverers of diplomatic signals and cultivators of their respective publics for the change in Sino-American relations. The media in both countries were also interrelated because they used each other as a source of information. By reading *People's Daily* closely, the U.S. media tried to find clues about the domestic and foreign policies of China. Similarly, many news stories in *Reference News* actually came from the U.S. media. There are ample instances where the media of the two countries moved in tandem. The most important feature they share is their ability to influence public opinion, although admittedly there were few dissenting opinions in China.

Sino-American rapprochement remains a fascinating topic for scholars. This study of the media's role offers an interesting but not definitive evaluation of this historic process. Nevertheless, it demonstrates the importance of the media for both governments in presenting their foreign policies to their respective publics. In a broader sense, it provides food for thought in the continuing debate about the government-media relationship in the United States. This study shows the wide range of roles the U.S. media played in Sino-American rapprochement. Before the government overtures to China, they were forerunners and proponents of policy renovations, and critics of its inflexibility. When breakthroughs occurred in Sino-American relations, they were cheerleaders who not only justified the government policies but also helped to cultivate the public opinion in that direction. In addition to being observers, they were also active participants or diplomats who were deeply involved in the people-to-people diplomacy between the two countries at the key moments of Sino-American rapprochement. At the same time, they might also become unwitting collaborators manipulated by the government due to their reliance on the latter for information in covering American foreign policies. These roles of the media show the complex dynamics between the media and the government, which is an important domestic context for the study of U.S. foreign relations.

The study of the Chinese newspapers challenges the idea that the media in Communist countries were used only for political indoctrination.[5] By showing how the Chinese government used different means of communication to legitimize its own policies to people at different levels of the political hierarchy, that is, from the higher Party leadership, to middle-level cadres, and then to the general public, it presents a more nuanced picture of the "propaganda state" of China. In particular, the *Reference News*'s relatively more objective coverage of China's international condition and especially the evolving relations between the United States demonstrated not only its unique contribution to Sino-American rapprochement but also the sophisticated ways in which the Chinese government handled public opinion. In other words, in addition to hard propaganda and Party directives, the Chinese government actually used "soft" ways to communicate its policies to the cadres and inner-circle intellectuals. Therefore, the complexities of the Chinese communication system in handling public opinion are useful factors for scholars to consider when they study the opaque politics of foreign policy making in China, particularly before more relevant documents are available.

Notes

Abbreviations

CWIHP	Cold War International History Project
FRUS	*Foreign Relations of the United States*
NYT	*New York Times*
PD	*People's Daily*
PPPUS	*Public Papers of the Presidents of the United States*
PRC	People's Republic of China
RN	*Reference News*
WP	*Washington Post*

Introduction

1. Richard Nixon, *The Real War* (New York: Warner, 1980), 134; Chen Jian, introduction to "All under Heaven Is Great Chaos: Beijing, the Sino-Soviet Border Clashes, and the Turn toward Sino-American Rapprochement, 1968–69," ed. Chen and David Wilson, CWIHP, Working Paper No. 11 (Washington, DC: Woodrow Wilson International Center for Scholars, 1998), 155.

2. For Cold War international settings, see Harold C. Hinton, *Peking-Washington: Chinese Foreign Policy and the United States* (Beverly Hills, CA: Sage, 1976); A. Doak Barnett, *China Policy: Old Problems and New Challenge* (Washington, DC: Brookings Institution, 1977); and Allen S. Whiting, *China and the United States, What Next?* (New York: Foreign Policy Association, 1976). For domestic politics in the United States, see Rosemary Foot, *The Practice of Power: US Relations with China since 1949* (Oxford, UK: Clarendon, 1995); and Foot, "Redefinitions: The Domestic Context of America's China Policy in the 1960s," in *Re-examining the Cold War: U.S.-China Diplomacy, 1954–1973,* ed. Robert Ross and Jiang Changbin (Cambridge: Harvard University Press, 2001). For public opinion in the United States, see Leonard A. Kusnitz, *Public Opinion and Foreign Policy: America's China Policy, 1949–1979* (Westport, CT: Greenwood, 1984); Steven W. Mosher, *China Misperceived: Amer-*

ican Illusion and Chinese Reality (New York: Basic, 1990); and Evelyn Goh, *Constructing the U.S. Rapprochement with China, 1961–1974: From "Red Menace" to "Tacit Ally"* (New York: Cambridge University Press, 2005). For domestic politics in China, see John W. Garver, *China's Decision for Rapprochement with the United States, 1968–1971* (Boulder, CO: Westview, 1982); Gong Li, *Kuayue honggou: 1969–1979 nian zhongmei guanxi de yanbian* [Bridging the chasm: The evolution of Sino-American relations, 1969–1979] (Zhengzhou, China: Henan renmin chubanshe, 1992); Qian Jiang, *Pingpong waijiao muhou* [Behind Ping-Pong Diplomacy] (Beijing: Dongfang chubanshe, 1997); and Yang Kuisong, "The Sino-Soviet Border Clash of 1969: From Zhenbao Island to Sino-American Rapprochement," *Cold War History* 1, no. 1 (August 2000); Gong Li, "Chinese Decision Making and the Thawing of U.S.-China Relations," and Zhang Baijia, "The Changing International Scene and Chinese Policy toward the United States, 1954–1970," in *Re-examining the Cold War: U.S.-China Diplomacy, 1954–1973,* ed. Robert Ross and Jiang Changbin (Cambridge: Harvard University Press, 2001); and Chen Jian, *Mao's China and the Cold War* (Chapel Hill: University of North Carolina Press, 2001). For activities at the high level, see Margaret MacMillan, *Nixon and Mao: The Week That Changed the World* (New York: Random House, 2007); and Chris Tudda, *A Cold War Turning Point: Nixon and China, 1969–1972* (Baton Rouge: Louisiana State University Press, 2012).

3. Melvin Small, *Covering Dissent: The Media and the Anti-Vietnam War Movement* (New Brunswick, NJ: Rutgers University Press, 1994), 7. See also John C. Pierce, Kathleen M. Beatty, and Paul R. Hagner, *The Dynamics of American Public Opinion: Patterns and Processes* (Glenview, IL: Scott, Foresman, 1982), 97, 13.

4. Harold D. Lasswell, "The Structure and Function of Communication in Society," in *The Process and Effects of Mass Communication,* ed. Wilbur Schramm and Donald F. Roberts (Urbana: University of Illinois Press, 1971), 84.

5. Small, *Covering Dissent,* 10.

6. Bernard C. Cohen, *The Press and Foreign Policy* (Princeton, NJ: Princeton University Press, 1963), 5, 13, 259.

7. Patrick O'Heffernan, *Mass Media and American Foreign Policy: Inside Perspectives on Global Journalism and the Foreign Policy Process* (Norwood, NJ: Ablex, 1991), 45–46.

8. Michael Lumbers, *Piercing the Bamboo Curtain: Tentative Bridge-Building to China during the Johnson Years* (Manchester, UK: Manchester University Press, 2008), 67.

9. David L. Altheide, *Media Power* (Beverly Hills, CA: Sage, 1985), 13–27.

10. Michel Oksenberg, "Methods of Communication within the Chinese Bureaucracy," *China Quarterly,* no. 57 (January–March 1974): 1–39.

11. See Russ Braley, *Bad News: The Foreign Policy of the "New York Times"* (Chicago: Regnery Gateway, 1984), 568–69. See also Nicholas O. Berry, *Foreign Policy and the Press: An Analysis of the New York Times' Coverage of U.S. Foreign Policy* (New York: Greenwood, 1990).

12. Small, *Covering Dissent,* 3.

13. Oksenberg, "Methods of Communication within the Chinese Bureaucracy," 1.

14. *NYT,* March 22, 1964, 13.

15. Yu Xinlu, "The Role of Chinese Media during the Cultural Revolution (1965–1969)" (PhD diss., Ohio University, 2001), 47–50.

16. Wei Guangyi, "Mao Zedong dingzhu: Ban yizhang tianxia duyiwuer de baozhi" [Mao Zedong's urge: Make the world's most unique newspaper], *Zongheng* [Across Time and Space], no. 4 (2000), 44–46; Zhang Xinmin, "Cankao xiaoxi: cong neibu kanwu dao gongkai faxing" [The *Reference News*: From internal publication to public circulation], *Dangshi bolan* [General Review of the Communist Party of China], no. 10 (2007), 5; Li Yang, "Cankao xiaoxi ruhe jiemi" [How to declassify the *Reference News*], *Zhongguo xinwen zhoukan* [China News Week], no. 42 (2008): 76.

17. Jörg Rudolph, *Cankao-Xiaoxi: Foreign News in the Propaganda System of the People's Republic of China* (Baltimore: School of Law, University of Maryland, 1984), 6–7.

18. Ibid. See also Wei, "Mao Zedong dingzhu," 44–46; Zhang, "Cankao xiaoxi: Cong neibu kanwu dao gongkai faxing" [*Reference News:* From internal publication to public circulation], *Dangshi bolan* [General Review of the Communist Party of China], no. 10 (2007) 5; Li Yang, "Cankao xiaoxi ruhe jiemi" [How to declassify *Reference News*], *Zhongguo xinwen zhoukan* [China News Week], no. 42 (2008): 76.

19. Small, *Covering Dissent,* 17, 13.

20. Yu, "The Role of Chinese Media during the Cultural Revolution (1965–1969)," 28–31.

21. Wu Lengxi, *Shinian lunzhan: 1956–1966 zhongsu guanxi huiyilu* [Ten years of polemics: A memoir of Sino-Soviet Relations, 1956–1966] (Beijing: Zhongyang wenxian chubanshe, 1999), 236.

22. Alastair Johnston and Robert Ross, *New Directions in the Study of China's Foreign Policy* (Stanford, CA: Stanford University Press, 2006), 127; Daniel Leese, *Mao Cult: Rhetoric and Ritual in China's Cultural Revolution* (New York: Cambridge University Press, 2011), 31.

23. Yu, "The Role of Chinese Media during the Cultural Revolution," 30.

24. In his interview with Snow on January 9, 1965, Mao told Snow: "Wherever there is revolution, we issue a statement and hold rallies to show support. . . . We like to fire empty cannons, but we don't send troops" (see Ministry of Foreign Affairs of the People's Republic of China, and Document Research Office of the CCP Central Committee, eds., *Mao Zedong waijiao wenxuan* [Selected works of Mao Zedong on diplomacy] [Beijing: Zhongyang wenxian chubanshe and shijie zhishi chubanshe, 1994], 558). During his second trip to Beijing in October 1971, Kissinger noticed several anti-American slogans on the city walls. When he asked Zhou Enlai about those slogans, Zhou said that was just "firing empty cannon" (see *FRUS, 1969–1976:* Vol. 17, *China, 1969–1972* [Washington DC: Government Printing Office, 1971], Document 163: "Memorandum from the President's Assistant for National Security Affairs [Kissinger] to President Nixon," October 29, 1971). All documents from the U.S. Department of State's *FRUS* series are henceforth cited in the format *Title* and document number. All are accessible at http://history.state.gov/historicaldocuments.

25. Small, *Covering Dissent,* 16.

26. Altheide, *Media Power,* 19; David Broder, *Behind the Front Page: A Candid Look at How the News Is Made* (New York: Simon and Schuster, 1987), 144–45.

27. Small, *Covering Dissent,* 16–17; Braley, *Bad News,* 570; Clarence Jones, *Winning with the News Media: A Self-Defense Manual When You're the Story* (Tampa, FL: Video Consultants, 1996), 340–41; John Vivian, *The Media of Mass Communication* (Boston: Allyn and Bacon, 2001), 242.

28. Robert M. Batscha, *Foreign Affairs News and the Broadcast Journalist* (New York: Praeger, 1975), 50; Philip Geyelin, "The Editorial Page," in *The Editorial Page*, ed. Laura Longley Babb (Boston: Houghton Mifflin, 1977), 18.

29. Small, *Covering Dissent*, 16–17.

30. Batscha, *Foreign Affairs News and the Broadcast Journalist*, 32, 142.

31. Small, *Covering Dissent*, 4, 13; Richard Nixon, *In the Arena: A Memoir of Victory, Defeat, and Renewal* (New York: Simon and Schuster, 1990), 254.

32. Steven M. Hallock, *Editorials and Opinion: The Dwindling Marketplace of Ideas in Today's News* (Westport, CT: Praeger, 2007), 23.

33. Small, *Covering Dissent*, 28.

34. Ibid., 13.

35. Michael Lumbers, "'Staying out of This Chinese Muddle': The Johnson Administration's Response to the Cultural Revolution," *Diplomatic History* 31, no. 2 (April 2007): 285.

1. The Depoliticization of the China Issue, 1963–1966

1. Michael Lumbers, "'Staying out of This Chinese Muddle': The Johnson Administration's Response to the Cultural Revolution," *Diplomatic History* 31, no. 2 (April 2007): 285.

2. See *NYT*, March 9, 1966, 1; *WP*, March 9, 1966, 1; Michael Lumbers, *Piercing the Bamboo Curtain: Tentative Bridge-Building to China during the Johnson Years* (Manchester, UK: Manchester University Press, 2008), 155.

3. John Foster Dulles, "Our Policies toward Communism in China," in *Department of State Bulletin* 37 (Washington, DC: Government Printing Office, 1957), 91–95. Available at http://home.heinonline.org.

4. Xia Yafeng, *Negotiating with the Enemy: U.S.-China Talks during the Cold War, 1949–1972* (Bloomington: Indiana University Press, 2006), 86, 98.

5. John F. Kennedy, "A Democrat Looks at Foreign Policy," *Foreign Affairs* 36, no. 1 (October 1957): 44–59.

6. Stephen Ambrose, *Nixon: The Education of a Politician: 1913–1962* (New York: Simon and Schuster, 1987), 579–80.

7. Roger Hilsman, *The Politics of Policy Making in Defense and Foreign Affairs: Conceptual Models and Bureaucratic Politics* (Englewood Cliffs, NJ: Prentice-Hall, 1987), 273.

8. For a detailed study of the China policy reform attempts during the Kennedy administration, see Rosemary Foot, "Redefinitions: The Domestic Context of America's China Policy in the 1960s," in *Re-Examining the Cold War: U.S.-China Diplomacy, 1954–1973*, ed. Robert Ross and Jiang Changbin (Cambridge: Harvard University Press, 2001), 264–65.

9. Roger Hilsman, "United States Policy toward Communist China," *Department of State Bulletin* 50 (Washington, DC: Government Printing Office, 1964): 11–17; accessible at www.heinonline.org.

10. *NYT*, December 14, 1963, 1; November 16, 1963, 3.

11. *NYT*, December 14, 1963, 1; *WP*, December 14, 1963, A5; December 15, 1963, E6.

12. Philip Geyelin, *Lyndon B. Johnson and the World* (New York: Praeger, 1966), 53.

13. *Newsweek,* December 30, 1963, 27.

14. *Time,* December 20, 1963, 22; March 6, 1964, 27.

15. Stephen J. Whitefield, *The Culture of the Cold War* (Baltimore: Johns Hopkins University Press, 1991), 160.

16. Seymour Topping, *On the Front Lines of the Cold War: An American Correspondent's Journal from the Chinese Civil War to the Cuban Missile Crisis and Vietnam* (Baton Rouge: Louisiana State University Press, 2010), 325. See also *NYT,* December 31, 1963, 22.

17. Roger Hilsman, *To Move a Nation: The Politics of Foreign Policy in the Administration of John F. Kennedy* (New York: Delta, 1968), 350–55.

18. Ibid., 355.

19. Nancy B. Tucker, *China Confidential: American Diplomats and Sino-American Relations, 1945–1996* (New York: Columbia University Press, 2001), 96.

20. Hilsman, *To Move a Nation,* 354–55.

21. Ibid., 355.

22. *FRUS, 1964–1968:* Vol. 30, *China* (Washington, DC: Government Printing Office, 1964), Document 63: "Memorandum from James C. Thomson, Jr., of the National Security Council Staff to the President's Special Assistant for National Security Affairs," October 28, 1964.

23. *PD,* December 15, 1963, 3.

24. *PD,* February 19, 1964, 3.

25. Joseph Fewsmith, *China since Tiananmen: The Politics of Transition* (New York: Cambridge University Press, 2001), 212.

26. *NYT,* March 22, 1964, 13.

27. *Red Flag,* no. 2–3 (1964): 33–45.

28. Ibid., no. 14 (July 1964): 34–39; no. 17–18 (September 1964): 1–27.

29. Song Yijun, "Xinzhongguo chengli hou zhongong lijie zhongyang lingdao jiti xingcheng shimo" [The formation of CCP's leading groups since the establishment of the PRC]. *Shiji qiao* [Bridge of Century], no. 6 (2013), 32.

30. Wu Lengxi, *Shinian lunzhan: 1956–1966 zhongsu guanxi huiyilu* [Ten years of polemics: A memoir of Sino-Soviet relations, 1956–1966] (Beijing: Zhongyang wenxian chubanshe, 1999), 779–81.

31. Roderick MacFarquhar and Michael Schoenhals, *Mao's Last Revolution* (Cambridge: Belknap Press of Harvard University Press, 2006), 7.

32. Lumbers, *Piercing the Bamboo Curtain,* 63. The treaty was tentatively concluded on July 25 and officially signed in Moscow on August 5, 1963 (see Xia, Negotiating with the Enemy: U.S.-China Talks during the Cold War, 1949–1972 [Bloomington: Indiana University Press, 2006], 117).

33. *NYT,* October 27, 1963, 13; November 21, 1963, 8; December 1, 1963, 7; December 28, 1963, 4; December 17, 1967, 3.

34. Charles de Gaulle, *Memoirs of Hope: Renewal and Endeavor,* trans. Terence Kilmartin (New York: Simon and Schuster, 1971), 201.

35. Franz Schurmann, *The Foreign Politics of Richard Nixon: Grand Design* (Berkeley: University of California, Institute of International Studies, 1987), 24. See also Edward A.

Kolodziej, *French International Policy under de Gaulle and Pompidou: The Politics of Grandeur* (Ithaca, NY: Cornell University Press, 1974), 323, 51–53.

36. Lumbers, *Piercing the Bamboo Curtain*, 63.

37. *NYT*, January 18, 1964, 1; *WP*, January 18, 1964, A1.

38. *PPPUS, Lyndon Johnson* (1963–64), book 1, 231; *Department of State Bulletin* 50 (1964), 260. Both the *Public Papers of the Presidents* and *Department of State Bulletin* are accessible at www.heinonline.org.

39. Lumbers, *Piercing the Bamboo Curtain*, 64.

40. *FRUS, 1964–1968:* Vol. 30, *China*, Document 2.

41. George Gallup, *The Gallup Poll: Public Opinion 1935–1971*, vol. 3 (New York: Random House, 1972), 1864, 1881.

42. *NYT*, January 18 1964, 1, 22; January 24, 1964, 26.

43. *WP*, January 19, 1964, E6; January 21, 1964, 13.

44. *Time*, January 24, 1964, 23–24; February 7, 1964, 60.

45. *Newsweek*, January 20, 1964, 27.

46. *Newsweek*, February 3, 1964, 31.

47. *NYT*, January 24, 1964, 26.

48. *WP*, January 19, 1964, E6; January 21, 1964, 13.

49. *FRUS, 1964–1968:* Vol. 30, *China*, Document 2.

50. *NYT*, January 18, 1964, 1; *WP*, January 28, 1964, A1.

51. *PD*, January 29, 1964, 1.

52. British recognition of China in January 1950 did not bring about immediate diplomatic ties between the two countries due to the disputes over the disposition of Nationalist property in Hong Kong and Britain's refusal to immediately support PRC's bid for a UN seat (see David C. Wolf, "'To Secure a Convenience': Britain Recognizes China–1950," *Journal of Contemporary History* 18, no. 2 [April 1983]: 318).

53. *PPPUS, Lyndon B. Johnson* (1963–64), book 2, 1357–58.

54. *WP*, October 23, 1964, A1.

55. *PD*, October 17, 1964, 1.

56. *NYT*, October 22, 1964, 1; October 24, 1964, 1. See "Mr. Rusk and Mr. Bundy Interviewed on Red China's Nuclear Testing," *Department of State Bulletin* 51 (1964): 615.

57. *NYT*, October 17, 1964, 28.

58. *WP*, October 17, A12.

59. *Newsweek*, October 26, 1964, 54.

60. *Time*, October 23, 1964, 36.

61. *NYT*, October 18, 1964, 3.

62. *PPPUS, Lyndon B. Johnson* (1963–64), book 2, 1377–80.

63. *NYT*, October 19, 1964, 1; *WP*, October 19, 1964, 1

64. *WP*, October 24, 1964, A1; *NYT*, October 23, 1964, 1; *Time*, October 30, 1964, 38.

65. *NYT*, October 24, 1964, 1; *WP*, October 24, 1964, 1.

66. *Time*, October 30, 1964, 39.

67. *NYT*, October 17, 1964, 11; October 26, 1964, 11; *WP*, October 23, 1964, 1.

68. *NYT*, October 23, 1964, 1.

69. Resolution 1762. Adopted on November 6, 1962, http://www.worldlii.org/int/other/UNGARsn/1962/21.pdf

70. *NYT,* October 25, 1964, E10, E11.

71. *WP,* October 24, 1964, A12.

72. Arthur S. Lall, "The Political Effects of the Chinese Bomb," *Bulletin of the Atomic Scientists* 21, no. 2 (1965): 21–24.

73. *FRUS, 1964–1968*: Vol. 30, *China,* Document 63, October 28, 1964.

74. Ibid., Document 64, November 5, 1964.

75. Ibid., Document 68, November 23, 1964.

76. Robert S. McNamara, *In Retrospect: The Tragedy and Lessons of Vietnam* (New York: Random House, 1995), 135, 139, 145, 174.

77. *PD,* February 28, 1964, 1; April 26, 1964, 1; June 20, 1964, 2. 1. The "five principles," proposed by Zhou Enlai at the Bandung Conference in 1955, include: mutual respect for each other's territorial integrity and sovereignty; mutual nonaggression; mutual noninterference in each other's internal affairs, equality and mutual benefit, and peaceful coexistence.

78. *PD,* January 11, 1964, 3; July 15, 1964, 3; September 6, 1964, 5.

79. Ibid., July 1, 1964, 3.

80. *PD,* August 6, 1964, 1; August 12, 1964, 1.

81. Ibid., March 25, 1965, 1, 2.

82. Document Research Office of the CCP Central Committee and PLA Academy of Military Science, eds., *Jianguo yilai Mao Zedong junshi wengao* [Mao Zedong's military writings since the establishment of the PRC], vol. 3 (Beijing: Junshi kexue shubanshe, 2010), 255.

83. Zhai Qiang, *China and the Vietnam Wars, 1950–1975* (Chapel Hill: University of North Carolina Press, 2000), 142.

84. Chen Jian, *Mao's China and the Cold War* (Chapel Hill: University of North Carolina Press, 2001), 214.

85. Zhai, *China and the Vietnam Wars, 1950–1975,* 143.

86. "Zhou Enlai and Pakistani President Ayub Khan," Karachi, April 2, in "Seventy-Seven Conversations between Chinese Leaders and Foreign Leaders on the Wars in Indochina, 1964–1977," ed. Odd Arne Westad, Chen Jian, Stein Tonneson, Vu Tung Nguyen, and James Hershberg, CWIHP, Working Paper No. 22 (Washington, DC: Woodrow Wilson International Center for Scholars, 1998), 82.

87. Chen, *Mao's China and the Cold War,* 217.

88. Ministry of Foreign Affairs of the People's Republic of China and Document Research Office of the CCP Central Committee, eds., *Mao Zedong waijiao wenxuan* [Selected works of Mao Zedong on diplomacy] (Beijing: Zhongyang wenxian chubanshe and shijie zhishi chubanshe, 1994), 554–58.

89. *PPPUS, Lyndon B. Johnson* (1965), book 1, 394–99.

90. *NYT,* April 9, 1965, 32.

91. *WP,* April 8, 1965, A24.

92. Ibid., April 21, 1965, A27; April 28, 1965, A24.

93. Donald A. Ritchie, *Reporting from Washington: The History of the Washington Press Corps* (New York: Oxford University Press, 2005), 250–51.

94. Guolin Yi, "The New York Times and Washington Post on Sino-American Rapprochement, 1963–1972," *American Journalism* 32, no. 4 (2015): 457. See also Ritchie, *Reporting from Washington,* 250–51.

95. Benjamin Bradlee, *A Good Life: Newspapering and Other Adventures* (New York: Simon and Schuster, 1995), 286–87.

96. *PPPUS, Lyndon B. Johnson* (1965), book 1, 395.

97. *PD,* September 3, 1965, 1–4.

98. *NYT,* September 4, 1965, 1, 2, 20.

99. *WP,* September 4, 1965, A4; September 9, 1965, A25.

100. *NYT,* September 24, 1965; October 2, 1965, SUA5_1; October 8, 1965, SU1_1; *Chicago Tribune,* October 15, 1965, 15.

101. *NYT,* October 2, 1965.

102. Lumbers, *Piercing the Bamboo Curtain,* 95, 59, 61, 67.

103. *WP,* April 20, 1965, 2; *NYT,* April 20, 1965, 18. Obviously the *Times* gave much lower prominence to this story than did the *Post.*

104. Lumbers, *Piercing the Bamboo Curtain,* 95.

105. Melvin Small, *Covering Dissent: The Media and the Anti-Vietnam War Movement* (New Brunswick, NJ: Rutgers University Press, 1994), 61–62.

106. *NYT,* February 8, 1966, 1; March 2, 1966, 1, 4; March 7, 1966, 1.

107. U.S. Congress, Senate, Committee on Foreign Relations, "The United States and China," 89th Cong. 2d Sess., March 7, 8, 10, *Congressional Record* (1966) vol. 112, parts 4, 5, accessible at http://home.heinonline.org/.

108. *Newsweek,* March 21, 1964, 25–26.

109. Small, *Covering Dissent,* 61–62.

110. They made the front pages of the *Times* on March 2, 7, 9, 11, 21, and 31; and of the *Post* on March 7, 9, 11, 17, and 19.

111. *NYT,* March 29, 1966, 1; *WP,* March 29, 1966, 1.

112. *NYT,* March 9, 1966, 1.

113. *WP,* March 10, 1966, A24; March 15, 1966, A14.

114. *NYT,* March 23, 1966, 46.

115. *Time,* March 18, 27; *Newsweek,* March 21, 1964, 25–26.

116. *NYT,* February 13, 1966, 176.

117. Small, *Covering Dissent,* 61–62; *Newsweek,* February 21, 1966, 27.

118. *NYT,* March 14, 1966, 1; *WP,* March 14, 1966, A1.

119. *Newsweek,* March 21, 1964, 25–26.

120. Lumbers, *Piercing the Bamboo Curtain,* 155.

121. Gallup, *The Gallup Poll: Public Opinion 1935–1971,* 1931–2, 2001–1.

122. *WP,* June 27, 1966, A13.

123. Stanley D. Bachrack, *The Committee of One Million: "China Lobby" Politics, 1953–1971* (New York: Columbia University Press, 1976), 232. Indeed, in a Gallup Poll in September 1966, those who were opposed to China's admission into the UN still accounted for 56 percent of the total (see Gallup, *The Gallup Poll: Public Opinion 1935–1971,* 2032–33).

124. *NYT,* display ad 50, October 31, 12; November 2, 1966, 28.

125. Ibid., December 18, 1966, 1.

126. *FRUS, 1964–1968:* Vol. 30, *China,* Document 112.

127. *PD,* May 10, 1966, 1.

128. *PD,* May 13, 1966, 1. The U.S. pilots claimed that while they were flying south of the Red River on May 12, they were attacked by unidentified aircraft and returned fire (see *FRUS, 1964–1968:* Vol. 30, *China,* Document 153).

129. Nguyen Vu Tung, "Interpreting Beijing and Hanoi: A View of Sino-Vietnamese Relations, 1965–1970," in "Seventy-Seven Conversations," ed. Westad et al., 63n104.

130. *PPPUS, Lyndon B. Johnson* (1966), book 2, 718–22.

131. *NYT,* July 13, 1966, 1, 40; *WP,* July 13, 1966, 1; July 14, 1966, A16.

132. Xu Guangqiu, *Congress and the U.S.-China Relationship, 1949–1979* (Akron, OH: University of Akron Press, 2007), 206, 302.

133. Niu Jun, "1962: The Eve of the Left Turn in China's Foreign Policy," CWIHP, Working Paper 48 (Washington, DC: Woodrow Wilson International Center for Scholars, 2005), 31–36; Li Jie, "Changing in China's Domestic Situation in the 1960s and Sino-American Relations," in *Re-Examining the Cold War,* ed. Ross and Jiang, 305, 453n9. See also Zhang Baijia, "The Changing International Scene and Chinese Policy toward the United States, 1954–1970," ibid., 61.

134. *PD,* April 12, 1966, 4; March 14, 1966, 3.

135. *PD,* January 7, 1966, 5; February 4, 1966, 5; March 27, 1966, 1, 3; April 24, 1966, 2; May 25, 1966, 6.

136. March 12, 1966, 4; March 13, 1966, 1; March 22, 1966, 4

137. March 24, 1966, 4; March 20, 1966, 4.

138. Hilsman, *To Move a Nation,* 349.

2. "All under Heaven Is Great Chaos," 1966–1968

1. Chen Jian and David Wilson, introduction to "All under Heaven Is Great Chaos: Beijing, the Sino-Soviet Border Clashes, and the Turn toward Sino-American Rapprochement, 1968–69," ed. Chen and Wilson, CWIHP, Working Paper No. 11 (Washington, DC: Woodrow Wilson International Center for Scholars, 1998), 155.

2. Michael Lumbers, *Piercing the Bamboo Curtain: Tentative Bridge-Building to China during the Johnson Years* (Manchester, UK: Manchester University Press, 2008), 202.

3. *PPPUS, Lyndon B. Johnson* (1967), book 1, 2–14. Accessible at www.heinonline.org.

4. *NYT,* January 18, 1967, 34.

5. Roderick MacFarquhar, *The Origins of the Cultural Revolution,* vol. 1: *The Coming of the Cataclysm 1961–1966* (New York: Columbia University Press, 1997), 468–71.

6. Mao Zedong, "Talks at the Yan'an Forum on Literature and Art," https://www.marxists.org/reference/archive/mao/selected-works/volume-3/mswv3_08.htm, accessed July 5, 2015.

7. Timothy Cheek, "Deng Tuo: Culture, Leninism and Alternative Marxism in the Chinese Communist Party," *China Quarterly,* no. 87 (September 1981): 484.

8. Ibid., 486; Won Ho Chang, *Mass Media in China: The History and the Future* (Ames: Iowa State University Press, 1989), 40–41.

9. Barbara Barnouin and Yu Changgen, *Ten Years of Turbulence: The Chinese Cultural Revolution* (London: Kegan Paul International, 1993), 46. See also Maurice Meisner, *Mao's China and After: A History of the People's Republic* (New York: Free Press, 1999), 286, 313.

10. Harry Harding, "The Chinese State in Crisis," in *The Cambridge History of China*, vol. 15, pt. 2, 137; Edgar Snow, *The Long Revolution* (New York: Random House, 1972), 17.

11. Harding, "The Chinese State in Crisis," 128.

12. Ibid. See *PD*, November 30, 1965, 5; December 15, 1965, 5; December 25, 1965, 5; January 19, 1966, 5.

13. Roderick MacFarquhar and Michael Schoenhals, *Mao's Last Revolution* (Cambridge: Belknap Press of Harvard University Press, 2006), 15–19; Barnouin and Changgen, *Ten Years of Turbulence*, 65. See also MacFarquhar, *The Origins of the Cultural Revolution*, 472–73.

14. Harding, "The Chinese State in Crisis," 128–33.

15. MacFarquhar and Schoenhals, *Mao's Last Revolution*, 41.

16. *PD*, May 17, 1967, 1; May 18, 1967, 1.

17. Julia Kwong, *Cultural Revolution in China's Schools: May 1966–April 1949* (Stanford, CA: Hoover Institution Press, 1988), 30.

18. Barnouin and Yu, *Ten Years of Turbulence*, 107–9; Harding, "The Chinese State in Crisis," 158–59.

19. The "Sixteen-Point Decision," in *The Search for Modern China: A Documentary Reader*, ed. Janet Chen, Pei-Kai Cheng, Michael Lestz, and Jonathan D. Spence (New York: Norton, 2014), 449–50.

20. Ma Jisen, *Cultural Revolution in the Foreign Ministry of China* (Hong Kong: Chinese University Press, 2004), 15. See also "Introduction to the Author," Chinese University Press, Hong Kong, http://www.chineseupress.com/asp/c_Book_card.asp?BookID=2059&Lang=C, last accessed, February 27, 2012.

21. *FRUS, 1964–1968*: Vol. 30, *China* (Washington, DC: Government Printing Office, 1964), Documents 234, 270.

22. Ibid., Document 180, 234, 270.

23. Ibid., Document 228, 234, 311.

24. *PD*, January 9, 1966, 5; June 9, 1967, 6; November 2, 1967, 6.

25. Ibid., July 5, 1966, 1; July 11, 1966, 1; July 23, 1966,1; July 24, 1966, 1; December 16, 1966, 1; April 26, 1967, 2; May 3, 1967, 2.

26. Ibid., August 3, 1966, 4; September 8, 1966,1.

27. *FRUS, 1964–1968*: Vol. 30, *China*, Documents 137, 180.

28. *NYT*, January 16, 1967, 1; *WP*, January 16, 1967, A1.

29. *PD*, February 2, 1967, 6.

30. Ibid., September 6, 1966, 1; December 18, 1966, 1; May 3, 1967, 2; July 7, 1967, 1.

31. Ibid., September 17, 1966, 2; September 18, 1966, 1; April 26, 1967, 1; August 30, 1967, 1; February 15, 1968, 1. According to a *Post* editorial, the United States admitted losing eight planes over or near China in three years (see *WP*, February 15, 1968, A24).

32. *PD*, August 22, 1967, 1, 4; August 30, 1967, 2.

33. *FRUS, 1964–1968:* Vol. 30, *China,* Documents 234, 270.

34. *PD,* December 6, 1966, 1.

35. Ibid., January 13, 1967, 5.

36. *RN,* January 11, 1967, 1; January 13, 1967, 4.

37. Roderick MacFarquhar and John K. Fairbank, eds., *The Cambridge History of China,* vol. 15: *The People's Republic,* pt. 2: *Revolutions within the Chinese Revolution 1966–1982* (New York: Cambridge University Press, 1991), 245–46.

38. MacFarquhar and Schoenhals, *Mao's Last Revolution,* 199–227; Harding, "The Chinese State in Crisis," 181–82.

39. *RN,* January 3, 1967, 4; January 4, 1967, 4; March 8, 1967, 4; March 10, 1967, 4.

40. *PD,* June 21, 1967, 5; August 8, 1967, 6; August 24, 1967, 5; August 15, 1968, 5; August 29, 1968, 5.

41. *RN,* September 14, 1967, 2; November 15, 1967, 2; November 5, 1968, 3; November 10, 1968, 3.

42. Michel Oksenberg, "Methods of Communication within the Chinese Bureaucracy," *China Quarterly,* no. 57 (January–March 1974): 35–36.

43. Michael Lumbers, "'Staying out of This Chinese Muddle': The Johnson Administration's Response to the Cultural Revolution," *Diplomatic History* 31, no. 2 (April 2007): 275.

44. Ibid., 260–65, 288.

45. Ibid., 273–74, 293.

46. *FRUS, 1964–1968:* Vol. 30, *China,* Document 236: "Memorandum from Alfred Jenkins of the National Security Council Staff to the President's Special Assistant (Rostow)," February 3, 1967.

47. Lumbers, "Staying out of This Chinese Muddle," 285.

48. *NYT,* June 4, 1966, 1; July 26, 1966, 1; *WP,* May 30, 1966, A16; June 4, 1966, A1.

49. *WP,* May 30, 1966, A16.

50. *NYT,* June 19, 18.

51. *PD,* July 25, 1966, 1.

52. *NYT,* July 26, 1966, 2; *WP,* July 26, 1966, 1.

53. *Time,* August 5, 1966, 27. At the beginning of the Cultural Revolution, the *Post* said the purge "foreshadowed another 'Great Leap'" Modernization; *Newsweek* used "Great Leap Outward" to describe the exodus to Hong Kong from Guangdong province during the Cultural Revolution (*Newsweek,* October 24, 1966, 57–60).

54. *Time,* August 5, 1966, 27; *Newsweek,* August 8, 1966, 36–37.

55. Melvin Small, *Covering Dissent: The Media and the Anti-Vietnam War Movement* (New Brunswick, NJ: Rutgers University Press, 1994), 11.

56. *NYT,* August 24, 1966, 1; *WP,* August 24, 1966, 1; *Time,* September 9, 1966, 29; *Newsweek,* September 12, 1966, 29.

57. *WP,* January 8, 1967, 1.

58. *NYT,* February 6, 1967, 1; *WP,* February 7, 1967, A1; *Newsweek,* February 20, 1967, 27.

59. *WP,* September 4, 1966, 1; January 12, 1967, 1.

60. *NYT,* August 26, 1966, 32; February 6, 1967, 27.

61. *WP,* August 25, 1966, 20.

62. *NYT*, September 5, 1966, 1; *Time*, September 16, 1966, 41.

63. *NYT*, November 2, 1966, 1.

64. *Time*, July 7, 1967, 31.

65. *Newsweek*, August 7, 1967, 46.

66. *WP*, September 30, 1966, A1; July 26, 1967, A1.

67. *Time*, January 13, 1967, 22–23.

68. *WP*, January 11, 1967, 1.

69. MacFarquhar and Schoenhals, *Mao's Last Revolution*, 236; Gao, *Wannian Zhou Enlai*, 233; Harding, "The Chinese State in Crisis," 169.

70. *NYT*, January 7, 1967, 24.

71. *Time*, January 13, 1967, 20.

72. *NYT*, January 18, 1967, 34.

73. *WP*, May 30, 1966, A16; June 18, 1966, A8.

74. Ibid., March 8, 1967, A16.

75. Nils Gilman, *Mandarins of the Future: Modernization Theory in Cold War America* (Baltimore: Johns Hopkins University Press, 2007), 3.

76. *WP*, January 24, 1967, A8; *NYT*, June 22, 1968, 32.

77. "Gallup Poll Index Report No. 34 April 1968," *Gallup Opinion Index, Political, Social and Economic Trends* (Gallup International, Inc., 1968), 3.

78. Michael Hunt, *Lyndon Johnson's War: America's Cold War Crusade in Vietnam, 1945–1968* (New York: Hill and Wang, 1996), 113–14.

79. Transcript of Rusk's press conference, *NYT*, October 13, 1967, 14.

80. *NYT*, October 13, 1967, 1, 14, 38; *WP*, October 13, 1967, 1.

81. *NYT*, October 17, 1967, 1; *WP*, October 17, 1967, A1, A17.

82. *NYT*, October 16, 1967, 1; *WP*, October 16, 1967, A5.

83. *NYT*, October 18, 1967, 4.

84. *WP*, March 2, 1967, 34; March 8, 1967, A16.

85. *NYT*, April 13, 1967, 1; *WP*, April 13, 1967, A1; *Time*, April 21, 1967, 40.

86. *WP*, April 14, 1967, A20.

87. Ibid., October 22, 1967, A1; *NYT*, October 28, 1967, 1; *Time*, July 19, 1968, 24; *Newsweek*, July 8, 1968, 38–39.

88. *NYT*, July 24, 1967, 32.

89. In July 1967, forces of the Wuhan Military Region mutinied and seized Minister of Public Security Xie Fuzhi and Wang Li, both prominent members of the Cultural Revolution Group. When Mao tried to mediate the situation in person, the mutiny went out of control and even threatened his life. Mao ended up being escorted to the airport at two in the morning (see MacFarquhar and Schoenhals, *Mao's Last Revolution*, 199–227; and Harding, "The Chinese State in Crisis," 181–82).

90. *NYT*, July 31, 1967, 26; *WP*, August 4, 1967, A18.

91. Lumbers, *Piercing the Bamboo Curtain*, 202.

92. *PD*, August 14, 1966, 1.

93. Ma, *Cultural Revolution in the Foreign Ministry of China*, 168–71; MacFarquhar and Schoenhals, *Mao's Last Revolution*, 222–23.

94. Sergey Radchenko, *Two Suns in the Heavens: The Sino-Soviet Struggle for Supremacy, 1962–1967* (Washington, DC: Woodrow Wilson Center, 2009), 181–84, 202.

95. Peter Jones and Sian Kevill, *China and the Soviet Union, 1949–1984* (New York: Facts on File, 1984), 91–92.

96. *RN*, November 10, 1966, 1; December 9, 1966, 4; December 17, 1966, 4; December 24, 1966, 4; February 5, 1967, 1; July 8, 1967, 1.

97. *NYT*, February 9, 1967, 1.

98. *WP*, February 10, 1967, A1; *Time*, February 17, 1967, 26; *Newsweek*, February 20, 1967, 27; February 13, 1967, 47–48.

99. *Newsweek* described the Soviets as showing "remarkable restraint" (September 12, 1966, 29); *Time* noted that the demonstrators in front of the Chinese embassy in Moscow were more behaved than the Red Guards surrounding the Soviet embassy in Beijing (see *Time*, February 17, 1967, 26).

100. *NYT*, September 17, 1966, 1; January 18, 1967, 34; *WP*, December 16, 1966, A28; *Newsweek*, September 12, 1966, 29.

101. *WP*, February 11, 1967, A12; *NYT*, February 11, 1967, 1, 27.

102. *Time*, December 2, 1966, 38, February 3, 1967, 25–26 .

103. *NYT*, February 6, 1967, 27; February 11, 1967, 1, 27.

104. Ibid., February 12, 1967, 1; *WP*, February 12, 1967, 1; *Time*, February 17, 1967, 26; *Newsweek*, March 6, 1967, 44.

105. It can be seen from the following titles: "China Dares Russia to End Ties, and Warns 'Graves Await You'" in the *Post*, February 9, 1967; "German Red Foreshadow Rift" in the *Times*, February 12, 1967, 2; "Close to a Final Split," in *Time*, February 17, 1967, 26. In an article entitled "Mao Baits the Russian Bear," *Newsweek* held that Mao was deliberately trying to "goad their former allies into a diplomatic break" (February 13, 1967, 48).

106. *NYT*, February 9, 1967, 1; *WP*, February 9, 1967, 1.

107. *NYT*, February 10, 1967, 2.

108. *WP*, February 13, 1967, A17; February 14, 1967, A17.

109. Lumbers, *Piercing the Bamboo Curtain*, 198.

110. *NYT*, June 23, 1967, 33; June 24, 1967, 22; June 25, 1967, E8; June 26, 1967, 32; *WP*, June 23, 1967, A20; June 25, 1967, C6; June 27, 1967, A16.

111. *NYT*, November 3, 1967, 1.

112. Lumbers, *Piercing the Bamboo Curtain*, 199.

113. Zhai Qiang, *China and the Vietnam Wars, 1950–1975* (Chapel Hill: University of North Carolina Press, 2000), 153.

114. Nicholas Khoo, "Breaking the Ring of Encirclement: The Sino-Soviet Rift and Chinese Policy toward Vietnam, 1964–1968," *Journal of Cold War Studies* 12, no. 1 (Winter 2010): 32–33.

115. "Zhou Enlai, Deng Xiaoping, Kang Sheng and Le Duan, Nguyen Duy Thrinh," April 13, 1966; "Zhou Enlai and Le Duan," March 23, 1966; "Zhou Enlai and Pham Van Dong, Hoang Tung," August 23, 1966, all in "Seventy-Seven Conversations," ed. Odd Arne Westad, Chen Jian, Stein Tonneson, Vu Tung Nguyen, and James Hershberg, CWIHP, Working Paper No. 22 (Washington, DC: Woodrow Wilson International Center for Scholars, 1998), 91–96.

116. *NYT*, May 12, 1966, 1; *Newsweek*, September 19, 1966, 51; *WP*, June 25, 1967, A1.

117. *WP,* April 10, 1968, A2; *NYT,* April 22, 1968, 1; April 28, 1968, E2; *Newsweek,* April 29, 1968, 15.

118. *WP,* July 13, 1968, 1; *NYT,* June 29, 1968, 1.

119. *WP,* July 6, 1968, A1; July 12, 1968, A1; *NYT,* July 10, 1968, 1. See also *Time,* December 6, 1968, 6.

120. *RN,* May 8, 1968, 2; May 11, 1968, 2, May 16, 1968, 2, May 24, 1968, 2.

121. Stanley D. Bachrack, *The Committee of One Million: "China Lobby" Politics, 1953–1971* (New York: Columbia University Press, 1976), 258.

122. The Democratic candidate Hubert Humphrey had talked about opening to China since 1966. In a news conference in Miami on August 6, the Republican candidate Richard Nixon declared that whoever became the American president would be prepared to talk with the next superpower, Communist China (*NYT,* August 7, 1968, 1).

123. *PD,* August 23, 1968, 1; August 24, 1968, 1; August 30, 1968, 1.

124. Nicholas Khoo, *Collateral Damage: Sino-Soviet Rivalry and the Termination of the Sino-Soviet Alliance* (New York: Columbia University Press, 2011), 157.

125. *PD,* October 1, 1968, 6; October 5, 1968, 3; November 7, 1968, 6.

126. Ibid., September 21, 1968, 5.

127. *RN,* October 12, 1968, 1.

128. *PD,* August 25, 1968, 3; October 1, 1968, 3, October 2, 1968, 2; October 1, 1967, 2; October 2, 1967, 2.

129. *WP,* October 2, 1968, A1. The *Times* did not pay much attention to this message, and it focused on the degraded role of the Red Guards shown in the celebration (*NYT,* October 2, 1968, 1).

130. *PD,* October 20, 1968, 1.

131. *NYT,* October 21, 1968, 10. The *Post* ignored the piece.

132. Ibid., November 7, 1968, 1.

133. *PD,* November 3, 1968, 5; November 5, 1968, 5; November 18, 1968, 6.

134. Odd Arne Westad, "History, Memory, and the Language of Alliance-Making," in "Seventy-Seven Conservations," ed. Westad et al., 11.

135. "Mao Zedong and Pham Van Dong" November 17, 1968, in "Seventy-Seven Conversations," ed. Westad et al., 141; Zhai, *China and the Vietnam Wars,* 179.

136. *PD,* November 27, 1968, 5. For previous statements, see *PD,* April 25, 1965, 5; July 2, 1965, 4; September 17, 1965, 4; December 17, 1965, 4; January 27, 1967, 5.

137. *NYT,* November 27, 1968, 1; November 29, 1968, 44; December 1, 1969, E1; December 22, 1968, E10.

138. *WP,* November 27, 1968, A16; November 28, 1968, A4; December 4, 1968, A19.

139. *CBS Evening News,* November 27, 1968, Vanderbilt Television News Archive, Record #198589. (All newscasts are hereafter cited in the format network, date, record number. All are accessible at Vanderbilt Television News Archive in Nashville, Tennessee.)

140. *ABC Evening News,* December 3, 1969, Record #1115.

141. *NBC Evening News,* December 13, 1968, Record #441090.

142. *Time,* January 17, 1969, 28–29; *Newsweek,* February 10, 1969, 43.

143. *FRUS, 1964–1968:* Vol. 30, *China,* Documents 330, 336.

144. Lumbers, *Piercing the Bamboo Curtain,* 202.

3. The Sino-Soviet Crisis: Danger and Opportunity in 1969

1. See *Life*, April 30, 1971, 4.

2. *PD*, November 27, 1968, 5.

3. Ibid., January 21, 1969, 5; January 22, 1969, 6.

4. Ibid., January 28, 1969, 1; January 29, 1969, 5; January 31, 1969, 5; February 1, 1969, 5; February 2, 1965, 5; February 3, 1969, 6.

5. *FRUS, 1969–1976*: Vol. 17, *China, 1969–1972* (Washington, DC: Government Printing Office, 1969), Document 6: "Memorandum from the President's Assistant for National Security Affairs (Kissinger) to President Nixon," February 12, 1969; Chen Jian, *Mao's China and the Cold War* (Chapel Hill: University of North Carolina Press, 2001), 245. For the statement of the Chinese Foreign Ministry, see *PD*, February 7, 1969, 6.

6. *NYT*, February 5, 1969, 1.

7. *PD*, February 7, 1969, 6.

8. Ibid., February 19, 1969, 5.

9. Chris Tudda, *A Cold War Turning Point: Nixon and China, 1969–1972* (Baton Rouge: Louisiana State University Press, 2012), 12, 8–9.

10. *FRUS, 1969–1976*: Vol. 17, *China, 1969–1972*, Document 6: "Memorandum from the President's Assistant for National Security Affairs (Kissinger) to President Nixon," February 12, 1969.

11. *CBS Evening News*, February 18, 1969, Vanderbilt Television News Archive, Record #202146; *NBC Evening News*, February 18, 1969, Record #444247; *ABC Evening News*, February 18, 1969, Record #3861; *WP*, February 19, 1969, A1, A20; *Newsweek*, March 3, 1969, 42.

12. *NYT*, January 29, 1969, 18; February 5, 1969, 1; February 20, 1969, 1, 46; *WP*, February 19, 1969, A1, A20. See also *Time*, February 14, 1969, 33.

13. Chen, *Mao's China and the Cold War*, 238. See also *PD*, January 28, 1969, 5.

14. "Mao Zedong's Comments on an Article by Commentator of *Renmin Ribao* (*People's Daily*) and *Hongqi* (*Red Flag*)," January 1969, in "All under Heaven Is Great Chaos: Beijing, the Sino-Soviet Border Clashes, and the Turn toward Sino-American Rapprochement, 1968–69," ed. Chen Jian and David Wilson, CWIHP, Working Paper No. 11 (Washington, DC: Woodrow Wilson International Center for Scholars, 1998), 161.

15. *PPPUS, Richard Nixon, 1969* (Washington, DC: Government Printing Office, 1971), 1–4. Accessible at www.heinonline.org.

16. Wu Xujun, "Mao Zedong de wubu gaoqi: Dakai zhongmei guanxi damen shimo" [Mao Zedong's five superior moves in opening Sino-American relations], in *Lishi de zhenshi—Mao Zedong shenbian gongzuo renyuan de zhengyan* [The true life of Mao Zedong—Eyewitness accounts by Mao's staff], by Xu Tao, Lin Ke, and Wu Xujun (Hong Kong: Liwen chubanshe, 1995), 312.

17. Richard Nixon, "Asia after Viet Nam," *Foreign Affairs* 46, no. 1 (October 1967): 121, 119.

18. Gong Li, "Chinese Decision Making and the Thawing of U.S.-China Relations," in *Re-Examining the Cold War*, ed. Robert Ross and Jiang Changbin (Cambridge: Harvard University Press, 2001), 332, 465n28.

19. Chen, *Mao's China and the Cold War*, 238–39.

20. Transcript of the Nixon press conference, *WP*, January 28, 1969, A8.

21. *Newsweek*, February 10, 1969, 44. The *Post* pointed out that Nixon's position might let down Americans who longed for Washington's flexibility but that it might "sweeten" the Russians who were worried that he may immediately "play the China card" (*WP*, January 28, 1969, A14).

22. *PD*, January 21, 1969, 5; January 22, 1969, 6; January 29, 1969, 6; February 3, 1969, 6; February 8, 1969, 5; February 18, 1969, 6.

23. Yang Kuisong, "The Sino-Soviet Border Clash of 1969: From Zhenbao Island to Sino-American Rapprochement," *Cold War History* 1, no. 1 (August 2000): 24–30.

24. *NYT*, March 3, 1969, 1; *WP*, March 4, 1969, A18.

25. *Time*, March 21, 1969, 23.

26. *Newsweek*, March 17, 16–17, 1969.

27. *CBS Evening News*, March 7, 1969, Record #202959; *ABC Evening News*, March 7, 1969, Record #4603; *NBC Evening News*, March 7, 1969, Record #444972.

28. *ABC Evening News*, March 7, 1969, Record #4603; *NYT*, March 8, 1969, 1; March 4, 1969, 1; *WP*, March 9, 1969, 1.

29. Barbara Barnouin and Yu Changgen, *Ten Years of Turbulence: The Chinese Cultural Revolution* (London: Kegan Paul International, 1993), 173–76.

30. Gong, "Chinese Decision Making and the Thawing of U.S.-China Relations," 324. See also Anne-Marie Brady, "Red and Expert: China's 'Foreign Friends' in the Great Proletarian Cultural Revolution, 1966–1969," in *China's Great Proletarian Cultural Revolution: Master Narratives and Post-Mao Counternarratives,* ed. Woei Lien Chong (Lanham, MD: Rowman and Littlefield, 2002), 96; Xia Yafeng, *Negotiating with the Enemy: U.S.-China Talks during the Cold War, 1949–1972* (Bloomington: Indiana University Press, 2006), 137.

31. *PD*, April 28, 1969, 1; "Mao Zedong's Speech at the First Plenary Session of the CCP's Ninth Central Committee, 28 April 1969," in "All under Heaven Is Great Chaos," ed. Chen and Wilson, 164.

32. *PD*, February 21, 1969, 1, March 15, 1969, 1; *Red Flag,* March 14, 1969, 5–9.

33. *WP*, January 2, 1969, A1; *NYT*, January 4, 1969, 1.

34. *WP*, April 2, 1969, A1; *NYT*, April 2, 1969, 1; *Newsweek*, April 14, 1969, 60; *Time*, April 11, 1969, 30.

35. *NYT*, April 2, 1969, 16; *NBC Evening News*, April 7, 1969, Record #445420.

36. *WP*, March 22, 1969, A1; March 19, 1969, A1; March 24, 1969, A25; March 30, 1969, 40, March 4, 1969, A18.

37. *NYT*, March 30, 1969, E13.

38. Ibid., March 21, 1969, 1; March 22, 1969, 7; *WP*, March 21, 1969, A1; March 22, 1969, A12; *NBC Evening News*, April 3, 1969, Record #445359.

39. Ma Jisen, *The Cultural Revolution in the Foreign Ministry of China* (Hong Kong: Chinese University Press, 2004), 320.

40. *NYT*, January 4, 1969, 4.

41. Gong, "Chinese Decision Making and the Thawing of U.S.-China Relations," 323. See *PD*, May 2, 1969, 1.

42. Xiong Xianghui, *Wode waijiao yu qingbao shengya* [My career in intelligence and diplomacy] (Beijing: Zhonggong dangshi chubanshe, 1999), 165; Gao Wenqian, *Wannian Zhou Enlai* [Zhou Enlai's later years] (New York: Mirrorbooks, 2003), 407–8.

43. Xiong, *Wode waijiao yu qingbao shengya,* 165–71.

44. "Report by Four Marshalls—Chen Yi, Ye Jianying, Xu Xiangqian, and Nie Rong-Zhen—to the Central Committee, 'a Preliminary Evaluation of the War situation' (excerpt), (11 July 1969)," in "All under Heaven Is Great Chaos," ed. Chen and Wilson, 167–68.

45. Xiong, *Wode waijiao yu qingbao shengya,* 178.

46. Gao, *Wannian Zhou Enlai,* 410. On June 27, 1950, President Harry Truman ordered the Seventh Fleet to neutralize the Taiwan Strait in response to the outbreak of the Korean War.

47. Xiong, *Wode waijiao yu qingbao shengya,* 169–73.

48. For border incidents, see *PD,* June 12, 1969, 1; July 9, 1969, 1. For editorials, see *PD,* June 7, 1969, 6; June 27, 1969, 6; July 3, 1969, 6; July 8, 1969, 6.

49. *FRUS, 1969–1976:* Vol. 17, *China, 1969–1972,* Document 11.

50. Henry Kissinger, *White House Years* (Boston: Little, Brown, 1979), 172–79.

51. *FRUS, 1969–1976:* Vol. 17, *China, 1969–1972,* Documents 14, 17.

52. *ABC Evening News,* July 21, 1969, Record #6284; *NBC Evening News,* July 21, 1969, Record #446568; *CBS Evening News,* Record #204654.

53. *NYT,* July 22, 1969, 1.

54. *WP,* July 22, 1969, A20.

55. *PPPUS, Richard Nixon* (1969), 544–56.

56. *WP,* September 10, 1965, A25.

57. *FRUS, 1969–1976:* Vol. 17, *China, 1969–1972,* Document 20. *NYT,* July 25, 1969, 8.

58. *ABC Evening News,* August 1, 1969, Record #6596, 6598.

59. *WP,* July 31, 1969, A19; *NYT,* August 5, 1969, 36.

60. *WP,* August 5, 1969, 1; *NYT,* August 4, 1969, 6; August 11, 1969, 7.

61. *PD,* July 31, 1969, 6; August 6, 1969, 6.

62. *RN,* April 6, 1969, 3; April 5, 1969, 3.

63. Ibid., July 1, 1969, 4; July 25, 1969, 1; July 30, 1969, 2; August 5, 1969, 1; August 10, 1969, 1.

64. Kissinger, *White House Years,* 180; Gao, *Wannian Zhou Enlai,* 410–11.

65. Yang, "The Sino-Soviet Border Clash of 1969," 34.

66. "Document No. 10, The CCP Central Committee's Order for General Mobilization in Border Provinces and Regions, 28 August 1969," in "All under Heaven is Great Chaos," ed. Chen and Wilson, 168–9.

67. *FRUS, 1969–1976:* Vol. 17, *China, 1969–1972,* Documents 25, 13.

68. Ibid., Documents 27, 29.

69. *Newsweek,* August 18, 1969, 38.

70. Elliot L. Richardson, "The Foreign Policy of the Nixon Administration: Its Aims and Strategy," *Department of State Bulletin* 61(Washington, DC: GPO, 1969), 260. Accessible at http://www.heinonline.org.

71. *NYT,* September 6, 1969, 1; *WP,* September 6, 1969, A1.

72. Kissinger, *White House Years,* 184; *FRUS, 1969–1976:* Vol. 17, *China, 1969–1972,* Document 38.

73. *RN,* September 9, 1969, 4.

74. *WP,* September 12, 1969, A1; *PD,* September 12, 1969, 2.

75. Gao, *Wannian Zhou Enali,* 412–13.

76. *NBC Evening News,* September 11, 1969, Record #447314.

77. *NYT,* September 12, 1969, 1, 46; *WP,* September 12, 1969, A1; September 14, 1969, 38.

78. Yang, "The Sino-Soviet Border Clash of 1969," 39–40.

79. "Report by Four Marshalls—Chen Yi, Ye Jianying, Xu Xiangqian, and Nie Rongzhen—to the Central Committee, 'Our Views of the Current Situation" (excerpt), (17 September 1969)" and "Further Thoughts by Marshal Chen Yi on Sino-American Relations," in "All under Heaven is Great Chaos," ed. Chen and Wilson, 170–71.

80. Xiong, *Wode waijiao yu qingbao shengya,* 181, 187. *PD,* September 17, 1969, 1; September 18, 1969, 1.

81. *PD,* September 21, 1969, 1; October 1, 1969, 2, 3; October 5, 1969, 2.

82. *RN,* October 1, 1969, 1, October 4, 1969, 1.

83. *PD,* October 8, 1969, 1; October 9, 1969, 2, 5.

84. *FRUS, 1969–1976:* Vol. 17, *China, 1969–1972,* Document 38.

85. *NYT,* October 9, 1969, 1.

86. *CBS Evening News,* October 9, 1969, Record #201041.

87. *RN,* October 12, 1969, 1.

88. *WP,* October 9, 1969, A1, A24.

89. *NYT,* October 9, 1969, 46.

90. *ABC Evening News,* October 9, 1969, Record #2929.

91. Gong, "Chinese Decision Making and the Thawing of U.S.-China Relations," 336–37.

92. *FRUS, 1969–1976:* Vol. 17, *China, 1969–1972,* Documents 50n4, 54.

93. *NYT,* December 25, 1969, 8; *WP,* December 25, 1969, D6.

94. Xia, *Negotiating with the Enemy,* 144–46.

95. Ibid.

96. Gong, "Chinese Decision Making and the Thawing of U.S.-China Relations," 336–37.

97. *NYT,* December 7, 1969, 1; *WP,* December 7, 1969, 1. The networks did not cover the story.

98. *PD,* December 8, 1969, 6; *RN,* December 9, 1969, 1.

99. Kissinger, *White House Years,* 188.

100. *ABC Evening News,* December 12, 1969, Record #3352; *CBS Evening News,* December 12, 1969, Record #201563; *NYT,* December 13, 1969, 1, 46; *WP,* December 13, 1969, A1; December 16, A14.

4. From Warsaw to Beijing: The "Intricate Minuet" of Signals, 1970–1971

1. Xia Yafeng, "China's Elite Politics and Sino-American Rapprochement, January 1969–February 1972," *Journal of Cold War Studies* 8, no. 4 (Fall 2006): 11.

2. *PD,* December 15, 1969, 5.

3. Henry Kissinger, *White House Years* (Boston: Little, Brown, 1979), 187.

4. *FRUS, 1969–1976:* Vol. 17, *China, 1969–1972* (Washington, DC: Government Printing Office, 1967), Document 51: "Memorandum from Helmut Sonnenfeldt of the National

Security Council Staff to the President's Assistant for National Security Affairs (Kissinger)," December 11, 1969.

5. Kissinger, *White House Years,* 188.

6. *WP,* January 9, 1970, A1; *NYT,* January 11, 1970, 167.

7. Kissinger italicized the word "appearance," in *FRUS, 1969–1976:* Vol. 17, *China, 1969–1972,* Document 59.

8. *NYT,* January 9, 1970, 1; *WP,* January 9, 1970, 1.

9. *NYT,* January 10, 1970, 29; January 11, 1970, 167; January 4, 1969, 1; April 3, 1969, 3; October 2, 1969, 3.

10. *RN,* January 10, 1970, 1.

11. *NYT,* January 9, 1970,1; January 10, 29; *WP,* January 9, 1970, A1, January 12, 1971, A18.

12. *NYT,* January 10, 1970, 1; *WP,* January 10, 1970, A1.

13. *Newsweek,* February 2, 1970, 40; *Time,* February 2, 1971, 24–25.

14. *FRUS, 1969–1976:* Vol. 17, *China, 1969–1972,* Document 62.

15. Kissinger, *White House Years,* 692. See also Pobzeb Vang, *Five Principles of Chinese Foreign Policies* (Bloomington, IN: AuthorHouse, 2008), 311.

16. *PD,* May 5, 1970, 1; Kissinger, *White House Years,* 694.

17. *PD,* May 11, 1970, 1; May 12, 1970, 1; May 13, 1970, 1.

18. Li Ping and Ma Zhisun, eds., *Zhou Enlai nianpu, 1898–1976* [A chronological record of Zhou Enlai, 1898–1976] (Beijing: Zhongyang wenxian chubanshe, 1997), 1284.

19. *PD,* May 19, 1970, 5. English version of the announcement in *NYT,* May 19, 1970, 1.

20. Moscow recognized the Sihanouk government on June 23 but retained diplomatic relations with the Lon Nol government in Phnom Penh (see Vang, *Five Principles of Chinese Foreign Policies,* 314).

21. *PD,* May 21, 1970, 1; May 22, 1970, 1.

22. *PD,* May 19, 1970, 5. English version in *NYT,* May 19, 1970, 1.

23. *FRUS, 1969–1976:* Vol. 17, *China, 1969–1972,* Document 80.

24. Li and Ma, eds., *Zhou Enlai nianpu,* 1287.

25. *PD,* June 21, 1970, 6.

26. *RN,* June 22, 1970, 1.

27. The Chinese government did not give prior notice to the U.S. consulate in Hong Kong about his release. Nor did the bishop himself understand why he was released at that particular time (see *NYT,* July 11, 1971).

28. *PD,* December 8, 1969, 6; July 11, 1970, 2.

29. *WP,* July 11, 1970, 1; *NYT,* July 11, 1970, 1, 19.

30. *ABC Evening News,* July 10, 1970, Vanderbilt Television News Archive, Record #11052; *CBS Evening News,* July 10, 1970, Record #210826.

31. *ABC Evening News,* July 16, 1970, Record #11139; *CBS Evening News,* July 16, 1970, Record #210944; *NBC Evening News,* July 16, 1970, Record #452085.

32. See page 64 of this book.

33. Edgar Snow, *Red Star over China* (New York: Garden City Publishing, 1939).

34. Huang Hua, *Qinli yu jianwen—Huang Hua huiyilu* [Personal experience and eyewitness account—Memoir of Huang Hua] (Beijing: Shijie zhishi chubanshe, 2007), 149–51;

Guolin Yi, "The 'Propaganda State' and Sino-American Rapprochement: Preparing the Chinese Public for Nixon's Visit," *Journal of American-East Asian Relations* 20, no. 1 (2013): 16.

35. See *PD,* August 19, 1970, 1, 2.

36. Edgar Snow, *The Long Revolution* (New York: Random House, 1972), 3,

37. *PD,* October 2, 1970, 1.

38. Ibid., December 25, 1970, 1, January 10, 1965, 1; *PLA Daily,* December 25, 1970, 1. The English version of the caption of the 1970 photo comes from *NYT,* January 22, 1971, 39.

39. Stanley Spangler, "The Sino-American Rapprochement, 1969–1972: A Study in Signaling" (PhD diss., University of North Carolina, Chapel Hill, 1978), 91; Nancy Tucker, *China Confidential: American Diplomats and Sino-American Relations, 1945–1996* (New York: Columbia University Press, 2001), 240; Tsan-Kuo Chang, *The Press and China Policy: The Illusion of Sino-American Relations, 1950–1984* (Norwood, NJ: Ablex, 1993), 72.

40. Chen, *Mao's China and the Cold War,* 255, 365n77.

41. Document Research Office of the CCP Central Committee, ed., *Jianguo yilai Mao Zedong wengao* [Manuscripts of Mao Zedong since the founding of the People's Republic of China], vol. 13 (Beijing: Zhongyang wenxian chubanshe, 1998), 150. (Hereafter cited as *Jianguo yilai Mao Zedong wengao*).

42. Yang Kuisong and Xia Yafeng, "Vacillating between Revolution and Détente: Mao's Changing Psyche and Policy toward the United States, 1969–1976," *Diplomatic History* 34, no. 2 (April 2010): 402–3.

43. Xiong Xianghui, *Wode waijiao yu qingbao shengya* [My career in intelligence and diplomacy] (Beijing: Zhonggong dangshi chubanshe, 1999), 198–213; Snow, *The Long Revolution,* 168.

44. Yang and Xia, "Vacillating between Revolution and Détente," 404.

45. *Time,* October 5, 1970, 25.

46. *WP,* September 28, 1970, A14.

47. *NYT,* October 27, 1970, 1; *WP,* October 27, 1970, A1.

48. *RN,* October 31, 1970, 4.

49. *NYT,* October 14, 1970, 1; *WP,* October 14, 1970, 1.

50. *WP,* November 21, 1970, A1; *NYT,* November 21, 1970, 1, 29.

51. *NYT,* November 13, 1970, 1, 35; *WP,* November 13, 1970, 1.

52. *FRUS, 1969–1976:* Vol. 17, *China, 1969–1972,* Document 94; Yi, "'Propaganda State' and Sino-American Rapprochement," 18.

53. Snow, *The Long Revolution,* 192, 9, 12. See also Anne-Marie Brady, *Making the Foreign Serve China: Managing Foreigners in the People's Republic* (Lanham, MD: Rowman and Littlefield, 2003), 178.

54. For the full text of the "minutes," see *Jianguo yilai Mao Zedong wengao,* vol. 13, 163–82.

55. *NYT,* December 11, 1970, 11; *WP,* December 11, B16. Snow, *The Long Revolution,* 159–63. Snow's version in this book was a combination of the two conversations he had with Zhou. The Italian magazine published only the first one. So is the Chinese translation of *Epoca* in the *Reference News* on June 7, 1971.

56. *NYT,* January 22, 1971, 39.

57. Paul Finkelman, ed., *Encyclopedia of African American History, 1896 to the Present:*

From the Age of Segregation to the Twenty-First Century, vol. 1 (New York: Oxford University Press, 2007), 374. See *PD,* August 9, 1966, 2, 3.

58. *Life,* April 30, 1971, 4, 46–51.

59. Snow, *The Long Revolution,* 9, 12; Brady, *Making the Foreign Serve China,* 178; Huang, *Huang Hua huiyilu,* 154–55.

60. Seymour Topping, *On the Front Lines of the Cold War: An American Correspondent's Journal from the Chinese Civil War to the Cuban Missile Crisis and Vietnam* (Baton Rouge: Louisiana State University Press, 2010), 325–26.

61. Kissinger, *White House Years,* 709.

62. Richard Nixon, *RN: The Memoirs of Richard Nixon* (New York: Grosset and Dunlap, 1978), 547.

63. On New Year's Eve of 1970, the consulate in Hong Kong sent an airgram to the Department of State reporting Zhou's interview with Snow as published in *Epoca.* Even though it argued that "it was apparent that Beijing considers Snow an important vehicle for carrying Chinese views and images to the West," it did not mention Mao's interview with Snow. Moreover, it could probably have failed to arouse the attention of Rogers and the White House because of the timing (see Chris Tudda, *A Cold War Turning Point: Nixon and China, 1969–1972* [Baton Rouge: Louisiana State University Press, 2012], 62, 229n19).

64. Gao Wenqian, *Wannian Zhou Enlai* [Zhou Enlai's later years] (New York: Mirrorbooks, 2003), 407.

65. *FRUS, 1969–1976:* Vol. 17, *China, 1969–1972,* Document 89.

66. Kissinger, *White House Years,* 700–701.

67. *FRUS, 1969–1976:* Vol. 17, *China, 1969–1972,* Document 100.

68. Ibid., Document 102. See also note 2 of the document.

69. *PD,* February 4, 1971, 1; February 14, 1971, 1.

70. Kissinger, *White House Years,* 706. See also Nixon, *The Memoirs of Richard Nixon,* 548.

71. *NYT,* February 13, 1971, 1; February 19, 1971, 1.

72. *WP,* February 13, 1971, A10.

73. *RN,* February 14, 1971, 1; February 20, 1971, 1.

74. *NYT,* February 26, 1971, 1; *WP,* February 26, 1971, A1, A14.

75. Kissinger, *White House Years,* 1052–3.

76. *NYT,* February 26, 1971, 1; *WP,* February 26, 1971, A1; *NBC Evening News,* February 25, 1971, Record #456162; *ABC Evening News,* February 25, 1971, Record #14415; *CBS Evening News,* February 25, 1971, Record #215118.

77. *RN,* February 27, 1971, 1; February 28, 1971, 1.

78. *PD,* March 5, 1971, 6.

79. Chen, *Mao's China and the Cold War,* 258–59. See also Xiong, *wode qingbao yu waijiao shengya,* 230–32.

80. *PD,* March 29, 1971, 6; April 2, 1971, 6.

81. Chen, *Mao's China and the Cold War,* 260–61.

82. Xiong, *Wode qingbao yu waijiao shengya,* 238–40.

83. Ibid.; Wu Xujun, "Mao Zedong de wubu gaoqi: dakai zhongmei guanxi damen shimo" [Mao Zedong's five superior moves in opening Sino-American relations], in *Li-*

shi de zhenshi—Mao Zedong shenbian gongzuo renyuan de zhengyan [The true life of Mao Zedong—Eyewitness Accounts by Mao's Staff], by Xu Tao, Lin Ke, and Wu Xujun (Hong Kong: Liwen chubanshe, 1995), 306–10.

84. *NYT*, April 11, 1; April 16, 1971, 1.

85. Chen, *Mao's China and the Cold War*, 261–62; Xia, "China's Elite Politics and Sino-American Rapprochement," 16n53.

86. *PD*, April 15, 1971, 1, 4.

87. This distinction was first proposed by Mao in 1965 when he met with a Japanese delegation. He was especially supportive of the American people when they opposed their own government. See Ministry of Foreign Affairs of the People's Republic of China and Document Research Office of the CCP Central Committee, eds., *Mao Zedong waijiao wenxuan* [Selected works of Mao Zedong on diplomacy] (Beijing: Zhongyang wenxian chubanshe and shijie zhishi chubanshe, 1994), 575–76.

88. *PD*, April 9, 1971, 6; April 27, 1971, 2.

89. *NYT*, March 16, 1971, 2; *WP*, March 16, 1971, 2.

90. *CBS Evening News*, April 7, 1971, Record #216587; *WP*, April 8, 1971, A1.

91. *NYT*, April 11, 1971, E3, 1.

92. *WP*, April 11, 1971, 1; *NYT*, April 15, 1971, 1.

93. Guolin Yi, "The New York Times and Washington Post on Sino-American Rapprochement, 1963–1972," *American Journalism* 32, no. 4 (2015): 472.

94. *Newsweek*, April 12, 1971, 57; May 17, 1971, 48.

95. *Time*, April 26, 1971, 26–8; *Life*, June 28, 1954, 116, 125.

96. *NYT*, April 15, 1971, 16; *WP*, April 12, 1971, A19; *Newsweek*, April 19, 1971, 62.

97. *Time*, April 26, 1971, 54.

98. *NBC Evening News*, April 14, 1971, Record #457079; April 16, 1971, Record #457126.

99. *ABC Evening News*, April 13, 1971, Record #15040.

100. *CBS Evening News*, April 16, 1971, Record #216151.

101. *NYT*, April 15, 1971, 1.

102. *RN*, April 23, 1971, 4; April 26, 1971, 4.

103. *NYT*, April 20, 1971, 1; April 21, 1971, 1; *WP*, April 20, 1971, 1; April 21, 1971, 1.

104. *CBS Evening News*, April 21, 1971, Record #216286.

105. Nixon, *RN: The Memoirs of Richard Nixon*, 549.

106. George H. Gallup, *The Gallup Poll: Public Opinion 1935–1971*, vol. 3 (New York: Random House, 1972), 2308.

107. *NYT*, May 30, 1971, 16; *WP*, May 30, 1971, 125.

108. *FRUS, 1969–1976*: Vol. 17, *China, 1969–1972*, Document 118.

109. Ibid., Documents 125, 122, 130, 132.

110. *NYT*, June 11, 1971, 1, 8; *WP*, June 11, 1971, 1.

111. *ABC Evening News*, June 10, 1971, Record #15843; *NBC Evening News*, June 10, 1971, Record #458199.

112. Kissinger, *White House Years*, 732.

113. *NYT*, June 28, 1971, 11.

114. John H. Holdridge, *Crossing the Divide: An Insider's Account of the Normalization*

of U.S.-China Relations (Lanham, MD: Rowman and Littlefield, 1997), 51–53; Margaret Mac-Millan, *Nixon and Mao: The Week That Changed the World* (New York: Random House, 2007), 187–91.

115. *FRUS, 1969–1976:* Vol. 17, *China, 1969–1972,* Document 140.

116. MacMillan, *Nixon and Mao,* 194–99. See also *FRUS, 1969–1976:* Vol. 17, *China, 1969–1972,* Document 142.

117. Nixon, *RN: The Memoirs of Richard Nixon,* 548–50.

118. *RN,* April 19, 1971, 1; May 2, 1971, 2.

119. Ibid., July 9, 1971, 1.

120. Kissinger, *White House Years,* 748.

121. *WP,* November 10, 1959, D2; March 28, 1960, A15.

122. Kissinger, *White House Years,* 747.

123. Eric J. Ladley, *Nixon's China Trip* (San Jose, CA: Writers Club Press, 2002), 101–2.

124. Words of Bernard Cohen, qtd. in Patrick O'Heffernan, *Mass Media and American Foreign Policy: Inside Perspectives on Global Journalism and the Foreign Policy Process* (Norwood, NJ: Ablex, 1991), 81.

5. Setting the Stage for the Show in Beijing, 1971–1972

1. Richard Nixon, *The Memoirs of Richard Nixon* (New York: Grosset and Dunlap, 1978), 544.

2. *NYT,* July 16, 1971, 1, 30; *WP,* July 17, 1971, A1, A14; *Time,* July 26, 1971; *Newsweek,* July 26, 1971, 16.

3. *NYT,* July 16, 1971, 1; July 17, 1971, 1; *WP,* July 16, 1971, 1 A16; *Time,* July 26, 1971, 16–17; *Newsweek,* July 26, 1971, 20–21.

4. *NYT,* July 16, 1971, 1, July 17, 1971, 1; *WP,* July 16, 1971, 1, July 17, 1971, 1.

5. *Time,* July 26, 1971, 12; *Newsweek,* July 26, 1971, 20.

6. *PD,* July 16, 1971, 1.

7. Ibid., August 10, 1971, 5.

8. *RN,* July 17, 1971, 1; July 18, 1971, 1, 2; July 19, 1971, 2, 4.

9. Ibid., July 20, 1971, 1; July 28, 1971, 4; August 10, 1971, 2; August 12, 1971, 4; August 13, 1971, 4.

10. *NYT,* July 20, 1971, 1.

11. Ibid., July 17, 1971, 1; July 19, 1971, 11.

12. *FRUS, 1969–1976:* Vol. 17, *China, 1969–1972* (Washington, DC: Government Printing Office, 1971), Document 147, "Memorandum from President Nixon to his Assistant for National Security Affairs (Kissinger)," July 19, 1971.

13. *PPPUS, Richard Nixon* (1971), 849–61. Accessible at www.heinonline.org.

14. Henry Kissinger, *White House Years* (Boston: Little, Brown, 1979), 772–73. See also *NYT,* August 4, 1971, 2.

15. *FRUS 1969–1976:* Vol. 17, *China, 1969–1972,* Document 167.

16. David Broder, *Behind the Front Page: A Candid Look at How the News Is Made* (New York: Simon and Schuster, 1987), 164–65.

17. Melvin Small, *The Presidency of Richard Nixon* (Lawrence: University Press of Kansas, 1999), 11.

18. Margaret MacMillan, *Nixon and Mao: The Week That Changed the World* (New York: Random House, 2007), 150–52.

19. Richard Nixon, *In the Arena: A Memoir of Victory, Defeat, and Renewal* (New York: Simon and Schuster, 1990), 123.

20. Joseph C. Spear, *Presidents and the Press: The Nixon Legacy* (Cambridge: MIT Press, 1984), 85.

21. Broder, *Behind the Front Page*, 164–65.

22. MacMillan, *Nixon and Mao*, 150.

23. John Ehrlichman, *Witness to Power* (New York: Simon and Schuster, 1982), 263–64.

24. H. R. Haldeman, *Haldeman Diaries: Inside the Nixon White House* (New York: Putnam's Sons, 1994), 364–66.

25. MacMillan, *Nixon and Mao*, 273–74.

26. Kissinger, *White House Years*, 757.

27. *WP*, February 20, 1972, B7.

28. *FRUS, 1969–1976*: Vol. E-13, *Documents on China, 1969–1972*, Document 40.

29. MacMillan, *Nixon and Mao*, 228, 273–74.

30. *NYT*, February 8, 1972, 5; *WP*, February 8, 1972, A2.

31. Spear, *Presidents and the Press*, 98.

32. *NYT*, February 8, 1972, 5; *WP*, February 8, 1972, A2; February 20, 1972, B7.

33. Max Frankel, *The Times of My Life and My Life with "The Times"* (New York: Random House, 1999), 348–49.

34. *WP*, February 15, 1972, A1; February 20, 1972, B7.

35. *NYT*, February 10, 1972, 20.

36. *WP*, February 15, 1972, 1; *NYT*, February 15, 1972, 1, February 11, 1972, 16. See also Nixon, *The Memoirs of Richard Nixon*, 557.

37. Xia Yafeng, "China's Elite Politics and Sino-American Rapprochement, January 1969–February 1972," *Journal of Cold War Studies* 8, no. 4 (Fall 2006): 17–20.

38. Li Ping and Ma Zhisun, eds., *Zhou Enlai nianpu, 1898–1976* [A chronological record of Zhou Enlai, 1898–1976] (Beijing: Zhongyang wenxian chubanshe, 1997), 1328–29.

39. *Jianguo yilai Mao Zedong wengao*, vol. 13, 182.

40. The conference convened between June 4 and 18, 1971 (see Li and Ma, eds., *Zhou Enlai nianpu*, 1329).

41. Xia, "China's Elite Politics and Sino-American Rapprochement," 21.

42. Wei Guangyi, "Mao Zedong dingzhu: Ban yizhang tianxia duyiwuer de baozhi" [Mao Zedong's urge: Make the world's most unique newspaper], *Zongheng* [Across Time and Space], no. 4 (2000): 44–46.

43. Wei Guangyi, "Mao Zedong, Zhou Enlai he cankao xiaoxi bao" [Mao Zedong, Zhou Enlai and the *Reference News*], *Yanhuang chunqiu* [Yanhuang Spring and Autumn], no. 4 (2000): 3–6.

44. *RN*, May 2, 1971, 1; June 7, 1971, 1; June 19, 1971, 1; June 20, 1971, 1.

45. Wei Guangyi, "Zhou Enlai zongli wenge qijian zhidao ban cankao xiaoxi" [Premier Zhou Enlai guided the *Reference News* during the Cultural Revolution], *Zongheng* [Across

Time and Space], no. 9 (2000), 7. In the 1980s, the circulation of the *Reference News* reached its peak at nine million.

46. Guolin Yi, " 'Propaganda State' and Sino-American Rapprochement: Preparing the Chinese Public for Nixon's Visit," *Journal of American-East Asian Relations* 20, no. 1 (2013): 24.

47. Ministry of Foreign Affairs of the People's Republic of China and Document Research Office of the CCP Central Committee, eds., *Mao Zedong waijiao wenxuan* [Selected works of Mao Zedong on diplomacy] (Beijing: Zhongyang wenxian chubanshe and shijie zhishi chubanshe, 1994), 575–76.

48. Snow, *The Long Revolution* (New York: Random House, 1972), 9, 12; Anne-Marie Brady, *Making the Foreign Serve China: Managing Foreigners in the People's Republic* (Lanham, MD: Rowman and Littlefield, 2003), 178.

49. "Minutes of Snow-Mao Conversation," in *Jianguo yilai Mao Zedong wengao*, vol. 13, 166; "Instruction on the Foreign Ministry's Report on Inviting Americans to Visit China," ibid., 211.

50. For example, see *PD*, April 30, 1971, 6; September 11, 1971, 6.

51. Sigrid Schmalzer, "Speaking about China, Learning from China: Amateur China Experts in 1970s America," *Journal of American-East Asian Relations* 16, no. 4 (Winter 2009).

52. Brady, *Making the Foreign Serve China*, 180–81. See also Yi, "'Propaganda State' and Sino-American Rapprochement," 21–22.

53. *PD*, May 25, 1971, 1; July 20, 1971, 1; July 25, 1971, 1; September 11, 1971, 6; September 19, 1971, 6; September 22, 6; October 2, 1971, 1; October 16, 1971, 1; October 30, 1971, 6; November 14, 1971, 1; December 29, 1971, 1; December 30, 1971, 6.

54. Seymour Topping, "Chinese Court U.S. Public Opinion." Hong Kong, June 26, 1971, in *The New York Times Report from China*, by Tillman Durdin, James Reston, and Topping (New York: Quadrangle, 1971), 52.

55. Frank Ching, introduction to *The New York Times Report from China*, 9.

56. Frankel, *The Times of My Life and My Life with "The Times,"* 348–49. See also Audrey Topping, "Premier Reminisces with an 'Old Friend,' Peking, May 1, 1971," in *The New York Times Report from China*, 20.

57. *RN*, August 5, 1971, 4.

58. Ibid., July 7, 1971, 4.

59. *NYT*, July 26, 1971, 1; July 19, 1971, 2.

60. Ibid., August 10, 1971, 14; August 11, 1971, 2.

61. Haldeman, *Haldeman Diaries*, 339.

62. *NYT*, August 4, 1971, 33.

63. *RN*, July 31, 1971, 4; August 4, 1971, 4; August 12, 1971, 1; August 15, 1971, 1; August 16, 1971, 1.

64. Gao Wenqian, *Wannian Zhou Enlai* [Zhou Enlai's later years] (Hong Kong: Mirrorbooks, 2003), 345–56.

65. *NYT*, September 22, 1971, 1; *WP*, September 22, 1971, A1.

66. *WP*, October 1, 1971, A1.

67. *NYT*, September 22, 1971, 1; September 23, 1971, 1; *WP*, September 22, 1971, A1; September 23, 1971, A1; *Newsweek*, October 4, 1971, 31; *Time*, October 4, 1971, 28–29; *NBC Evening News*, October 1, 1971, Vanderbilt Television News Archive, Record #454163.

68. *WP,* September 23, 1971, A19; September 24, 1971, A26; October 3, 1971, 25.

69. *NYT,* October 4, 1971, 38; *WP,* October 3, 1971, 31.

70. *NYT,* October 3, 1971, 1; October 4, 1971, 38; *WP,* October 3, 1971, 25.

71. Kissinger, *White House Years,* 768, 770.

72. *FRUS, 1969–1976:* Vol. 17, *China, 1969–1972,* Documents 143, 151, 155, 156.

73. *FRUS, 1969–1976:* Vol. E-13, *China, 1969–1972,* Document 25.

74. *NYT,* October 6, 1971, 1, 46; *WP,* October 6, 1971, A1, A15.

75. *FRUS, 1969–1976:* Vol. 17, *China, 1969–1972,* Document 163.

76. Ibid.

77. *PD,* October 21, 1971, 1; October 27, 1971, 1; October 28, 1971, 1.

78. Ibid., October 21, 1971, 1, 2; October 27, 1971, 1.

79. Edgar Snow, *The Long Revolution,* 3.

80. John H. Holdridge, *Crossing the Divide: An Insider's Account of the Normalization of U.S.-China Relations* (Lanham, MD: Rowman and Littlefield, 1997), 71.

81. *NYT,* October 22, 1971, 3; *WP,* October 22, 1971, A20; *NBC Evening News,* October 22, 1971, Record #454417.

82. *NYT,* October 26, 1971, 1; October 29, 1971, 40.

83. *ABC Evening News,* October 26, 1971, Record #13037; *NBC Evening News,* October 26, 1971, Record #454479; *CBS Evening News,* October 26, 1971, Record #213485.

84. *NYT,* October 26, 1971, 1; October 27, 1971, 46; *WP,* October 26, 1971, 1; October 27, 1971, A20; *Time,* November 8, 1971; *Newsweek,* November 8, 1971, 22.

85. *NYT,* October 27, 1971, 16.

86. Ibid., October 28, 1971, 1; October 31, E1; *WP,* October 28, 1971, 1.

87. *WP,* October 27, 1971, A20; *NYT,* October 27, 1971, 46, 47.

88. *WP,* October 27, 1971, 1; *NYT,* October 31, 1971, E1.

89. *FRUS, 1969–1976:* Vol. 17, *China, 1969–1972,* Document 161.

90. *WP,* October 28, 1971, 1.

91. *NYT,* October 28, 1971, 1; *WP,* October 28, 1971, 1; *Time,* November 8, 1971, 26–27.

92. *FRUS, 1969–1976:* Vol. E-13, *Documents on China, 1969–1972,* Document 60.

93. *PD,* November 21, 1971, 1; November 24, 1971, 1; November 27, 1971, 1; November 28, 1971, 1; November 30, 1971, 1.

94. Ibid., February 17, 1972, 1, 2; February 20, 1972, 1.

95. *NBC Evening News,* February 15, 1972, Record #462432; *ABC Evening News,* February 15, 1972, Record #19313; *NYT,* February 16, 1972, 1; February 17, 1972, 36, 40; *WP,* February 16, 1972, 1; February 18, 1972, B10.

96. CBS special program, February 17, 1972, Record #659061; ABC special program, February 17, 1972, Record #19360; NBC special program, February 17, 1972, Record #659443; *NYT,* February 18, 1972, 1; *WP,* February 18, 1972, 1.

97. Kissinger, *White House Years,* 1054.

98. *Newsweek,* March 6, 1972, 27.

99. *WP,* February 21, 1972, 1; *NYT,* February 21, 1972, 1; ABC special program, February 20, 1972, Record #658981.

100. ABC special program, February 20, 1972, Record #658981.

101. James Reed, "In Memoriam: James C. Thomson Jr.," *American Historical Association (AHA)*, http://www.historians.org/perspectives/issues/2003/0302/0302mem1.cfm last updated February 6, 2008.

102. MacMillan, *Nixon and Mao*, 65, 71.

103. Haldeman, *Haldeman Diaries*, 415–16.

104. *WP*, February 22, 1971, 1.

105. *CBS Evening News*, February 21, 1972, Record #221667.

106. *WP*, February 22, 1972, 1; *Time*, March 6, 1972, 11; *Newsweek*, March 6, 1972, 15.

107. Haldeman, *Haldeman Diaries*, 416.

108. Spear, *Presidents and the Press*, 98.

109. *Newsweek*, March 6, 1972, 3, 14–29; *Time*, March 6, 1972, 10–28.

110. *ABC Evening News*, February 22, 1972, Record #19427; *NBC Evening News*, February 22, 1972, Record #462573; *CBS Evening News*, February 22, 1972, Record #221686; *NYT*, February 23, 1972, 1; *WP*, February 23, 1972, 1.

111. *WP*, February 22, 1972, 1; *NYT*, February 22, 1; February 23, 1972, 1; *Newsweek*, March 6, 1972, 16; *Time*, March 6, 1972, 16.

112. Kissinger, *White House Years*, 776.

113. *RN*, September 14, 1971, 4; September 19, 1971, 1; January 28, 1972, 1; February 11, 1972, 1; February 22, 1972, 1; February 24, 1972, 4; February 26, 1972, 2; February 28, 1972, 1, 2; February 29, 1972, 1.

114. Ibid., January 30, 1972, 4; February 19, 1972, 4. In an ABC footage, when the Chinese Ping-Pong team visited Detroit in April 1972, using a bullhorn McIntire shouted that Mao killed more Christians than Hitler killed Jews and urged the Chinese players to defect. He was ignored (see *ABC Evening News*, April 13, 1972, Record #20178).

115. *RN*, February 22, 1972, 2.

116. Kissinger, *White House Years*, 1075.

117. Ibid., 1076–80.

118. *WP*, February 28, 1972, A2.

119. *WP*, February 28, 1972, A1; *NYT*, February 28, 1972, 1.

120. *WP*, February 29, 1972, 1; *ABC Evening News*, February 28, 1972, Record #19504; *CBS Evening News*, February 28, 1972, Record #221782; *NBC Evening News*, February 28, 1972, Record #462696.

121. Haldeman, *Haldeman Diaries*, 423.

122. Spear, *Presidents and the Press*, 100.

123. *NYT*, February 29, 1972, 16. Nixon claimed these points as the "heart of the communiqué" in the cabinet meeting the next day (see Haldeman, *Haldeman Diaries*, 424).

124. *WP*, February 29, 1972,1, A18; *NYT*, February 28, 1972, 30.

125. *Time*, March 6, 1972, 10–12; *Newsweek*, March 13, 1972, 18–19.

126. *PD*, March 1, 1972, 1.

127. *NYT*, March 1, 1972, 1. See also *Time*, March 13, 1972, 18–19.

128. Broder, *Behind the Front Page*, 144–45.

129. *NYT*, February 19, 1972, 30.

130. *WP*, February 20, 1971, B7; March 4, 1972, A19.

131. Spear, *Presidents and the Press,* 98.

132. *Time,* March 6, 1972, 10–12.

133. *Newsweek,* March 6, 1972, 27.

134. *WP,* February 20, 1971, B7; March 4, 1972, A19; February 28, 1972, A20.

135. *WP,* March 3, 1972, A26.

Conclusion

1. Nicholas O. Berry, *Foreign Policy and the Press: An Analysis of the "New York Times"" Coverage of U.S. Foreign Policy* (New York: Greenwood, 1990), ix; Robert M. Entman, *Projections of Power: Framing News, Public Opinion, and U.S. Foreign Policy* (Chicago: University of Chicago Press, 2004), 4.

2. Patrick O'Heffernan, *Mass Media and American Foreign Policy: Inside Perspectives on Global Journalism and the Foreign Policy Process* (Norwood, NJ: Ablex, 1991), 37.

3. Robert M. Batscha, *Foreign Affairs News and the Broadcast Journalist* (New York: Praeger, 1975), 36–46.

4. Guolin Yi, "The New York Times and Washington Post on Sino-American Rapprochement, 1963–1972," *American Journalism* 32, no. 4 (2015): 453–75.

5. Anne-Marie Brady, *Marketing Dictatorship: Propaganda and Thought Work in Contemporary China* (Lanham, MD: Rowman and Littlefield, 2008), 1; Timothy Cheek, *Propaganda and Culture in Mao's China: Deng Tuo and the Intelligentsia* (New York: Oxford University Press, 1998), 1.

Bibliography

ARCHIVAL SOURCES

Vanderbilt University Television News Archive, Nashville, Tennessee

PUBLISHED PRIMARY MATERIALS

Newspapers and Magazines

Cankao Xiaoxi [Reference News]
Hong Qi [Red Flag]
New York Times
Newsweek
Renmin Ribao [People's Daily]
Time
Washington Post

Documents

Chen, Janet, Pei-Kai Cheng, Michael Lestz, and Jonathan D. Spence, eds. *The Search for Modern China: A Documentary Reader*. New York: Norton, 2014.

Chen, Jian, and David Wilson, eds. "All under Heaven Is Great Chaos: Beijing, the Sino-Soviet Border Clashes, and the Turn toward Sino-American Rapprochement, 1968–69." Cold War International History Project (hereafter CWIHP), Working Paper No. 11. Washington, DC: Woodrow Wilson International Center for Scholars, 1998.

Document Research Office of the CCP Central Committee, ed. *Jianguo yilai Mao Zedong wengao* [Manuscripts of Mao Zedong since the founding of the People's Republic of China]. Vol. 13. Beijing: Zhongyang wenxian chubanshe, 1998.

Document Research Office of the CCP Central Committee and PLA Academy of
Military Science, eds. *Jianguo yilai Mao Zedong junshi wengao* [Mao Zedong's
military writings since the establishment of the PRC]. Vol. 3. Beijing: Junshi
kexue shubanshe, 2010.

Gallup, George. *The Gallup Poll: Public Opinion, 1935–1971*. Vol. 3. New York: Random House, 1972.

"Gallup Poll Index Report No. 34 April 1968." In *Gallup Opinion Index, Political,
Social and Economic Trends*. Gallup International, Inc., 1968.

Li Ping, and Ma Zhisun, eds. *Zhou Enlai nianpu, 1898–1976* [A chronological record of Zhou Enlai, 1898–1976]. Beijing: Zhongyang wenxian chubanshe, 1997.

Ministry of Foreign Affairs of the People's Republic of China, and Document Research Office of the CCP Central Committee, eds. *Mao Zedong waijiao wenxuan*
[Selected works of Mao Zedong on diplomacy]. Beijing: Zhongyang wenxian
chubanshe and shijie zhishi chubanshe, 1994.

———, eds. *Zhou Enlai waijiao wenxuan* [Selected works of Zhou Enlai on diplo-
macy]. Beijing: Zhongyang wenxian chubanshe, 1990.

Perlstein, Rick, ed. *Richard Nixon: Speeches, Writings, Documents*. Princeton, NJ:
Princeton University Press, 2008.

Public Papers of the Presidents of the United States. Washington, DC: Government
Printing Office, 1963–72. Available at: http://home.heinonline.org

U.S. Congress. *Congressional Record*. Washington, DC: Government Printing Office, 1963–72. Available at: http://home.heinonline.org

U.S. Department of State. *Department of State Bulletin*. Washington, DC: Government Printing Office, 1963–72. Available at: http://home.heinonline.org

———. *Foreign Relations of the United States*. Washington, DC: Government Printing Office, 1963–72. Available at: http://history.state.gov/historicaldocuments.

Westad, Odd Arne, Chen Jian, Stein Tonneson, Vu Tung Nguyen, and James Hersh-
berg, eds. "Seventy-Seven Conversations between Chinese Leaders and Foreign
Leaders on the Wars in Indochina, 1964–1977." CWIHP, Working Paper No. 22.
Washington, DC: Woodrow Wilson International Center for Scholars, 1998.

Zhai, Qiang. "Beijing and the Vietnam Peace Talks, 1965–68: New Evidence from
Chinese Sources." CWIHP, Working Paper No. 18. Washington, DC: Woodrow
Wilson International Center for Scholars, 1997.

Zhang, Shuguang, and Chen Jian, eds. *Chinese Communist Foreign Policy and the
Cold War in Asia: New Documentary Evidence, 1944–1950*. Chicago: Imprint
Publications, 1996.

Memoirs and Autobiographies

Bradlee, Benjamin. *A Good Life: Newspapering and Other Adventures*. New York:
Simon and Schuster, 1995.

Bundy, William. *A Tangled Web: The Making of Foreign Policy in the Nixon Presidency.* New York: Hill and Wang, 1998.

De Gaulle, Charles. *Memoirs of Hope: Renewal and Endeavor.* Translated by Terence Kilmartin. New York: Simon and Schuster, 1971.

Ehrlichman, John. *Witness to Power.* New York: Simon and Schuster, 1982.

Frankel, Max. *The Times of My Life and My Life with "The Times."* New York: Random House, 1999.

Graham, Katharine. *Katharine Graham's Washington.* New York: Knopf, 2002.

———. *Personal History.* New York: Knopf, 1997.

Green, Marshall, John H. Holdridge, and William N. Stoke. *War and Peace with China: First-Hand Experience in the Foreign Service of the United States.* Bethesda, MD: Dacor, 1994.

Haig, Alexander Meigs, and Charles McCarry. *Inner Circles: How America Changed the World: A Memoir.* New York: Warner, 1992.

Haldeman, H. R. *Haldeman Diaries: Inside the Nixon White House.* New York: Putnam's Sons, 1994.

Hilsman, Roger. *To Move a Nation: The Politics of Foreign Policy in the Administration of John F. Kennedy.* New York: Delta, 1968.

Holdridge, John H. *Crossing the Divide: An Insider's Account of the Normalization of U.S.-China Relations.* Lanham, MD: Rowman and Littlefield, 1997.

Huang Hua. *Qinli yu jianwen—Huang Hua huiyilu* [Personal experience and eyewitness account—Memoir of Huang Hua]. Beijing: Shijie zhishi chubanshe, 2007.

Kissinger, Henry. *White House Years.* Boston: Little, Brown, 1979.

Kong, Dongmei. *Gaibian shijie de rizi—Yu Wang Hairong tan Mao Zedong waijiao wangshi* [In the era of a changing world: Talking about Mao Zedong's diplomatic past with Wang Hairong]. Beijing: Zhongyang wenxian chubanshe, 2006.

Nixon, Richard. *In the Arena: A Memoir of Victory, Defeat, and Renewal.* New York: Simon and Schuster 1990.

———. *RN: The Memoirs of Richard Nixon.* New York: Grosset and Dunlap, 1978.

———. *Six Crises.* Garden City, NY: Doubleday, 1962.

Paley, William S. *As It Happened: A Memoir.* Garden City, NY: Doubleday, 1979.

Rusk, Dean. *As I Saw It.* New York: Norton, 1990.

Topping, Seymour. *On the Front Lines of the Cold War: An American Correspondent's Journal from the Chinese Civil War to the Cuban Missile Crisis and Vietnam.* Baton Rouge: Louisiana State University Press, 2010.

Wang, Bingnan. *Nine Years of Sino-U.S. Talks in Retrospect.* Washington, DC: Joint Publications Research Service, 1985.

Wu Faxian. *Wu Faxian huiyi lu* [The memoirs of Wu Faxian]. Hong Kong: Star North Books, 2006.

Wu Lengxi. *Shinian lunzhan: 1956-1966 zhongsu guanxi huiyilu* [Ten years of po-

lemics: A memoir of Sino-Soviet relations, 1956–1966]. Beijing: Zhongyang
    wenxian chubanshe, 1999.

Wu Xujun. "Mao Zedong de wubu gaoqi: Dakai zhongmei guanxi damen shimo"
    [Mao Zedong's five superior moves in opening Sino-American relations]. In
    Lishi de zhenshi—Mao Zedong shenbian gongzuo renyuan de zhengyan [The
    true life of Mao Zedong—Eyewitness accounts by Mao's staff], by Lin Ke, Xu
    Tao, and Wu, 287–320. Hong Kong: Liwen chubanshe, 1995.

Xiong Xianghui. *Wode waijiao yu qingbao shengya* [My career in intelligence and
    diplomacy]. Beijing: Zhonggong dangshi chubanshe, 1999.

SECONDARY SOURCES

Books

Altheide, David L. *Creating Reality: How TV News Distorts Events.* Beverly Hills:
    Sage, 1976.

———. *Media Power.* Beverly Hills: Sage, 1985.

Ambrose, Stephen. *Nixon: The Education of a Politician, 1913–1962.* New York: Si-
    mon and Schuster, 1987.

———. *Nixon: The Triumph of a Politician 1962–1972.* New York: Simon and Schus-
    ter, 1989.

Appy, Christian G. *Cold War Constructions: The Political Culture of United States
    Imperialism, 1945–1966.* Amherst: University of Massachusetts Press, 2000.

Armstrong, J. David. *Revolutionary Diplomacy: Chinese Foreign Policy and the
    United Front Doctrine.* Berkeley: University of California Press, 1977.

Aronson, James. *The Press and the Cold War.* Indianapolis: Bobbs-Merrill, 1970.

Babb, Laura Longley, ed. *The Editorial Page.* Boston: Houghton Mifflin, 1977.

———, ed. *Of the Press, by the Press, for the Press (and Others, Too): A Critical Study
    of the Inside Workings of the News Business, from the News Pages, Editorials,
    Columns and Internal Staff Memos of the Washington Post.* Washington, DC:
    Washington Post, 1974.

Bachrack, Stanley. *The Committee of One Million: "China Lobby" Politics, 1953–1971.*
    New York: Columbia University Press, 1976.

Ball-Rokeach, Sandra J., and Muriel G. Cantor. *Media Audience and Social Struc-
    ture.* Beverly Hills, CA: Sage, 1986.

Barkin, Steve Michael. *American Television News: The Media Marketplace and the
    Public Interest.* Armonk, NY: Sharpe, 2003.

Barnds, William J., ed. *China and America: The Search for a New Relationship.* New
    York: New York University Press, 1977.

Barnett, A. Doak. *China Policy: Old Problems and New Challenge.* Washington, DC: Brookings Institution, 1977.

——. *Communist China and Asia: Challenge to American Policy.* New York: Harper, 1960.

——. *The Making of Foreign Policy in China: Structure and Process.* Boulder, CO: Westview, 1985.

Barnouin, Barbara, and Yu Changgen. *Ten Years of Turbulence: The Chinese Cultural Revolution.* London: Kegan Paul International, 1993.

Batscha, Robert M. *Foreign Affairs News and the Broadcast Journalist.* New York: Praeger, 1975.

Baum, Matthew. *Soft News Goes to War: Public Opinion and American Foreign Policy in the New Media Age.* Princeton, NJ: Princeton University Press, 2003.

Beaubien, Michael P., and John S. Wyeth Jr., eds. *Views on the News: The Media and Public Opinion.* New York: New York University Press, 1994.

Berry, Nicholas O. *Foreign Policy and the Press: An Analysis of the New York Times' Coverage of U.S. Foreign Policy.* New York: Greenwood, 1990.

Block, Herbert. *Herblock Special Report.* New York: Norton, 1974.

Blum, Robert. *Drawing the Line: The Origin of the American Containment Policy in East Asia.* New York: Norton, 1982.

Bogart, Leo. *Press and Public: Who Reads What, When, Where, and Why in American Newspapers.* Hillsdale, NJ: Lawrence Erlbaum, 1989.

Borg, Dorothy, ed. *Historians and American Far Eastern Policy.* New York: Columbia University Press, 1966.

Brady, Anne-Marie. *Making the Foreign Serve China: Managing Foreigners in the People's Republic.* Lanham, MD: Rowman and Littlefield, 2003.

——. *Marketing Dictatorship: Propaganda and Thought Work in Contemporary China.* Lanham, MD: Rowman and Littlefield, 2008.

——. "Red and Expert: China's "Foreign Friends" in the Great Proletarian Cultural Revolution, 1966–1969." In *China's Great Proletarian Cultural Revolution: Master Narratives and Post-Mao Counternarratives,* edited by Woei Lien Chong. Lanham, MD: Rowman and Littlefield, 2002.

Braley, Russ. *Bad News: The Foreign Policy of the "New York Times."* Chicago: Regnery Gateway, 1984.

Broder, David. *Behind the Front Page: A Candid Look at How the News Is Made.* New York: Simon and Schuster, 1987.

Burke, Peter. *What Is Cultural History?* Cambridge, UK: Polity, 2008.

CBS News. "CBS News Daily News Broadcasts." Ann Arbor, MI: University Microfilms International [etc.], 1963.

Chang, Gordon. *Friends and Enemies: The United States, China and the Soviet Union, 1948–1972.* Stanford, CA: Stanford University Press, 1990.

Chang, Tsan-Kuo. *The Press and China Policy: The Illusion of Sino-American Relations, 1950–1984.* Norwood, NJ: Ablex, 1993.

Chang, Won Ho. *Mass Media in China: The History and the Future.* Ames: Iowa State University Press, 1989.

Cheek, Timothy. *Propaganda and Culture in Mao's China: Deng Tuo and the Intelligentsia.* New York: Oxford University Press, 1998.

Chen, Jian. *China's Road to the Korean War: The Making of the Sino-American Confrontation.* New York: Columbia University Press, 1994.

———. *Mao's China and the Cold War.* Chapel Hill: University of North Carolina Press, 2001.

Cohen, Bernard C. *The Press and Foreign Policy.* Princeton, NJ: Princeton University Press, 1963.

———. *The Public's Impact on Foreign Policy.* Boston: Little, Brown, 1973.

Cohen, Warren. *America's Response to China: A History of Sino-American Relations.* New York: Columbia University Press, 2000.

———. *America's Response to China: An Interpretative History of Sino-American Relations.* New York: Wiley, 1971.

Cohen, Warren, and Nancy B. Tucker, eds. *Lyndon Johnson Confronts the World: American Foreign Policy, 1963–1968.* New York: Cambridge University Press, 1994.

Cowan, Geoffrey, and Nicholas J. Cull, eds. *Public Diplomacy in a Changing World.* Thousand Oaks, CA: Sage, 2008.

Curtin, Michael. *Redeeming the Wasteland: Television Documentary and Cold War Politics.* New Brunswick, NJ: Rutgers University Press, 1995.

Dinh, Tran Van. *Communication and Diplomacy in a Changing World.* Norwood, NJ: Ablex, 1987.

Dower, John. "Ten Points of Note: Asia and the Nixon Doctrine." In *The Great Nixon Turnaround: America's New Foreign Policy in the Post-Liberal Era (How a Cold Warrior Climbed Clean out of His Skin),* edited by Lloyd C. Gardner. New York: New Viewpoints, 1973.

Dulles, Foster Rhea. *American Policy toward Communist China, 1946–1969.* New York: Crowell, 1972.

Durdin, Tillman, James Reston, and Seymour Topping. *The New York Times Report from China.* New York: Quadrangle, 1971.

Entman, Robert M. *Projections of Power: Framing News, Public Opinion, and U.S. Foreign Policy.* Chicago: University of Chicago Press, 2004.

Epstein, Edward Jay. *Between Fact and Fiction: The Problem of Journalism.* New York: Vintage, 1975.

Fairbank, John King. *China Perceived: Images and Policies in Chinese-American Relations.* New York: Knopf, 1974.

———. Introduction to *American Policy toward Communist China, 1946–1969*, by Foster Rhea Dulles. New York: Crowell, 1972.

———. *The United States and China*. Cambridge: Harvard University Press, 1983.

Felsenthal, Carol. *Power, Privilege, and the Post: The Katharine Graham Story*. New York: Putnam's, 1993.

Fewsmith, Joseph. *China since Tiananmen: The Politics of Transition*. New York: Cambridge University Press, 2001.

Finkelman, Paul, ed. *Encyclopedia of African American History, 1896 to the Present: From the Age of Segregation to the Twenty-First Century*. Vol. 1. New York: Oxford University Press, 2007.

Foot, Rosemary. *The Practice of Power: U.S. Relations with China since 1949*. Oxford, UK: Clarendon, 1995.

———. "Redefinitions: The Domestic Context of America's China Policy in the 1960s." In *Reexamining the Cold War: U.S.-China Diplomacy, 1954–1973*, edited by Robert S. Ross and Jiang Changbin. Cambridge: Harvard University Press, 2001.

Friedman, Leon, and William F. Levantrosser, eds. *Cold War Patriot and Statesman: Richard Nixon*. Westport, CT: Greenwood, 1993.

Gaiduk, Ilya V. *The Soviet Union and the Vietnam War*. Chicago: Ivan R. Dee, 1996.

Gallup, George. *The Gallup Poll: Public Opinion 1935–1971*. Vol. 3. New York: Random House, 1972.

Gans, Herbert. *Deciding What's News: A Study of "CBS Evening News," "NBC Nightly News," "Newsweek," and "Time."* New York: Random House, 1980.

Gao Wenqian. *Wannian Zhou Enlai* [Zhou Enlai's later years]. New York: Mirrorbooks, 2003.

Gardner, Lloyd C., ed. *The Great Nixon Turnaround: America's New Foreign Policy in the Post-Liberal Era (How a Cold Warrior Climbed Clean out of His Skin)*. New York: New Viewpoints, 1973.

Garson, Robert A. *The United States and China since 1949: A Troubled Affair*. Madison, NJ: Fairleigh Dickinson University Press, 1994.

Garver, John W. *China's Decision for Rapprochement with the United States, 1968–1972*. Boulder, CO: Westview, 1982.

Gellman, Irwin F. *The Contender, Richard Nixon: The Congress Years, 1946–1952*. New York: Free Press, 1999.

Geyelin, Philip. "The Editorial Page." In *The Editorial Page*, edited by Laura Longley Babb. Boston: Houghton Mifflin, 1977.

———. *Lyndon B. Johnson and the World*. New York: Praeger, 1966.

Gilman, Nils. *Mandarins of the Future: Modernization Theory in Cold War America*. Baltimore: Johns Hopkins University Press, 2007.

Goh, Evelyn. *Constructing the U.S. Rapprochement with China, 1961–1974: From "Red Menace" to "Tacit Ally."* New York: Cambridge University Press, 2005.

Gong, Li. "Chinese Decision Making and the Thawing of U.S.-China Relations." In *Re-Examining the Cold War: U.S.-China Diplomacy, 1954–1973,* edited by Robert Ross and Jiang Changbin. Cambridge: Harvard University Press, 2001.

———. *Kuayue honggou: 1969–1979 nian zhongmei guanxi de yanbian* [Bridging the chasm: The evolution of Sino-American relations, 1969–1979]. Zhengzhou, China: Henan renmin chubanshe, 1992.

Green, Marshall, John H. Holdridge, and William N. Stoke. *War and Peace with China: First-Hand Experience in the Foreign Service of the United States.* Bethesda, MD: Dacor, 1994.

Gregor, A. James. *The China Connection: U.S. Policy and the People's Republic of China.* Stanford, CA: Hoover Institution Press, 1986.

Halberstam, David. *The Powers That Be.* New York: Knopf, 1979.

Hallock, Steven M. *Editorials and Opinion: The Dwindling Marketplace of Ideas in Today's News.* Westport, CT: Praeger, 2007.

Handel, Michael. *The Diplomacy of Surprise: Hitler, Nixon and Sadat.* Cambridge: Harvard University Press, 1981.

Hanhimaki, Jussi M. "An Elusive Grand Design." In *Nixon in the World: American Foreign Relations, 1969–1977,* edited by Fredrik Logevall and Andrew Preston. New York: Oxford University Press, 2008.

Harding, Harry. "The Chinese State in Crisis," In *The People's Republic,* pt. 2: *Revolutions within the Chinese Revolution 1966–1982,* edited by Roderick MacFarquhar and John K. Fairbank. New York: Cambridge University Press, 1991.

———. *A Fragile Relationship: The United States and China since 1972.* Washington, DC: Brookings Institution, 1992.

Herring, George. *LBJ and Vietnam: A Different Kind of War.* Austin: University of Texas Press, 1994.

Hilsman, Roger. *The Politics of Policy Making in Defense and Foreign Affairs: Conceptual Models and Bureaucratic Politics.* Englewood Cliffs, NJ: Prentice-Hall, 1987.

Hinton, Harold. *Communist China in World Politics.* Boston: Houghton Mifflin, 1966.

———. *Peking-Washington: Chinese Foreign Policy and the United States.* Beverly Hills, CA: Sage, 1976.

Humes, James. *Nixon's Ten Commandments of Statecraft.* New York: Scribner, 1997.

Hunt, Michael. *The Genesis of Chinese Communist Foreign Policy.* New York: Columbia University Press, 1996.

———. *Lyndon Johnson's War: America's Cold War Crusade in Vietnam, 1945–1968.* New York: Hill and Wang, 1996.

Iriye, Akira. "Culture and International History." In *Explaining the History of American Foreign Relations,* edited by Michael J. Hogan and Thomas Patterson. New York: Cambridge University Press, 2004.

Isaacs, Harold. *Scratching on Our Minds: American Images of China and India.* New York: John Day, 1958.

Johnston, Alastair, and Robert Ross, eds. *New Directions in the Study of China's Foreign Policy.* Stanford, CA: Stanford University Press, 2006.

Jones, Clarence. *Winning with the News Media: A Self-Defense Manual When You're the Story.* Tampa, FL: Video Consultants, 1996.

Jones, Peter, and Sian Kevill. *China and the Soviet Union, 1949–1984.* New York: Facts on File, 1984.

Keith, Ronald. *The Diplomacy of Zhou Enlai.* New York: St. Martin's, 1989.

Kengor, Paul. *Wreath Layer or Policy Player? The Vice President's Role in Foreign Policy.* Lanham, MD: Lexington, 2000.

Khoo, Nicholas. *Collateral Damage: Sino-Soviet Rivalry and the Termination of the Sino-Soviet Alliance.* New York: Columbia University Press, 2011.

Kirby, William C., Robert S. Ross, and Gong Li, eds. *Normalization of U.S.-China Relations: An International History.* Cambridge: Harvard University Press, 2005.

Klinkner, Philip A. *The Losing Parties: Out-Party National Committees: 1956–1993.* New Haven: Yale University Press, 1994.

Kochavi, Noam. *A Conflict Perpetuated: China Policy During the Kennedy Years.* Westport, CT: Praeger, 2002.

Koen, Ross Y. *The China Lobby in American Politics.* New York: Octagon, 1974.

Kolodziej, Edward A. *French International Policy under De Gaulle and Pompidou: The Politics of Grandeur.* Ithaca, NY: Cornell University Press, 1974.

Kunz, Diane B., ed. *The Diplomacy of the Crucial Decade: American Foreign Relations during the 1960s.* New York: Columbia University Press, 1994.

Kusnitz, Leonard A. *Public Opinion and Foreign Policy: America's China Policy, 1949–1979.* Westport, CT: Greenwood, 1984.

Kwong, Julia. *Cultural Revolution in China's Schools: May 1966–April 1949.* Stanford, CA: Hoover Institution Press, 1988.

Ladley, Eric J. *Balancing Act: How Nixon Went to China and Remained a Conservative.* Lincoln, NE: iUniverse, 2007.

———. *Nixon's China Trip.* San Jose, CA: Writers Club Press, 2002.

Lasswell, Harold D. "The Structure and Function of Communication in Society." In *The Process and Effects of Mass Communication,* edited by Wilbur Schramm and Donald F. Roberts. Urbana: University of Illinois Press, 1971.

Lauren, Paul Gordon, ed. *The China Hands' Legacy: Ethics and Diplomacy.* Boulder, CO: Westview, 1984.

Leese, Daniel. *Mao Cult: Rhetoric and Ritual in China's Cultural Revolution.* New York: Cambridge University Press, 2011.

Lewis, John Wilson, and Xue Litai. *China Builds the Bomb.* Stanford, CA: Stanford University Press, 1988.

Li, Jing. *China's America: The Chinese View of the United States, 1900–2000*. New York: State University of New York Press, 2011.

Linden, Frank van der. *Nixon's Quest for Peace*. Washington: Robert B. Luce, 1972.

Lu, Ning. *The Dynamics of Foreign-Policy Decision-Making in China*. Boulder, CO: Westview, 2000.

Lumbers, Michael. *Piercing the Bamboo Curtain: Tentative Bridge-Building to China during the Johnson Years*. Manchester, UK: Manchester University Press, 2008.

Ma, Jisen. *The Cultural Revolution in the Foreign Ministry of China*. Hong Kong: Chinese University Press, 2004.

MacFarquhar, Roderick. *The Origins of the Cultural Revolution*. Vol. 1: *The Coming of the Cataclysm 1961–1966*. New York: Columbia University Press, 1997.

———. *The Politics of China: The Eras of Mao and Deng*. New York: Cambridge University Press, 1997.

MacFarquhar, Roderick, and John K. Fairbank, eds. *The Cambridge History of China*, vol. 15: *The People's Republic*, pt. 2: *Revolutions within the Chinese Revolution 1966–1982*. New York: Cambridge University Press, 1991.

MacFarquhar, Roderick, and Michael Schoenhals. *Mao's Last Revolution*. Cambridge: Belknap Press of Harvard University Press, 2006.

MacMillan, Margaret. "Nixon, Kissinger, and the Opening to China." In *Nixon in the World: American Foreign Relations, 1969–1977*, edited by Fredrik Logevall and Andrew Preston. New York: Oxford University Press, 2008.

———. *Nixon and Mao: The Week That Changed the World*. New York: Random House, 2007.

Mann, James. *About Face: A History of America's Curious Relationship with China*. New York: Knopf, 1999.

Mayer, William G. *The Changing American Mind: How and Why American Public Opinion Changed between 1960 and 1988*. Ann Arbor: University of Michigan Press, 1992.

Mazo, Earl, and Stephen Hess. *Nixon: A Political Portrait*. New York: Harper and Row, 1968.

McGregor, Charles. *The Sino-Vietnamese Relationship and the Soviet Union*. London: International Institute for Strategic Studies, 1988.

McMahon, Robert J. *Dean Acheson and the Creation of an American World Order*. Washington, DC: Potomac, 2009.

McNamara, Robert S. *In Retrospect: The Tragedy and Lessons of Vietnam*. New York: Random House, 1995.

Meisner, Maurice. *Mao's China and After: A History of the People's Republic*. New York: Free Press, 1999.

Mosher, Steven W. *China Misperceived: American Illusion and Chinese Reality*. New York: Basic, 1990.

Nacos, Brigitte L., Robert Y. Shapiro, and Pierangelo Isernia, eds. *Decisionmaking in a Glass House: Mass Media, Public Opinion, and American and European Foreign Policy in the 21st Century.* Lanham, MD: Rowman and Littlefield, 2003.

Neils, Patricia. *China Images in the Life and Times of Henry Luce.* Lanham, MD: Rowman and Littlefield, 1990.

Nixon, Richard. *The Real War.* New York: Warner, 1980.

O'Heffernan, Patrick. *Mass Media and American Foreign Policy: Inside Perspectives on Global Journalism and the Foreign Policy Process.* Norwood, NJ: Ablex, 1991.

Pierce, John C., Kathleen M. Beatty, and Paul R. Hagner. *The Dynamics of American Public Opinion: Patterns and Processes.* Glenview, IL: Scott, Foresman, 1982.

Pollack, Jonathan D. "The Opening to America." In *The People's Republic,* pt. 2: *Revolutions within the Chinese Revolution 1966–1982,* edited by Roderick Mac-Farquhar and John K. Fairbank. New York: Cambridge University Press, 1991.

Qian Jiang. *Pingpong waijiao muhou* [Behind Ping-Pong Diplomacy]. Beijing: Dongfang chubanshe, 1997.

Radchenko, Sergey. *Two Suns in the Heavens: The Sino-Soviet Struggle for Supremacy, 1962–1967.* Washington, DC: Woodrow Wilson Center Press, 2009.

Reston, James. *The Artillery of the Press: Its Influence on American Foreign Policy.* New York: Harper and Row, 1967.

Ritchie, Donald A. *Reporting from Washington: The History of the Washington Press Corps.* New York: Oxford University Press, 2005.

Roberts, Priscilla, ed. *Behind the Bamboo Curtain: China, Vietnam, and the World beyond Asia.* Washington, DC: Woodrow Wilson Center Press, 2006.

Rosenberg, Morris, and Ralph H. Turner. *Social Psychology: Sociological Perspectives.* New Brunswick, NJ: Transaction, 1990.

Ross, Robert, ed. *China, the United States, and the Soviet Union: Tripolarity and Policy Making in the Cold War.* London: M. E. Sharpe, 1993.

———. *Negotiating Cooperation: The United States and China, 1969–1989.* Stanford, CA: Stanford University Press, 1995.

Ross, Robert, and Jiang Changbin, eds. *Re-Examining the Cold War: U.S.-China Diplomacy, 1954–1973.* Cambridge: Harvard University Press, 2001.

Roy, Denny. *China's Foreign Relations.* Lanham, MD: Rowman and Littlefield, 1998.

Rudolph, Jörg. *Cankao-Xiaoxi: Foreign News in the Propaganda System of the People's Republic of China.* Baltimore: School of Law, University of Maryland, 1984.

Schaller, Michael. *The United States and China in the Twentieth Century.* New York: Oxford University Press, 1979.

Schurmann, Franz. *The Foreign Politics of Richard Nixon: Grand Design.* Berkeley: Institute of International Studies, University of California, Berkeley, 1987.

Shapiro, Robert Y., and Lawrence R. Jacobs. "Who Leads and Who Follows? U.S. Presidents, Public Opinion, and Foreign Policy." In *Decisionmaking in a Glass*

House: Mass Media, Public Opinion, and American and European Foreign Policy in the 21st Century, edited by Shapiro, Brigitte L. Nacos, and Pierangelo Isernia. Lanham, MD: Rowman and Littlefield, 2003.

Shen, Zhihua, and Li Danhui. *After Leaning to One Side: China and Its Allies in the Cold War.* Washington, DC: Woodrow Wilson Center Press, 2011.

Sheng, Michael M. *Battling Western Imperialism: Mao, Stalin, and the United States.* Princeton, NJ: Princeton University Press, 1997.

Small, Melvin. *Covering Dissent: The Media and the Anti-Vietnam War Movement.* New Brunswick, NJ: Rutgers University Press, 1994.

———. *Democracy & Diplomacy: The Impact of Domestic Politics on U.S. Foreign Policy, 1789–1994.* Baltimore: John Hopkins University Press, 1996.

———. *Johnson, Nixon, and the Doves.* New Brunswick, NJ: Rutgers University Press, 1988.

———. *The Presidency of Richard Nixon.* Lawrence: University Press of Kansas, 1999.

Snow, Edgar. *The Long Revolution.* New York: Random House, 1972.

———. *Red Star over China.* New York: Garden City Publishing, 1939.

Snyder, Alvin A. *Warriors of Disinformation: American Propaganda, Soviet Lies, and the Winning of the Cold War.* New York: Arcade, 1995.

Spear, Joseph C. *Presidents and the Press: The Nixon Legacy.* Cambridge: MIT Press, 1984.

Steel, Ronald. *Walter Lippmann and the American Century.* Boston: Little, Brown, 1980.

Stueck, William. *Rethinking the Korean War—A New Diplomatic and Strategic History.* Princeton, NJ: Princeton University Press, 2002.

Sutter, Robert G. *The China Quandary: Domestic Determinants of U.S. China Policy, 1972–1982.* Boulder, CO: Westview, 1983.

———. *U.S. Policy toward China: An Introduction to the Role of Interest Groups.* Lanham, MD: Rowman and Littlefield, 1998.

Teiwes, Frederick C., and Warren Sun. *The Tragedy of Lin Biao: Riding the Tiger during the Cultural Revolution, 1966–1971.* Honolulu: University of Hawai'i Press, 1996.

Tucker, Nancy B. *China Confidential: American Diplomats and Sino-American Relations, 1945–1996.* New York: Columbia University Press, 2001.

———. "Threats, Opportunities, and Frustrations in East Asia." In *Lyndon Johnson Confronts the World: American Foreign Policy, 1963–1968,* edited by Warren Cohen and Tucker. New York: Cambridge University Press, 1994.

Tudda, Chris. *A Cold War Turning Point: Nixon and China, 1969–1972.* Baton Rouge: Louisiana State University Press, 2012.

Tyler, Patrick. *A Great Wall: Six Presidents and China.* New York: PublicAffairs, 1999.

Vang, Pobzeb. *Five Principles of Chinese Foreign Policies.* Bloomington, IN: Author-House, 2008.

Vivian, John. *The Media of Mass Communication.* Boston: Allyn and Bacon, 2001.

Waldron, Arthur. "From Nonexistent to Almost Normal: U.S.-China Relations in the 1960s." In *The Diplomacy of the Crucial Decade: American Foreign Relations during the 1960s,* edited by Diane B. Kunz. New York: Columbia University Press, 1994.

Walker, Anne Collins. *China Calls: Paving the Way for Nixon's Historic Journey to China.* Lanham, MD: Madison, 1992.

Wang Nianyi. *Da dongluan de niandai: Wenhua da geming shinian shi* [Years of turmoil: The ten-year history of the Cultural Revolution]. Zhengzhou, China: Henan renmin chubanshe, 2005.

Westad, Odd Arne. *Brother in Arms: The Rise and Fall of the Sino-Soviet Alliance 1945–1963.* Stanford CA: Stanford University Press, 1998.

Whitefield, Stephen J. *The Culture of the Cold War.* Baltimore: Johns Hopkins University Press, 1991.

Whiting, Allen S. *China and the United States, What Next?* New York: Foreign Policy Association, 1976.

Xia, Yafeng. *Negotiating with the Enemy: U.S.-China Talks During the Cold War, 1949–1972.* Bloomington: Indiana University Press, 2006.

Xu, Guangqiu. *Congress and the U.S.-China Relationship, 1949–1979.* Akron, OH: University of Akron Press, 2007.

Young, Kenneth. *Negotiating with the Chinese Communists: The United States Experiences, 1953–1967.* New York: McGraw-Hill, 1968.

Zhai, Qiang. *China and the Vietnam Wars, 1950–1975.* Chapel Hill: University of North Carolina Press, 2000.

Zhang, Baijia. "The Changing International Scene and Chinese Policy toward the United States, 1954–1970." In *Re-Examining the Cold War: U.S.-China Diplomacy, 1954–1973,* edited by Robert Ross and Jiang Changbin. Cambridge: Harvard University Press, 2001.

Zhang, Shuguang. *Deterrence and Strategic Culture: Chinese-American Confrontations, 1949–1958.* Ithaca, NY: Cornell University Press, 1992.

———. *Economic Cold War: America's Embargo against China and the Sino-Soviet Alliance, 1949–1963.* Washington, DC: Woodrow Wilson Center Press; Stanford, CA: Stanford University Press, 2001.

Articles

Astarita, Claudia. "The Evolution of the Image of China in the United States during the Cold War." *China Report* 45, no. 1 (January–March 2009): 23–34.

Burr, William, and Jeffrey T. Richelson. "Whether to 'Strangle the Baby in the Cradle': The United States and the Chinese Nuclear Program, 1960–64." *International Security* 25, no. 3 (Winter 2000): 54–99.

Caldwell, Dan. "The Legitimation of the Nixon-Kissinger Grand Design and Grand Strategy." *Diplomatic History* 33 no. 4 (September 2009): 633–52.

Cheek, Timothy. "Deng Tuo: Culture, Leninism and Alternative Marxism in the Chinese Communist Party." *China Quarterly*, no. 87 (September 1981): 470–91.

Christensen, Thomas J. "Worse Than a Monolith: Disorganization and Rivalry within Asian Communist Alliances and U.S. Containment Challenges, 1949–69." *Asian Security* 1, no. 1 (January 2005): 80–127.

Connolly, Chris. "The American Factor: Sino-American Rapprochement and Chinese Attitudes to the Vietnam War, 1968–72." *Cold War History* 5, no. 4 (November 2005): 501–27.

Goodman, Robyn S. "Prestige Press Coverage of US-China Policy during the Cold War's Collapse and Post-Cold War Years: Did a Deteriorating Cold War Paradigm Set the Stage for More Independent Press Coverage?" *International Communication Gazette* 61, no. 5 (1999): 391–410.

Griffith, Robert. "The Cultural Turn in Cold War Studies." *Reviews in American History* 29, no. 1 (March 2001): 150–57.

He, Di. "The Most Respected Enemy: Mao Zedong's Perception of the United States." *China Quarterly*, no. 137 (March 1994): 144–58.

Hunt, Michael. "The Long Crisis in U.S. Diplomatic History: Coming to Closure." *Diplomatic History* 16, no. 1 (January 1992): 115–40.

Kaufman, Victor. "A Response to Chaos: The United States, the Great Leap Forward, and the Cultural Revolution, 1961–68." *Journal of American-East Asian Relations* 7, no. 1–2 (Spring-Summer 1998): 73–92.

Kennedy, John F. "A Democrat Looks at Foreign Policy." *Foreign Affairs* 36, no. 1 (October 1957): 44–59.

Khoo, Nicholas. "Breaking the Ring of Encirclement: The Sino-Soviet Rift and Chinese Policy toward Vietnam, 1964–1968." *Journal of Cold War Studies* 12, no. 1 (Winter 2010): 3–42.

Kochavi, Noam. "Mist across the Bamboo Curtain: China's Internal Crisis and the American Intelligence Process, 1961–1962." *Journal of American-East Asian Relations* 5, no. 2 (Summer 1996): 135–55.

Lall, Arthur S. "The Political Effects of the Chinese Bomb." *Bulletin of the Atomic Scientists* 21, no. 2 (1965): 21–24.

Li Yang. "Cankao xiaoxi ruhe jiemi" [How to declassify *Reference News*]. *Zhongguo xinwen zhoukan* [China News Week], no. 42 (2008): 76–78.

Liao, Kuang-Sheng. "Linkage Politics in China: Internal Mobilization and Articulated External Hostility in the Cultural Revolution, 1967–1969." *World Politics* 28 (July 1976): 590–610.

Lumbers, Michael. "'Staying out of This Chinese Muddle': The Johnson Administration's Response to the Cultural Revolution." *Diplomatic History* 31, no. 2 (April 2007): 259–94.

Niu, Jun. "1962: The Eve of the Left Turn in China's Foreign Policy." CWIHP, Working Paper 48. Washington, DC: Woodrow Wilson International Center for Scholars, 2005.

Nixon, Richard. "Asia after Viet Nam." *Foreign Affairs* 46, no. 1 (October 1967): 111–25.

Oksenberg, Michel. "Methods of Communication within the Chinese Bureaucracy." *China Quarterly*, no. 57 (January–March 1974): 1–39.

Schram, Stuart R. "Mao Zedong a Hundred Years On: The Legacy of a Ruler." *China Quarterly*, no. 137 (March 1994): 125–43.

Schwartz, Thomas. "Explaining the Cultural Turn—or Detour." Review of *Explaining the History of American Foreign Relations*, edited by Michael J. Hogan and Thomas G. Patterson. *Diplomatic History* 31, no. 1 (January 2007): 143–47.

Song, Yijun. "Xinzhongguo chengli hou zhongong lijie zhongyang lingdao jiti xingcheng shimo" [The formation of CCP's leading groups since the establishment of the PRC]. *Shiji qiao* [Bridge of Century], no. 6 (2013): 29–37.

Stevenson, Adlai E. "Putting First Things First: A Democratic View." *Foreign Affairs* 38, no. 2 (January 1960): 191–208.

Wei Guangyi. "Mao Zedong, Zhou Enlai he cankao xiaoxi bao" [Mao Zedong, Zhou Enlai, and *Reference News*]. *Yanhuang chunqiu* [Yanhuang Spring and Autumn], no. 4 (2000): 2–6.

———. "Mao Zedong dingzhu: Ban yizhang tianxia duyiwuer de baozhi" [Mao Zedong's urge: Make the world's most unique newspaper]. *Zongheng* [Across Time and Space], no. 4 (2000): 44–47.

———. "Zhou Enlai zongli wenge qijian zhidao ban cankao xiaoxi" [Premier Zhou Enlai guided *Reference News* during the Cultural Revolution]. *Zongheng* [Across Time and Space], no. 9 (2000): 4–9.

Wolf, David C. "'To Secure a Convenience': Britain Recognizes China–1950." *Journal of Contemporary History*, 18, no. 2 (April 1983): 299–326.

Xia, Yafeng. "China's Elite Politics and Sino-American Rapprochement, January 1969–February 1972." *Journal of Cold War Studies* 8, no. 4 (Fall 2006): 3–28.

Yang, Kuisong. "Changes in Mao Zedong's Attitude toward the Indochina War, 1949–1973." CWIHP, Working Paper No. 34. Washington, DC: Woodrow Wilson International Center for Scholars, 2002, 1–44.

———. "The Sino-Soviet Border Clash of 1969: From Zhenbao Island to Sino-American Rapprochement." *Cold War History* 1, no. 1 (August 2000): 21–52.

Yang, Kuisong, and Xia Yafeng. "Vacillating between Revolution and Détente: Mao's Changing Psyche and Policy toward the United States, 1969–1976." *Diplomatic History* 34, no. 2 (April 2010): 395–423.

Yi, Guolin. "The New York Times and Washington Post on Sino-American Rapprochement, 1963–1972." *American Journalism* 32, no. 4 (2015): 453–75.

———. "'Propaganda State' and Sino-American Rapprochement: Preparing the Chinese Public for Nixon's Visit." *Journal of American-East Asian Relations* 20, no. 1 (2013): 5–28.

Zhang Xinmin. "Cankao xiaoxi: Cong neibu kanwu dao gongkai faxing" [*Reference News:* From internal publication to public circulation]. *Dangshi bolan* [General Review of the Communist Party of China], no. 10 (2007): 4–9.

Dissertations

Spangler, Stanley Eugene. "The Sino-American Rapprochement, 1969–1972: A Study in Signaling." PhD diss., University of North Carolina, Chapel Hill, 1978.

Yu, Xinlu. "The Role of Chinese Media during the Cultural Revolution (1965–1969)." PhD diss., Ohio University, 2001.

Index

CPSIA information can be obtained
at www.ICGtesting.com
Printed in the USA
LVHW091624091020
668436LV00007B/115

9 780807 172650